SYSTEM OF A DOWN

RIGHT HERE IN HOLLYWOOD ★ BEN MYERS

Published in 2006 by
INDEPENDENT MUSIC PRESS
Independent Music Press is an imprint of I.M. P. Publishing Limited
This Work is Copyright © I. M. P. Publishing Ltd 2006

System Of A Down: Right Here In Hollywood
by Ben Myers

British Library Cataloguing-in-Publication Data.
A catalogue for this book is available from The British Library.

ISBN 0-9549704-6-2

Cover Design by Fresh Lemon.
Edited by Martin Roach.

Printed in the UK.

INDEPENDENT MUSIC PRESS
P.O. Box 69,
Church Stretton, Shropshire
SY6 6WZ

Visit us on the web at: www.impbooks.com

For a free catalogue, e-mail us at: info@impbooks.com
Fax: 01694 720049

SYSTEM OF A DOWN

RIGHT HERE IN HOLLYWOOD

by Ben Myers

Independent Music Press

Contents

Acknowledgements

Thanks to the following people for assisting in the researching and writing of this book:

Simon Hargreaves and Nick Worsley at James Grant, Andy 'Ontronik' Khachaturian, Lisa Johnson, Tom Morello, Paul Brannigan, Caroline Fish, Luke Lewis, Bobbie Lane and all at *Kerrang!,* Martin, Kaye and Alfie Roach, Mark 'Barney' Greenway, George Horne, Andrew Sonnetti, Roland Hyams at Work Hard PR, Kathryn and Richard, Davey James, my parents, Kara Cooper and the Captains Of Industry. And thanks also to David Benveniste and System Of A Down. Just because.

Some extracts from the author's own interviews have previously appeared in *Kerrang!* magazine. Thanks to them.

Author's Note

This is a book about System Of A Down. But you probably know that already. If you don't … well, there is still time to turn back.

This is the first full-length account of this most interesting of bands – the first to delve into their past and to fully contextualise the importance of their music within their surroundings, their epoch. In some small way it is also a book about current affairs, the state of the world in recent years. And in a smaller way still it is about war. Actual war and musical/cultural war, two man-made conceits that will never dissipate.

Though I have been following System Of A Down closely since 1998, have interviewed the band members on a number of occasions for various magazines and seen them play numerous times, this nonetheless is an unofficial and unauthorised account. It is a biography written by a fan – which, lest we forget, is short for 'fanatic'. When you're fanatical you become passionate, which automatically renders your opinions and interpretations subjective and open to debate. But that's OK. This is rock 'n' roll we're discussing; an entity that is worthless without passion, hollow and unoriginal without discourse.

Accordingly, any opinions expressed are the author's own and any factual inaccuracies lie with myself. I hope I have done System Of A Down justice. I hope they keep doing their bit for political and religious harmony – and heavy metal.

Because someone has to.

Because, to paraphrase some old hippy somehow, if you're not part of the solution, you're surely part of the problem.

Ben Myers
February 2006

Introduction: The Falling Of Christ

Jesus Christ wasn't born in Armenia, but it was the first country in which he was accepted when Christianity first took root there. Some also believe Armenia to have been the origin of the Garden Of Eden, the paradise that was doing just fine until it became populated by man; a Utopia humans have been blindly striving for ever since.

Amazingly, it was a heavy metal band that led me to this fact. There's more: Armenia is a landlocked country lying between the Black and Caspian seas and bordered by Turkey, Georgia, Azerbaijan and Iran. It has a rich history stretching to some of the earliest recorded civilisations against which 'newer' countries such as the US or Australia pale by comparison. In 1200BC its mountainous region was known as Nairi – "land of rivers", while the first known use of the name Armenia is recorded as dating back to before 500BC.

Because of its strategic positioning between the two continents of Europe and Asia, Armenia benefited from trade routes yet was also susceptible to attack from invading neighbours such as the Greeks, Romans, Arab, Turks, Assyrians, Persians (now Iranians) and Mongols. Perhaps it was because of such an influx of passing foreigners – ranging from marauders to missionaries – that Armenia became the first state to officially adopt Christianity as its main religion in AD301, having first been preached there by two of Jesus's twelve apostles circa AD50.

Over the centuries that followed, Armenia was ruled by various foreign dynasties who took it upon themselves to command control of the country – whether the advanced Romans or the hardy Mongols. In a sign of things to come in the 1500s, the Ottoman Empire divided Armenia with the Safavid Persians.

Armenia has never been a great empire building country. Its small population of largely passive people, mountainous terrain and relatively traditional (and arguably primitive, by some Western standards) methods of living prevented it from being a major force in the Middle East and it found itself the victim of imperialism, such as in the 1800s when it was temporarily incorporated into the expanding Russian Empire.

Armenian mines are rich with copper, zinc, gold, and lead but natural energy resources are few as the country has relied on neighbours such as the former Soviet Union for imported fuel. Literacy levels amongst its modern people are high, with many citizens speaking Russian as a second language and English as an increasingly popular third language. Today the country is populated by close to three million people, the majority of whom are ethnic Armenians. But it is a population that would be much larger were it not for events of the early twentieth century from which Armenia has never full recovered, its population vastly depleted through emigration and – worse – genocide.

Between the years of 1915 and 1922, the long-standing Turkish Ottoman Empire, an area whose catchment included many places containing classical antiquities and landmarks of great historical importance, imposed itself upon Armenia. While the history of the Ottoman Empire is vast and complex, it is these final years of the Empire that we are interested in. In an effort to retain power as their empire slipped away as a result of various factors (World War I, the changing borders of the Balkan States, the Russian Revolution) the Ottomans engaged in a series of battles, including with the British over the Suez Canal and with the Russians during World War I. Many Armenians were caught in the middle. Having suffered a humiliating defeat at the hands of the Russians who gained control of much of the Ottoman-run Armenian territories, Ottoman war lords laid blame at the feet of the Armenians and in a mass movement of scapegoating ordered many citizens fighting in the Ottoman forces to be disarmed and sent to labour camps. Few survived and many were executed. As many Armenian intellectuals were arrested and executed, hundreds of thousands more of their countrymen were forcefully evacuated from their own land – an act of ethnic cleansing of huge proportions. Many of them were alleged to have been raped, robbed and killed while being escorted away by the Ottoman troops.

Details surrounding this period remain the subject of great dispute today. Over a million Armenians were displaced during the forced evacuation to nearby Syria and Mesopotamia. Many historians suggest that, as with the mass murders of Jews at the hands of the Nazi party some three decades later, 'evacuation' was actually a cover up for mass execution, a point that Turkey still disputes but which some history books state as fact. Over a million Armenians disappeared somewhere along the line and no one has been held accountable – they must have gone somewhere? Indeed, the Armenian 'genocide' (another term still hotly disputed by descendents of its perpetrators and not yet officially recognised as the correct historical term) was believed by some to have been a model for Hitler, a sign that if the Ottomans could get away with such an act unchallenged by international law, then so could he.

Whatever the political stance, the facts were unavoidable: Armenia has been raped, plundered and gutted by either the Ottomans or Turkish and Kurdish bandits, its citizens completely disenfranchised as they were either placed in a number of concentration camps – or callously dispensed of. And there was little the world did about it. Those who survived often did so without their families. Many fled abroad in the hope of restarting their lives.

"It was a true genocide whose lessons should have been learned, and all our parents and grandparents are survivors of it," says System Of A Down singer Serj Tankian. "Hitler got pointers from it because he saw that nobody was doing anything about it. It opened a door for me. I thought: 'I know this genocide is true, but for political reasons it's being denied by supposedly democratic countries, so how many other lies are there?'"

As a result of the atrocities of 1915-1922, Armenia has a widespread diaspora with eight million citizens now scattered around the globe. By the census of 2000 there were believed to be 385,000 Armenians living in the US, though taking into account mixed ancestry, some sources have the figure closer to one million.

The Armenian emigration to the US continued throughout the second half of the twentieth century, its relocated citizens taking with them a rich culture. A process of reinvention of sorts occurred as Armenians began new lives in new lands, assimilating their own culture into that of their new homes. It was a rich culture of traditional folk music played on a number of non-Western instruments, of internationally renowned classical composers, of opera, of arts and crafts and a long tradition of goldsmithery.

Many of the first generation émigrés fled to the US and in particular to New York and the Californian Valley, settling in growing areas there such as Fresno and Glendale. Today the latter is predominantly populated by foreign-born residents and home to some 80,000 Armenian-Americans working and studying across all social sectors, almost all of them there as a direct result of the genocide, with many more living in nearby neighbourhoods. Glendale houses one of the most concentrated populations of Armenians outside of their home country.

"My grandfather told me a lot about it, how he managed to escape and his whole family got killed. I grew up with it and it influenced my thinking," says Serj. "The fact that the band shares the same roots, the same Armenian heritage is a common bond. In a way we're all outsiders and see things from the position as an outsider. We look at things from an outside perspective and that perspective is often more clear."

Though Armenians have been integrating into US society for decades – centuries even – and the country has produced many renowned composers, their contribution to burgeoning pop culture was limited. Perhaps the most famous exponent was singer Cher (born Cherilyn Sarkisian), who emerged in the 1960s and whose father was of Armenian descent, though there is little evidence of her heritage in her work. Besides, she was also part-Scots-Irish and Cherokee Indian.

That was all soon to change though. Soon Armenia was going to be put on the map and in the minds of millions of young music fans the world over thanks to a once-in-a-generation rock 'n' roll band whose success few could have predicted.

"We were the first country to officially accept Christianity as the national religion and we've been fucked ever since," said Serj. "The nation has always been a place for everyone else to have a war, like the Turks and also Russia. Now Armenia's free from Soviet rule, it's getting some breathing space as a nation."

From persecution and conflict to integration, assimilation and worldwide success, this is the story of Armenia's most famous sons.

This is the story of System Of A Down.

Chapter 1: Old School Hollywood

It was into another era of conflict that Serj Tankian was born on April 21, 1967. Following the Ottoman genocide, it was Beirut, capital city of Lebanon, that became the largest adopted home in the world for displaced Armenians, who fled there in their droves. But Beirut was no safe haven. In fact it was one of the political hot-spots of modern times as the heartland of the Middle East. And though it provided a home for Armenians, many of them moved on to the growing communities in and around LA.

In 1967 when Serj was born, Lebanon was facing a period of great upheaval. Granted independence from French rule (and before that, Ottoman rule) following World War II, Beirut became the capital city of the country and indeed intellectual capital of the Arab world. In echoes of the influx of Armenians, following the Arab-Israeli war of the same year, the city became home to many Palestinian refugees under the leadership of Yasser Arafat's PLO organisation. As a city Beirut quickly grew into a popular tourist destination and a commercial and economic success. However this period of post-War stability was to be short-lived when in April 1975 civil war broke out over disagreements concerning the increase of Palestinian refugees in the south.

As the government quickly became ineffectual and powerless and various militia fought coalition forces, Beirut became divided between the predominantly Muslim part of the city in the west and the Christian community in the east. The centre of the city, once capable of drawing visitors from around the globe became the epitome of a No Man's Land. This once-popular hub of modernity had been half-destroyed by persecution and pointless conflict that claimed thousands of lives.

Once again, following a similar pattern to the flight of Armenians from their land, many moved abroad again, including scholars, academics and intellectuals. In the case of the Tankians, whose parents' parents had been victims of the Armenian genocide the first time around, it was a move to LA, where various family and friends spoke of a safe and prosperous community for their country folk.

"I was eight years old when I came to LA so I don't have a lot of memories of my time there, but I do have some, like where our house was and that of my school and my grandparents' house," Serj told me of his days in Beirut. "They're visual memories really. I also remember the beginnings of the civil war. I'd learnt some English at school when I was young but moving to LA was still somewhat of a culture shock after the Lebanon."

Though leaving it behind at a young age, the conflict witnessed in Beirut had an undeniable effect on Serj and would inform his world outlook throughout his life. "One thing I can say is that if you've ever heard bombs fall in a city, you will have a different sensitivity to dropping bombs on a city," he once commented.

The Tankians relocated to Hollywood in 1975 with their two sons Serj and his brother Sevag – a world apart from the one they left behind. A town with a different set of values, ideals and structure. Though it may often present itself as the heart of the United States and the centre of the universe, Hollywood is only a recent addition to the rich psycho-geography of a country that only officially announced itself on July 4, 1776. A mere twelve years later and the United States' Constitution confirmed a new vision for the country. America became the United States and a new way of life was born.

Unlike many other sizeable cities, Los Angeles is not divided into official districts, so the exact demarcation of Hollywood is not visible in the huge smoggy sprawl of a city of extremes of wealthy and poverty. The film industry has been a major part in perpetuating the myth of the town in which the majority of American cinema is filmed, financed by or centred around in some way. To most, Hollywood is post-Oscar ceremony parties, the Walk of Fame outside Mann's Chinese theatre, it's Cecil B DeMille and Orson Welles. It's Tom and Julia and Brad and Leo and Angelina. And so on – an endless parade of perfectly dentured clones smiling for the camera. It's Hollywood and it's as alluring as any religion, as untouchable as any god.

On screen perhaps.

But in reality, Hollywood is nothing more than a neighbourhood within a city, a collection of streets newer than most in London, Paris or Rome. The concept of the Hollywood of stage and screen is just that – a projected idyll to be beamed around the world, a place where everyone is beautiful and free to be who they want to be, it's the American dream amplified and pumped with false colour. It's the entertainment wing of an ever-powerful empire that has economic, political and financial foot-holds in more places than any of us could truly know. Despite ideological divisions between the traditionally conservative corridors of the White House in the East and the liberal sex-and-drugs-and-silicone world on the West Coast, Hollywood nevertheless remains the greatest publicist and propaganda machine the US could hope for, reaching round the world to sell an idea of the Land of The Free.

The young Serj was sensitive and intelligent, softly spoken and showing a keen aptitude for education from a small age. He enrolled at a nearby private school that catered for children of Armenian-Americans, The Rose & Alex Pilibos School. Though no one could have known it at the time the school was the starting point in System Of A Down's rich history.

A simple two-storey building in the heart of so-called Little Armenia was for students entering at all levels – pre-school, kindergarten, elementary and high school – Rose & Alex Pilibos was one of a number of institutions under the auspices of the Western Prelacy of the Armenian Apostolic Church of America. The teachings of Christianity ranked high on its agenda. Situated on North Alexandria Avenue, the school opened in 1969 specifically to cater to the educational needs of the children of first and second generation Armenian immigrants, as well as other Eastern European or Middle Eastern nationals. Over the intervening years it has gained an impressive reputation for a high standard of achievement. Alex Pilibos himself was, in 1950, also a founder member of the Educated Armenian Foundation, an organisation launched to assist needy students of Armenian origin, to promote Armenian study programmes in colleges and universities across America and so forth.

Though two fellow pupils at school would later join Serj in forming one of the most important rock bands of the modern age, their age difference meant contact was initially minimal – by the time Serj was in 12th grade, future System Of A Down band-mate Shavo Odadjian was in the 5th and Daron Malakian in the 4th. They did however appear in the same yearbook, in all their geeky glory. Though Serj excelled academically, the anti-authoritarian streak that would come to define his later work was already apparent.

"Academically speaking I was good, but I was also always a nonconformist though," he said. "You don't need to have to destroy things to be anti-conformist. I'd argue with my history teachers all the time. I remember one time we were doing American history and we were discussing the Boston Tea Party and the Boston Massacre. This is an Armenian school, where we all know about history and the genocide. To us, that's a massacre – one and a half million people! When I pointed out that something like five people had died in the Boston Massacre, the whole class laughed."

In the right hands, non-conformity can be a powerful asset when backed up by a certain level of intelligence. Serj's future band mates were also academically intelligent although still generally more concerned with skateboarding, comics, Kiss and Motley Crue than formal education (though bassist Shavo Odadjian would also attended college); Serj was a promising student who did well across the board – whether in literature, science or business.

In an interesting aside, in 1982 when Serj was a student at Rose & Alex Pilibos, the FBI arrested and charged four youths in LA who were members of the Armenian Youth Federation over allegations of 'conspiring to transport explosives' with reference to an alleged plot against the Philadelphia Honorary Turkish Consul General. No bombings were ever committed, no attack took place and no one was hurt.

Nonetheless, the four were jailed, but later gained PhDs, renounced violence and went on to have successful careers despite their dissident past. One of the main figures, Viken Yacoubian, a 19-year-old from Glendale, was sentenced to and served two years under the federal youth corrections act – his conviction was later expunged. Academically gifted, he later obtained a doctorate in counselling psychology from the University of California, and went on to enjoy a career today as a teacher and principal at … Rose And Alex Pilibos School. Though such events were completely unrelated to the then-adolescent members of System Of A Down, the case of Yacoubian and his cohorts illustrated feelings within certain quarters of the community towards the unacknowledged genocide. Dr. Yacoubian is now considered a valued member of East Hollywood's Little Armenian community. As the *LA Examiner* reported in 2001: "The attack never took place, and no one was hurt. In Little Armenia, not surprisingly, he is considered a hero."

Meanwhile the young Serj's artistic interests were expanding, though his tastes were different to his metal-loving future bandmates. He read voraciously, devouring poetry from TS Eliot to the beat generation, political and philosophical books and novels. Crucially he had little exposure to, or interest in rock, punk and metal during his adolescence, later citing traditional Armenian music, pop music and Billy Joel as favourites ahead of the expected rock bands of the day.

"Unlike Shavo and Daron, who were metalheads from a young age, my early inspirations were completely different to theirs," he one laughed. "I enjoyed the reckless years later. I've always tried to listen to a lot of different music from around the world. I like African music, and I'm a huge Ravi Shankar fan. And Harout Pamboukijian is one of the biggest Armenian folk singers in the world. In the 1970s he was making these records that were really Zeppelin-influenced."

In fact, Serj claimed his introduction to music came via the perennially uncool Bee Gees – he started with their *Saturday Night Fever* soundtrack and worked backwards, discovering all that came before it.

From a young age Serj was also keenly aware of his heritage: the events that had happened, why they had happened and the implications of the misuse of power and continued wide-scale war-mongering. Seeing something such as genocide from the perspective of a grandson of a surviving victim adds levels of insight that are never going to be obtained from a newspaper clipping or a TV news story, which was about all the Armenian genocide had warranted in the mainstream. When the deaths of a million people is still denied by certain circles, naturally to the curious mind it gives a whole new insight into concepts such as truth and justice and media representation.

To an intelligent and curious teenager such things can only fuel any smouldering indignation. As a teenager Serj joined the aforementioned Armenian Youth Federation, the youth wing of the Armenian Revolutionary Federation, an organisation founded in 1890 for "social justice, democracy and national self-determination for the Armenian people." Following the genocide and the Sovietization of Armenia in 1920, the ARF leadership was exiled, though continued to expand a cultural framework for preserving Armenian identity in the face of great change. It remains an influential force within Armenian business, communities and culture the world over.

"Being in AYF throughout my youth opened my eyes to activism and the importance of fighting injustice," Serj explained in 2005. "It's very important not to be myopic in cases of activism, though. Because all injustice, as the world, is one."

At the close of his teens Serj won a place at California State University to study Marketing & Business. "It's probably not typical of a rock singer, but then I don't know what a typical *anything* is," Serj laughed when I interviewed him in 2005. "What's a typical plumber? I guess I *was* a nerd though…" Serj's inherent nerdiness meant he was a latecomer to the rock party – many of the key punk, hardcore and metal acts System Of A Down would initially be compared to in reviews, Serj had yet to hear. The Beatles were another huge influence but again Serj came to them relatively late, only truly discovering them in his twenties. "I was listening to them like nuts and ended up getting every album," he said. "I realized that I'd heard every song as a kid but just never knew they were by The Beatles. Musically, they are as universal as music gets. I love all their albums, though *Revolver* was where they started to turn into something unique. It's a good place to start because it's a nice bridge between the early and late Beatles."

At college, he continued his academic climb with aplomb and also pursued a growing interest in activism and politics that would increase over the coming years. "One time when I was younger, I was in a demonstration against the Armenian genocide which took place outside the Turkish embassy," he remembered. There was a line of police pushing everyone about – including old ladies – and then they started arresting people for no reason. I guess I was just lucky they didn't get me."

Serj's politicization continued, a position informed by his own reading and studies and the anomalies he saw in American life as a transplanted outsider. "I also used to be in some Armenian organisations and I've been part of an Armenian political party that had its roots in the late nineteenth century and had its own soldiers," he explained. "Of course in America it's more non-violent and we'd do stuff like go from house to house getting money during the Armenian earthquake [of 1988]. I wasn't encouraged by my parents in that. They understood why I wanted to do it, my grandfather has totally given his life to the Armenian cause, and when you give your life to something – whether it's music or whatever – you can't do other things successfully."

All the while Serj's tastes were expanding as he heard bands like Bauhaus and Alien Sex Fiend for the first time, both later cited as influences on System. Formed in Northampton, England, Bauhaus combined post-punk with goth and synthesizers to create a bleak sound that helped them achieve large success during their relatively short career in the early 1980s, particularly in the US. From the same era and country, Alien Sex Fiend were goth punks with a similar synthesizer fetish who enjoyed parallel success. Though not glaringly obvious today, both bands would prove to be as influential on System Of A Down as the more commonly quoted Slayer or Dead Kennedys, neither of whom Serj actually grew up listening to. During this time, the singer had also learnt to play the keyboards and become reasonably proficient enough to make his first steps towards playing music with friends.

After graduating from college, Serj worked in various jobs in manufacturing and retail (including a brief stint at Hollywood Guitar Centre, LA's premier music equipment shop – "As soon as they asked me to clean the toilets I left," he recalled. "I'd heard 'Stairway To Heaven' too many times….") Over the years that followed he would live in a variety of locations in the city – Hollywood, Studio City, North Hollywood and Sherman Oaks.

"LA is completely decentralised," he told me. "Because it's such a big city and everything is spread out then people become localised, socially. And work-wise too." Serj worked for a computer software company before setting up his own business developing Propriety Vertical Industry Modular Accounting Software.

"I developed customised accounting software systems for the jewellery industry in California," he said. "We worked manufacturing a wholesale, fully-integrated accounting system for jewellers and also a metal accounting system for the metal industry – for manufacturers of gold, silver and so forth. It was pretty interesting."

Going into business brought a number of responsibilities but it also provided a degree of freedom and flexibility. For starters, he was his own boss, which meant he could make time to spend on his other interests – like his tentative steps towards playing music at the relatively late age of his early-to-mid-twenties.

It was while running the business that Serj joined his first band with a number of friends from the Armenian-American community, some of whom were into metal, while others had more esoteric tastes. So while a young Daron was listening to Vince Neil yelp in and out of tunes about strippers and blow, Serj was drawing vocal inspiration from wider sources – and, crucially for the evolution of their future musical direction – the non-Western influences he had grown up with.

"I've been influenced a lot less by music than by life itself, however there are a lot of singers who have influenced me over time – almost too many to get into!" Serj told me. "I guess if I were to go back, my dad was an influence. My dad is an amazing singer and every time he sings it provokes a lot of emotion. It makes me want to cry. He sings mostly old Armenian folk songs. Maybe that's where my singing comes from."

But it wasn't Serj's distinctive voice that he was lending to this new band, who had recently settled on the name of Forever Young and jammed together in Hollywood circa 1994. Instead he played keyboards for the group. "We shared rehearsal space with another band who had [future SOAD-er] Daron as their singer. Actually, he played guitar and sang. That's how we met."

Shavarsh Odadjian was born in Yerevan, the capital city of Armenia, on April 22, 1974. His first five years were spent in the troubled country – just enough time to form a few fleeting memories of the place. When he was five years old, his parents moved to Rome for six months; at the time – the height of the Cold War – Armenia was a republic of the former Soviet Union and therefore didn't have open borders with the US, the Odadjian's preferred final destination.

Shavo's mother was a college lecturer with a Masters degree under her belt and wanted the best start for her son. As with all political regimes, the communist politics that ruled the country had dissipated into the usual systems of control with the benevolent rulers dictating to the proletariat – a far cry from the original ideals. Shavo's parents preferred the idea of meritocracy: the idea of just rewards for just actions. You take out what you put in. "When communism started off back in the day it was for the people, by the people," explained Shavo. "It wasn't a government regime but it became one. The government has a way of taking something that is righteous and smacking you with it and turning it on its head."

In short, communism was failing its citizens. The obvious action against such a system was relocation, which the Odadjians finally did when they received US citizenship in 1979 and moved to the beating, blackened heart of America's entertainment industry, Hollywood. Though historically viewed by America's right-wing as an area and industry full of decadence, communists, homosexuals etc, since the growth of the movie industry in the 1920s and 1930s the film industry had also been portraying and reflecting the idea of America as the emerging economic and political force. Furthermore the movie industry tapped into the American psyche and beamed it around the world in tandem with United State's rapid economic growth throughout the second half of the twentieth century as it rose to become the world's only true superpower. American culture played a huge part in selling the idea of the country as some sort of new Utopia available to all who invested time and effort in it – rock 'n' roll, Coca Cola, Levis, McDonald's and movies were the rewards.

Compared to Armenia, which was living in the twin shadows of recent genocide and USSR-led communism, Hollywood was a culture shock. Fortunately though, the Odadjian's were prepared. Before relocating, Shavo's mother taught her son English in preparation for their new life in America "so that I wasn't that foreigner kid moving into the neighbourhood." Along with his parents was Shavo's grandmother, who would be a strong influence in his upbringing.

The right-wing were correct about certain things – Hollywood as a place and industry *was* one of the most liberal areas in America. Compared to the conservative heartland it was practically Sodom & Gomorrah. But the notion that it was an area of great wealth was, like the American Dream itself, misleading. Sure, the film business was a self-serving industry that generated vast sums of money, but by the 1970s most of its exponents preferred to live in the safer neighbourhood of the Hollywood Hills, affluent areas such as Beverley Hills or in some of the more upmarket beach communities, away from the glare of the media and LA's hoi polloi. But the film business had done its job in propagating the notion that Hollywood was a dream factory, a place when anyone could 'make it'. As such, throughout the second half of the twentieth century it continued to become a Mecca for starlets and wannabes as well as the lost and disaffected, its promise of fame, fortune and a better life magnetically drawing people from across the continent – and indeed, the globe. Of course, the dream was a silver screen lie. For every young actress who made it, there were fifty more who didn't; fifty more waitresses to feed the very movie executives whose eyes they sought to catch. Fifty more entrants into the service industry, the dream of success rapidly fading. Hollywood was that rare place: an élite club where acceptance was everything but failure more likely. The result was an area of great wealth – Hollywood in the 1970s was a whacked-out, coke-fuelled peak of excess – but equally of poverty and struggle, a skewed microcosm of Los Angeles at large. American movies and literature are littered with such tales of glorious failure and the bulk of Hollywood's residents were essentially there to prop up the ruling rich with the hope that they might be thrown some crumbs from the big table.

"My parents always tried to protect me from the evils that Hollywood holds and that is probably why I see it as a special place," Shavo said in 2006. "Daron grew up in the same neighbourhood as me and his fondest and worst memories of all time are about Hollywood as well. Growing up there is not like growing up in any other place because you are exposed to so much shit. It definitely makes you grow up differently and *think* differently."

School for the young Shavo was a time spent forming important friendships that would last over the years to come – although not necessarily with those who he would go on to find fame with. "I have a friend called Vahe who I've known since first grade," he later recalled. "There's also Jack and Manoly who I still hang out with a lot. I might as well give them a namecheck. I can trust those guys with anything, even my girlfriend." As is common with many talented future artists, though intelligent and articulate Shavo wasn't enamoured with the rigours of study and was instead already taking his first steps to being an entertainer. "I was the joke of the class always getting sent to the headmaster's office," he laughed. "I'd draw caricatures of the teachers and show them to the rest of the class."

Shavo's earliest musical memories are of seeing the band Kiss on TV in the late 1970s. Drawing from the early glam scene instigated by the calamitous New York Dolls, Kiss styled themselves as *the* band for American teenagers, inspired by their theatrical outlandishness. They soon expanded their look into a highly lucrative merchandise mini-empire for kids to buy into and throughout the decade and on into the 1980s established themselves as more than just a band; they were a *brand* whose stock was in rock 'n' roll escapism and showmanship. And it was always rising.

"I was five when I first saw Kiss on TV, and I made my Mom let me stay up to see it," he enthused. "The funny thing was, Daron made his

Mom stay up to see the same show and he was a year younger than me."

Though music provided that much needed escape, adjusting to life in LA wasn't easy. Shavo later described the new neighbourhood in which he found himself living as "really terrible." "There was a Shakey's Pizza, a hooker motel and a strip club on my block," he says. "Isn't that great? Awesome. The best and worst of everything. And I think I learned more from the worst. It was on the border of three gangs, an Armenian gang, a gang from El Salvador and a white gang," he explained. "Since I was local no one really bothered me, but a lot of the friends I grew up with are either dead, in jail or still in the gangs. I just did what I wanted to do and I wasn't into fighting or sitting on the corner throwing [gang] signs at people. I always thought that was dumb. I was really into music and skating.

All of my friends were gang bangers and they wouldn't let me join gangs, even when I wanted to. I was impressionable and I wanted to fit in but they were like 'Oh no, you're the kid who is not supposed to join.'"

What 'the kid' was supposed to do exactly was unclear, but music and skateboarding certainly offered salvation from a young age in Hollywood. Clearly, the streets were far from paved with gold. Shavo often wondered who the ladies were who stood out on the street at 7.30am as he was being driven to school and he later claimed that his first glimpses of sex came at the age of eight when he heard noises while passing a motel room window on his skateboard and, his interest piqued, saw a hooker and her john getting it on. "It tripped me out, I saw sex, live in my face," he remembers. "I was like, 'Whoah, what is he doing? Is he killing her?'" It was his twin passions for music and skating – at which he was becoming increasingly adept – and his mother and grand-mother's watchful eyes that kept Shavo safe and grounded during his formative years. The interest in Messrs Simmons, Stanley and Co. led to Shavo getting his first guitar at the age of ten – after much begging, Shavo's mother reluctantly relented. Reluctant because she was a realist.

"I never took lessons," he later revealed. "I sat in my room and played. They thought I was gonna play it for a few months and then it would collect dust, but I still play the same guitar when I go home. My mom said she knew this was going to happen and she didn't want it to happen because artists usually live such a fucked up life and only half of one per cent of them make it," he said. "My mother was very conservative about it…she wanted me to be a doctor or a lawyer."

In the pursuit of a respectable career, Shavo was enrolled as a student at the Alex Pilibos School. Seven school years behind Serj, his path didn't cross with his band's future frontman, though he was in the year above fellow music fan and budding musician Daron Malakian.

Anyone who has a problem with ethnic diversity and the immigrant integration would be wise to consider Little Armenia as a case study. The contribution offered by this new wave of Armenians within the lifetime of System Of A Down's members has been considerable. Though street prostitution and drug deals still go on today, the community has been successful in cleaning up the area as a whole to make it a better place today. Also, its close proximity to the Los Feliz and Silverlake areas has brought a welcome knock-on effect of recent gentrification. Sharing borders with the nearby neighbourhoods of Thai Town and Virgil Village also ensured East Hollywood remains one of the most ethnically diverse areas in Los Angeles, if not the US.

Then at the age of fifteen, Shavo left the Alex Pilibos school and entered a more multi-cultural school, where being Armenian-American was much more of a rarity. "It was hard at first because you're thrown into this group of all nationalities," he remembered. "I made friends with everybody, but I wasn't part of any social group. I'm skinny so they poked fun at me, but I got over that by expressing myself with words and fists."

Shavo spent his spare hours skating, a lifestyle-defining pastime that would also lead to an interest in video-making that he would later put to good use directing some of System Of A Down's promo clips. "It's always been a passion," he said. "When I was a kid, I used to make skateboarding videos, and I would pretend to be in a band and make rock videos that I'd edit with two VCRs. So, I guess I've had it in me for a long time. Now when I hear a song, I close my eyes and see a lot of stuff happen, and I love making those visuals come to life."

The entry points of Kiss, Def Leppard and their ilk took the young Shavo into a whole other world of possibilities, a place where freakishness was an asset and the cool guys, the heroes, were not the track and field stars or the book-ish academics. Like generations before them, rock showed that through music you can be yourself – and be rewarded for it. Through his adolescence and early teen years, his tastes broadened, taking in the classic rock and metal bands that had gone before, including investigating the extreme ends of the genre ("As a teenager I used to fall asleep listening to Cannibal Corpse and Deicide", a similarly inspired Daron once commented) to listening to a lot of the big bands of the day – may of whom were right on their doorstep. "My walls were covered with pictures of metal bands – Iron Maiden, Kiss, Ozzy, Twisted Sister," said Shavo. "I had a *whole wall* dedicated to Kiss."

This was the mid-to-late 1980s when rock music fell into two categories – the pouting, strutting, other-worldly excess and decadence of the glam rock scene (though given glam had already taken place in the UK in the 1970s, and some of the newer bands were far from pretty, 'hair metal' was always a more appropriate term) whose spiritual centre was the nearby Sunset Strip. Many hair metal bands were born out of venues such as The Roxy, The Whisky, The Cathouse, but their influence and appeal spread across the US and indeed around the world.

Inspired by bands like Finnish quintet Hanoi Rocks, who mixed the style of the New York Dolls, the guitars of The Clash and the swagger of Keith Richards to great effect, as well as the recent mainstream success of records such as Def Leppard's *Pyromania* and *1984* by Van Halen, bands such as local boys Motley Crue kickstarted a scene with their 1981 debut *Too Fast For Love* that only grew in popularity and absurdity throughout the decade. Soon WASP, Quiet Riot, Fastway, Ratt, Twisted Sister, and Cinderella were filling the clubs and getting signed. And getting increasingly absurd. To far-flung rock fans in places such as the dreary British suburbs, hair metal provided a fantastical escape from the mundane as expressed by the straight-faced appropriation of spandex as a fashion item, latent lyrical misogyny, drugs and *massive* primped-and-ruffled hair with ozone-damaging levels of hairspray. For a while it seemed like the ailing state of the earth's ozone layer was solely down to these self-important Sunset cliques who to the rest of the world were clearly having the time of their lives in the playground of LA. 1980s glam rock was a time when rock stars had to look the business; as is evident in much of the recorded output of the time, the music was merely a secondary concern. As the 1980s progressed, more bands emerged from the scene to varying levels of success – Poison, Warrant, Dokken and kings of the Strip, Guns N' Roses.

The antithesis of the hairspray rockers were the true metal bands, raised on a diet of British bands like Black Sabbath, Iron Maiden and Motorhead, but also inspired by the harsher, more underground sounds of bands such as black metal founding-fathers Venom, whose early works inspired a new generation of scowling bands playing brutal music designed to shock the senses and offend sensibilities: Celtic Frost, Slayer, Testament, Metallica and Morbid Angel were just some of the bands helping turn metal into thrash, and its many sub-genres (black, death, doom etc).

With hair metal on his doorstep in Hollywood, it wasn't long before a thirteen-year-old Shavo's path crossed with the next best thing to his formative heroes Kiss – Motley Crue. "They did their videotaping for [single] 'Girls Girls Girls' right across from where we lived," he remembers. "My Mom and I were in the parking lot there, at the supermarket across from the club. My Mom says 'That guy next to us looks like the guy on your wall.' I looked, and it was Nikki Sixx and I was starstruck. I went home, grabbed my *Too Fast For Love* album and I wanted him to sign it. Nikki and Tommy [Lee, drummer] saw me and called me over. They all signed it, and Nikki asked if I'd heard 'Girls Girls Girls' which was their new song. He told me to go inside, but I was too young, so he told the bouncer that I was family and to let me in!"

Growing up in and around Hollywood presented a number of contradictions that would inform so much of System Of A Down's later work. As we know, on the one hand was the fake glamour of the film and rock industry always close by but yet somehow unobtainable except to the élite few; on the other, the stark reality of the poverty that defined large parts of the area. Living in close proximity to both a world of wealth and Hollywood's forgotten underclass – the likes of which have been best documented in the gutter tales of local author Charles Bukowski – would certainly raise questions within enquiring minds. If Hollywood is the zenith of the American Dream, that area which attracts a nation's worth of budding screen stars out to make their mark, then it was also home to the American nightmare. It was where people scraped by holding down two or three jobs, where immigrants formed their own communities for self-preservation, where the false promise of wealth and comfort and stability for all-comers was tantalisingly just out of reach.

"They were weird areas that I wouldn't walk through now because they're not too safe," Shavo said of the neighbourhoods he and Daron Malakian grew up in. "When I was living there I wasn't scared at all, but

I know there's a lot of shit goes on because every time I drive by there's something going on. It's got cleaner, it's got dirtier. It's like a rollercoaster. I always drive through my old neighbourhood just to get the vibe. There were helicopters outside every night and you'd hear gunshots."

The neighbourhood may have been far from salubrious – how can it not be when Nikki Sixx is loitering nearby? – but Shavo came from a good family, was intelligent and naturally creative. At the age of seventeen and inspired by the LA metal scene, Shavo joined his first band playing guitar in an outfit called Polaris, named after a Megadeth song. "It was *metal* metal," recalls Shavo. "*Kill 'Em All*, Metallica metal. We covered Sepultura and stuff like that." It was around about this period that Shavo became the first of the future band members to do something *bona fide* rock 'n' roll when, at the age of eighteen, he appeared as an extra in a video for AC/DC's 1993 single 'Big Gun'. Amazingly, he appeared alongside Austrian beefcake actor and future right-wing Governor of California Arnold Schwarzenegger, whose movie *Last Action Hero* featured the song. Look carefully and you can briefly see the young Shavo sporting not only a backwards baseball cap but hair too. "You see me full-on," Shavo proudly remembered. "It just happened where Arnold Schwarzenegger came next to me. It was bad lighting, because they had more light on me than they did Arnold. And I'm watching it going, 'Whoa, dude – I'm on TV!' It was really strange."

Higher education beckoned however and Shavo went to college for three years to study, with a view to becoming either a psychologist or an architect. By this point though, his interest in music had expanded into DJ-ing at rave parties, playing a mix of metal, techno and hip-hop under the name DJ Tactic. He also continued to play guitar in a couple of other bands. Towards the end of his college days, at the age of 21, Shavo smoked marijuana for the first time. Weed and music have always made for complementary bed fellows and as former school mate Daron Malakian was discovering at the same time, he developed something of a taste for it.

Away from the legalities of marijuana or the moral stance taken by anti-drugs campaigners, the drugs-in-art debate has been one that has raged for decades. Many would argue that marijuana has no positive effect – and it certainly can have a negative side effect if abused – but the millions of people around the world who smoke it every day may argue otherwise, including those who reason that it heightens senses and perception and therefore helps achieve a state of clarity or a level of concentration that is conducive to the production of great art. One only has to consider the various artistic works created under the influence of drugs to see that this argument holds some weight – whether the literature of Baudelaire or Kerouac and the Beat generation, the music of Bob Dylan, The Beatles, Bob Marley, The Clash (and ten thousand other bands besides), the comedy of Bill Hicks … the list goes on. Think of the influence of weed on jazz, reggae, punk, hip-hop.

We can now add System Of A Down to that list for the band are voracious smokers – certainly Shavo and Daron – whose music had surely been shaped in some way by the amount of sticky green stuff they have smoked over the years.

"It was always around me and marijuana slows down your thinking process if you do it when you're young," Shavo said during an interview around the time of the band's first album. "When you reach a certain mental level you can experiment with it, have fun with it. It's very nice for relaxing, and I like playing music when I'm high – not onstage though. Daron writes a lot of the music and he smokes weed. And the tracks I wrote were done when I was smoking. I smoke a little, grab a guitar and start playing without thinking, and it turns out to be something. I tape it, sleep on it, then come back to it."

But that was all still to come, for the members of System Of A Down had not yet started to play together. That would soon change when the various graduates of Alex Pilibos school found themselves in the same musical circles. What they needed was a genius professor – someone with that extra spark – to bring them together musically. Enter former school mate Daron Malakian.

"As a child, I had a lot of dark, dark moments," Daron Malakian told *Rolling Stone* journalist Neil Strauss in 2002. "I had to be an adult very quick. I've done acid once in my life, and I watched *The Exorcist,* and everyone in the room with me was freaking out. I was like, 'I know how to handle this, because I've been in hell before…'"

The 'hell' the guitarist and youngest member of System Of A Down was aware was of the same strange world that is modern America – specifically Hollywood – which his band mates and their families were greeted with when relocating there. A world that has the best and worst of everything; a spend–happy culture ruled by prescription drugs, TV adverts, lame 1980s pop music, fast food, gas-guzzling automobiles, racism from all angles, B-movie stars reinvented as right-wing leaders and the ultimate hollow promise of freedom through purchase power. Tellingly, of the four future SOAD members, it was only Daron who was born in the US after his artist parents moved from Armenia to LA, settling in Hollywood in 1974. A year later they had their only child on July 18.

Daron's parents were both artistically-inclined, his father Vartan a prolific painter and his mother a keen sculptor. Growing up, he was surrounded by art and spent a lot of time being taken to museums and exhibitions. "My biggest inspiration is my father," he later said. "He's why I am what I am. He's my biggest mentor and teacher."

Money was quite short in the Malakian household. Home was a one-bedroom apartment in one of Hollywood's "ghetto neighbourhoods" for the first thirteen years of Daron's life, eventually saving enough money to buy a house in which their son had his own bedroom for the first time.

A combination of being an only child and living in close confines, much of Daron's formative years were spent in his own imagination. "Although my two cousins were like my best friends, I was an only child. I had my toys, but I was pretty much alone. But that was cool because I write a lot of music for this band alone. I'm used to it."

Daron claims to have started collecting records at the age of four – a young start by anyone's standards. As mentioned, the first band to truly ignite the flame of his fertile mind was the consummate showmanship of Kiss.

"Seeing Kiss posters in my cousin's bedroom aged about four years old weirded me out, but I was also really attracted to them," he remembers. "When me and Shavo first saw Kiss we both said 'We wanna do that!' Later we saw each other at school and said 'Hey, you look cool' and 'Damn, you play good bass and you're a pretty good guitarist!'"

Music was Daron's first love, but there was the small matter of education to endure in the meantime. Already seduced by the glamour and fantastical allure of music, the rigidity of the education system paled by comparison and the creative young Daron reacted by rebelling.

"All my teachers would call me Damien, from *The Omen* movies," he laughs. "Thinking about it, that was my nickname at school – that's what my teachers called me anyway. I really fucked around a lot at school. I always wanted to be in a band so I never considered school work to be very important." Daron's family moved to Glendale when he was 11 and he went to Roosevelt Middle School, then the Rose and Alex Pilibos School, then Glendale High School – former home to that none-more-American icon Marion Morrison, better known as John Wayne. It was also around this time that he began to devour music after his mother bought him his first record, a copy of Def Leppard's *Pyromania*, first released in 1983. From there his 'studies' continued…

"I was a bad student," Daron confessed during an interview on the website of his *alma mater*, Glendale High. "I wouldn't want anyone to follow my example. I cut class and when I did go to class I didn't pay much attention. I didn't take it as seriously as I now know I should have. What I've learned is that if a student doesn't go to class or doesn't do anything in school, that's probably the pattern they're going to continue later on in life, and then where will they be? But I always had a plan, a strategy. I just knew school wasn't for me."

As puberty and metal combined, Daron's schooling suffered. While his school mates were busying themselves with extra-curricular activities of buying up the latest MC Hammer tunes, by the age of 15 Daron was skipping most activities (including, later, his High School Prom – though he did turn up to get his picture taken for the Yearbook because "you gotta leave your mark somehow"), instead pursuing his own education, which primarily involved playing guitar and drums and, as with Shavo, fighting for survival on the local streets, an area defined by the many street gangs that grew out of the poorer neighbourhoods and Hispanic barrios. While notorious hardcore gangs like the Crips ruled East LA, over in Hollywood smaller, less organised groups of streetwise kids banded together for self-preservation. Safety in numbers. For a teenager it was a fiercely territorial time defined by race and who you knew. For Daron – always small for his age, but with hormones raging – it was a case of fight or flight and confrontations inevitably arose. Mainly though it was timeless, teenage territorial nonsense that most grow out of.

"I used to pick on people twice my height," he told *Kerrang!* in 1998. "I stood up for my friends a lot and people would back down just from attitude. I came from a pretty rough background so I wouldn't take shit. I had friends that were gang members, so it made me open my eyes. I've had enough knives and crowbars pulled on me, but I try to avoid stuff like that now. It's just better to make friends than act like a complete jerk. And we would [act like jerks] – we'd wait for someone to do something and then we'd jump 'em."

One of Daron's friends at the time was future System Of A Down drum tech Sako Karaian, who would later be immortalized in their debut single 'Sugar'. "I went through a lot of shit with him…" Daron later said, cryptically. Far from purely being a put-upon victim though, Daron was always quick to stand his ground. "In high school there was a rumour that this guy was talking shit about me and my friends so I just went up to him and hit him," he recalled. "He fell on the floor and I started smacking his head into the concrete. That's probably the worst thing I've done to anybody. He actually moved out of the city after that. I had some pretty crazy moments in school when it came to that sort of thing. We used to get into fights and start a lot of shit, but I'm a much nicer guy now than I was before all this [the band] happened. After a couple of my friends got shot … I went to three funerals in high school and one of my friends went blind."

The Armenian-American community was not without its troubles too. As with most areas of LA there was the gang scene to offer protection on the streets and, though tight-knit, Daron would later lament the fact that amongst sub-cultures and America as a whole, separation was often as likely as integration.

"There are a lot of different cultures in America, but I wish they'd combine instead of being so separate," said Daron in 1998. "People don't react here. The problem is, we've never been bombed. It takes things like that to bring people together. Every time there's an earthquake in LA, everyone comes together, but apart from that I've never talked to my neighbours at all. Humans beings are becoming real sad …"

Two other facts that united Daron and Shavo were that they were close to their grandmothers, both of whom featured heavily in their upbringing. Equally, both suffered when they passed away. "I totally lost faith in everything," Shavo is on record on the band's official website as saying. "I was pissed. I used to pray every night and I haven't ever since. Not once. It doesn't mean I don't believe in God any more, but I believe in *my* god." (for more see: *www.systemofadown.com*)

"A lot of fighting," was Daron's explanation as to how he handled his loss as a teenager. "I kicked a lot of people's fuckin' asses. I realized that

I had a lot of aggression in me. I've had to learn to keep it in check. If someone turns around to look at my chick, I want to fucking kill them. If someone fucks with my homeboys, I want to fucking kill them. I've got to keep it in check now."

For an intelligent guy with a growing knowledge of music – other particular long-standing favourites now included the likes of Dire Straits and Christopher Cross – and a burgeoning ability at playing both drums and guitar, Daron was never destined for a full-time life on the mean streets. Though he later claimed to have turned up to school drunk on a number of occasions, by the age of 17 he was calming down – or at least directing his energy towards more fruitful pursuits.

"The fighting went beyond school fighting and got more serious, so I didn't wanna be involved in anything like that," said Daron. "I've never been a fan of fighting. I get nervous if I know I'm about to fight and I don't like that feeling. Hopefully as life goes on I'll never fight again. If you have any intelligence you realize that what you're doing is wrong but that was part of life and it helped me be who I am now. I put all that energy or anger or whatever it is into music."

Despite enjoying his science class, in his junior year Daron was summoned into the principal's office for a stern talking to. "When I got there these very concerned looking adults sat me down and asked me what I wanted to do with my life because I was barely passing any of my classes," Daron remembered. "It was like in the Twisted Sister video – I told them 'I wanna rock!' They looked at all my report cards and said, 'but you've never taken any music classes here,' and I said, 'I teach myself,' and they just shook their heads ... they didn't understand."

Though perfectly placed in the heart of Hollywood to catch any up-and-coming bands, Daron's first exposure to live music came at the age of thirteen when he went to see arena-filling metal in all its glory. With their 1988 album *...And Justice For All* Bay Area quartet Metallica had established themselves as the new leaders of thrash and metal. Though the album suffered from poor production and the band neglected to play many of the songs live – approaching ten minutes in length they were deemed too long – it was nevertheless a milestone record in the genre, and clearly a vast stylistic departure from reigning rock bands like Motley Crue and Poison – the very artists Daron could see hanging around the Strip on any given day. For the show, Metallica had a little known up-and-coming fellow San Franciscan band called Faith No More opening for them. It was, to Metallica's credit, one of the first times a resolutely heavy metal act had taken a band out with them who were doing something quite different within this genre – in Faith No More's case playing weird dark pop songs injected with funk bass, atmospheric post-punk keyboards and Mike Patton's unique (and later to be proven highly influential) vocals.

Formed in 1981, though still very much an underground band by the end of the 1980s Faith No More had already been through their share of trials and tribulations, a working relationship informed by their conflicting personalities (they had a metal fiend on guitar, a gay keyboardist, not to mention an early incarnation also featuring Courtney Love). After making two challenging rock records with original frontman Chuck Mosely, the singer was replaced by the unknown Patton (Mosely later resurfaced briefly fronting the equally as influential DC hardcore icons Bad Brains – another influence on System Of A Down), who provided the much-needed injection of youth and personality that would make them one of the most important rock bands of the 1990s.

"Nobody really knew who Faith No More were and it was still a very closed-minded time in music, and mixing rap with rock was not necessarily accepted at that point," Daron told me. "So when Mike Patton came out and started rapping it did not sit well in front of 13,000 Metallica fans. At that time, Metallica hadn't put out their ballads and were very much still on the *...And Justice For All* tip, so the fans were pretty hard on them."

It's significant that Daron's first show was seeing an extreme-sounding metal band who had managed to sell millions of albums *and* a rising act unafraid to risk ridicule in front of a relatively conservative rock crowd. Something clearly stuck with the young Daron that night in December 1988 for when his own band would release their debut album a decade later they would manage to combine the facets displayed by both bands – widespread commercial success with a wilfully uncompromising musical stance.

Interestingly, independently of his future band mates, Faith No More also had an impact on Serj. In fact, above all else, it was they who turned him onto rock music at a time when a career as a heavy metal front man was looking the likeliest of career options.

"They were probably the first rock band I heard," he said in *Spin*. "They're what made me go back and listen to Slayer and Metallica. *Angel Dust* [1992] wasn't as commercially viable as [Patton's 1989 debut and breakthrough album] *The Real Thing*, but I think it's probably their best album. I'm a huge fan of Mike Patton. I first met him when we toured with Mr Bungle in 2000. The guy would never do any vocal warm-ups, and would instead eat, like, a full steak dinner right before the show and then just go straight onstage!"

It wasn't all street fights and teenage drinking for Daron. Endless hours spent playing along in his bedroom to the greats and not-so-greats was turning him into an accomplished and inventive player. At the age of sixteen he formed his first band, Snowblind ("And we weren't even a Black Sabbath cover band!").

Just as Nirvana was giving hard rock a long-overdue overhaul, Daron played his first ever live show, at the Night Rock Café in LA. Though Snowblind's career was short-lived, Daron was already sold on the emotive powers of music — music as an outlook, music as a saving grace.

"When I used to hang around with a group of tough guys I would take my acoustic guitar to parties and sing songs that I'd written. Even though they were often ballads, some of the tough dudes would end up crying. Writing songs that could touch people made me believe I could do anything with my music."

Though clearly in love with rock music that placed the guitar at the centre point, Daron was already broadening his musical scope and diversifying his burgeoning talents, something which would serve him and his band well in late life. When heard for the first time, Malakian's guitar sound on *System Of A Down* almost sounds like it was played with the approach of a drummer — all syncopated rhythms, clipped riffs and strange flourishes to fill the gaps.

"I'm really not that focused on the guitar exclusively," he told me in 2005. "I play five different instruments, so I'm inspired by music as a whole, art and my dad, who has been in front of me my whole life as an artist. That all inspired me, as opposed to any one guitarist. A guitar is a great tool to write songs, but I don't care whether those songs are written on a guitar, behind a keyboard or a drum kit. So long as songs come out is all that matters, rather than, you know, great guitar solos of the past or whatever."

Daron graduated high school but with qualifications that were not going to set academia alight. "I don't regret shit, I don't feel like a dumb dude," he reflected years later to *Metal Hammer*'s Amelia Daarke. "Although this isn't a great message to send out, I'm more successful than all my friends that graduated from high school. If you've got the character and you try hard enough you'll always get what you want."

After finishing college and during the very earliest days of the band that would evolve into System Of A Down, Shavo held a number of jobs, most notably selling kebabs, delivering flowers ("That was cool – I could get stoned all day") and as a bank teller. Though earning a steady income to subsidise his musical interests, Shavo's entry into the working world merely served to alert him that the nine-to-five 'Working for The Man' life was not for him; a shared trait amongst the members of the band, save perhaps for Serj, who worked for himself.

"I actually went through a bank robbery," said Shavo. "While working as a teller, I got robbed at gunpoint. These guys came in and before we knew it, they were on our side of the counter, holding guns to our heads. I was the only guy working there so they put most of their attention on me. It was crazy. It all happened so fast, I didn't have time to think. They told me to get down, so I got down and they took off with all the money. They made a lot of noise and scared everyone, and it freaked me out for a while. I had thought that I might die. And I kept thinking 'Is this is how it's gonna be? This sucks!'"

Daron's working career meanwhile was somewhat chequered and even less assured than that of Shavo, who had at least had the necessary skills and college degree to hold down a job at a bank – even if his life was on the line.

"Look at me – who would hire me?" chuckled Daron in 2003. "The only jobs I could get were in, like, telemarketing or places where I'd be hidden away from public view. I delivered jungle jumps [bouncy castles] for kids once. And I sold carpet cleaner over the phone for a week or two. I just couldn't hold down a job… I know it really frightened my parents."

"Being a musician is all I've ever dreamed of being and playing the guitar or drums is all I've ever done. I don't have a plan B. I don't do anything else. I can't repair a car. I can't fix a leaky faucet. I couldn't even build a box when I was in wood shop there. But I can write you a song. I realized early on that I could do something not many people could do.

No one taught me how to do it – I just did it."

Fortunately, they had other things on the go, creative outlets to distract from the potential horror of a lifetime serving someone else just to make a wage to survive; once again, the American nightmare in full effect.

Music provided that escape route.

Central to the earliest incarnation of System Of A Down was the Armenian community and various alumni of the Rose And Alex Pilibos school of East Hollywood. All tinkering about individually with ideas and instruments, a pool of aspiring musicians came together circa 1993 via mutual acquaintances to jam, most of it centred around the Nightingale Studios, a small hive of musical activity in Burbank, twenty minutes north of Hollywood.

Though former school mates, it took a reintroduction for Serj and Shavo to pair off and begin practising together. Serj's band Forever Young was fizzling out, though they had never been a serious proposition anyway, more of a communal gathering.

During these tentative early days Odadjian switched from bass to guitar and back again as he tried to decide which instrument to devote himself to. "The guys there would tease me, since I was always changing my mind: 'Hey, Shavo, you gonna play the triangle in your new band?!'"

The guys in question included other former school mates such as another budding bassist Dave Hagopyan and a talented drummer, Andy Khachaturian, both of whom had designs on playing music full time. It was Hagopyan who was the most pro-active in moving things up a level. When he announced that he was forming a proper band, one of the first to pay him a visit was Daron Malakian, keen to put his use of bedroom noodling along to his favourite glam and thrash bands to good use. It was either that or get a job. Sporting long flowing locks and wide, wandering eyes, the guitarist also revealed that he could sing, capable of replicating the guttural growl of vocalists like Slayer's Tom Araya or harmonising in a strangely affecting and distinctive high-pitch.

"When Daron started to play guitar, as well as sing, Dave asked me what I thought," says Shavo. "I said, 'Dude, get rid of your other guitarist!' Daron was really good." Daron and Dave soon began playing together, along with a drummer named Domingo – affectionately known as 'Dingo' on occasions.

Another person coming into his own was Serj, until then pegged as something of a business whiz, decent keyboard player and all-round budding Zen-master. But not a singer. At some point though the singer, who had been writing poetry throughout his teenage years and already in his mid-twenties had a worldlier outlook than some of his younger more excitable friends, stepped up to the mic. He had always written lyrics in the form of poems and grew up listening to his father sing; now he made the leap himself.

It quickly became apparent to those who spent their nights hanging out at the Nightingale Studios that Serj had a unique voice. Growing up on Armenian folk music had given him the ability to fill his voice with the type of emotion that immediately provided a connection to the various musicians' Armenian cultural heritage, yet at the same time he could also sing in the abrasive bark synonymous with thrash and hardcore-leaning punk bands. Clearly, Serj had more to offer than merely being keyboard player; he could sing and scream and shout and a whole lot more. Though his bark has a prophetic, pulpit-bashing quality that could strip paint at ten paces, it was always one of a unique cadence for metal, possessing an underlying warmth that seemed to encapsulate the timeless humanitarian qualities that Serj himself tried to live his life in accordance with.

As brutal as Slayer's Tom Araya, as apoplectically expressive as Jello Biafra and as melodious and spiritual as Cat Stevens, it was a rare and powerful asset. "I'm not angry," Serj would tell *Rolling Stone*. "Just because you raise your voice does not mean it's anger. But earlier in the band's career there was definitely more true anger coming through. I had a lot of feelings that I had to work with."

With Daron deciding to concentrate solely on his guitar playing, Dave Hagopyan invited Serj to join him, Daron and Domingo. The bassist christened this latest musical endeavour Soil and a band was born.

They began writing and honing a set of songs at Nightingale. Though the band was destined to be short-lived, it was during 1994-1995 that the true foundations for System Of A Down were laid in something of a meeting of creative minds. Musically, Soil were challenging from the start, mixing a love of metal and art-rock bands with the Armenian folk element simmering somewhere underneath.

Arguably the coolest of them all, Shavo offered to manage this fledging project that his friends had put together. His first job was securing them a gig, which he did, booking them a show at the Café

Club Fais Do-Do on West Adams Boulevard in the mid-city area between Culver City and downtown LA. Still there today, it seemed like the perfect venue for this strange mix of personalities united by musical ambition and Armenian heritage to play, described as it is as "a gumbo of eclectic music and diverse people coming together to build a stronger community by offering exposure to new cultures, foods, sounds, and philosophies" (in the 1960s it was also a hangout of legendary musicians such as Sam Cooke, Billy Preston and John Coltrane).

The venue also goes down in history for another reason – it was the place that housed the one and only Soil show. Though the low-key gig went well enough and the band concocted an interesting combination of musical ingredients, a clash of personalities – the textbook rock 'n' roll 'creative tensions' – prevented them from taking things further. We could romanticise things, but really Soil were just one more LA band of wannabes falling at the first hurdle. On one side were Daron and Serj, two very different people but yet both ambitious, talented and keen to express themselves in as original way as possible; on the other Domingo and Dave Hagopyan who both saw little future in Soil. The band parted ways.

"Daron came to me and said 'I've got good news and bad news,'" said Shavo. "'We want you for the band. Unfortunately we don't have a drummer anymore.' I was still friends with Dave, so it was a little uncomfortable taking his place."

Chapter 2: Lost In Hollywood

The year 1995. Democrat Bill Clinton was finally US President after years of Republican ruling, OJ Simpson was acquitted of a double murder in the trial of the century and a band called Soil was looking for a drummer.

In the mid-1990s American rock was going through something of a fallow period. The grunge scene that began with so much promise in or around Seattle at the dawn of the 1990s had been diluted down to a new wave of angst-ridden rock bands with only the strongest of the old guard surviving and diversifying into rock pomposity, smacked-out introspection or just good old radio-friendly rock – bands like Smashing Pumpkins, Alice in Chains and Foo Fighters, who released some of the biggest rock albums of the year. Below them were a plethora of tedious bands cashing in on the last traces of grunge all with little or nothing to do with the garage punk promise made by the likes of Nirvana, Tad or Mudhoney. Now it was all about hoarse Kurt-like vocals and wearing your pain on your sleeve. In Wal-Mart usually.

The more challenging albums of the year that did well in the mainstream seemed to be coming from Europe – Bjork, Tricky, Radiohead, Portishead, The Aphex Twin – while the UK rock scene was waving its own dusty flag for revisionist bands like Blur and Oasis. All well and good, but highly parochial in their outlook and therefore never destined to do hugely well Stateside.

The world of major label alternative rock – the place we look to for epoch-making icons – wasn't in a healthy state either. After an awesome debut, Rage Against The Machine was already floundering amid much acrimony while attempting to write a second album, Faith No More had just released their below-par *King For A Day...* album, Metallica were increasingly losing sight of why people liked them and had failed to release a record in five years, Green Day were huge but not exactly breaking down boundaries and Red Hot Chili Peppers released their worst album with *One Hot Minute,* ironically their one album with Dave Navarro from Jane's Addiction – the last freakishly brilliant band to burst forth from the City of Angels.

Even metal – that one genre that up until then had seemed to be impervious to outside trends – wasn't in the best of states, its better exponents seemingly existing in their own hermetically-sealed niches – bands like Pantera, Tool and Sepultura.

The fantasy land of 1980s Sunset glam was long dead, killed off by grunge bands who made glam's wanton hedonism and endless partying almost seem a criminal offence. Even Daron's beloved Motley Crue had tried to save their skins with 1994's self-titled grunge-leaning, commercial flop. In 1995, the exciting stuff was happening elsewhere – whether in the rough and ready rap collective Wu-Tang Clan, in emerging forms like drum 'n' bass or imbedded deep in the independent rock underground best epitomised by bands like Fugazi.

On the upside, rock music was due a new movement.

One band of note to emerge and quickly achieve commercial success were Korn, from Bakersfield, California. Their self-titled debut, released the previous year, had casually gone platinum with little media exposure. Despite this success, few predicted that it was this scowling rag-tag bunch that would be leaders of such a new movement. Yet in aggressively mixing up metal, rap and some of funk rock's dynamics and singing about subjects their fans could relate to – the turmoil of adolescence, basically – they created a fresh outlet for musical catharsis, a new hybrid sound that broadened metal's scope without diluting its power or resonance. Korn became huge quickly and the effects were felt right across California where new bands were formed by teenagers picking up guitars for the first time while some up-and-coming bands were reconsidering their position.

In Hollywood in the same year things were finally coming together. There was no sudden event, major realisation or significant turning point but rather, as is so often the way, things just fell together over time. Friendships had been forged, others had been broken and a wide pool of people had been gradually distilled into a small group of individuals who felt their chemistry was compatible enough to turn this into a band, as opposed to the jam sessions or interchangeable bands who seemed to exist with a revolving door policy. In this case, a core trio remained: Serj, Shavo and Daron, still labouring under the name of Soil. The earliest version of System Of A Down was born.

"Though I started my company before the band started, I still owned and operated it when things began to get busier on the musical front," Serj told me a decade later. "I would work during the day in the thousand foot warehouse that I rented in north Hollywood. I had a little office space in there to run the company from, then a huge open air room for the band's rehearsal space. So I would work nine-to-five on business, then five-to-nine – or sometimes more like five-to-twelve! – on the band. It was a lot of fun in the warehouse space. When the band began to progress, we went from having a rehearsal space to having none at all and tended to rehearse in ad hoc rehearsal rooms or sound stages before going on tour, so it's important to have those memories of places where we became closely-knit – not just playing music but also hanging out and enjoying each other."

Hanging out and enjoying each other, as the singer puts it, was key to the development of the band. If a group of musicians can't get on when they're a new, young band with no pressures other than those that are self-imposed, then it's unlikely things are going to be any easier when things get hectic – when there are journalists waiting to be appeased, lawyers to be paid, deals to be brokered and arenas full of fans waiting to be entertained. Which is precisely why bands that are born out of friendships are more likely to survive than those born out of classified ads in the back of *The LA Weekly, Village Voice* or *NME*. Not always, of course, but with a solid foundation and any differences ironed out early on, a band has so much greater chance of achieving success if their internal relationships are water-tight and insecurities addressed away from the public eye. Given that their frontman was twenty-eight, a relatively mature age to embark on the slow process of climbing the hierarchical ladder of the music business, the nascent Soil no doubt benefited from a more mature approach than some of their LA contemporaries.

"It was all progressive, the ways the things slowly developed," says Serj. "We used to have little parties for friends who would come over, and we'd all hang out and make music." Whether deliberate or not, such considerations rose to prominence during the early days of the band as they dedicated themselves to channelling their personalities and energy into one common musical voice that played to its individual strengths. For example, Shavo's switch from part-time guitarist to full-time bassist was as much out of practical necessity as anything.

"Bass players are funny because it is hard to find one who doesn't show off but still doesn't suck," says Shavo. "So a lot of bassists have this complex about not being guitarists, but I don't mind. So I thought

I would play bass and do what I thought an ideal bass player should do."

Though the members of the fledgling band later claimed never to have heard Korn's output until after they had got signed and were making their own debut some four years after the Bakersfield band's, an aesthetic and sonic change was clearly in the air – not least in and around LA where a new breed of bands unafraid to incorporate rap into their music or include DJs in their ranks were mobilising themselves and making tentative trips to the Strip for their first shows.

The new hang out was on North Hollywood's Lankershim Boulevard and provided a perfect HQ for Soil. They spent as much time there as possible, customising the space to suit their creative needs, covering the walls with paint splattering and making its hard floors comfortable to sleep on, as they often did. "We had a lot of good times in that place," says Shavo. "We'd stay there every night and just hang out, even if there wasn't a rehearsal. We'd talk about what we were going to do next."

Though the band already existed in the minds of its creators and, thanks to Serj and Daron's unique styles, there were suggestions of an interesting sound emerging, they could do nothing without that one vital missing component for a rock band: a drummer.

Fortunately LA is full of aspiring drummers but unfortunately most of them either failed to grasp Soil's sounds and ideas or didn't fit in, personality-wise. The trio auditioned a number of players, watching as a succession of wannabes passed through. Growing frustrated and keen to push things forward, the band decided to recruit their friend Andy Khachaturian. He made perfect sense – they already knew him, he was a decent drummer and, in a move of perfect, if accidental, symmetry, he was also Armenian-America.

★

"We weren't as focused on songs then," Daron would comment years later, of the Soil days. "It was all prog-rock and musical masturbation, but it was the root of the System sound. A change came into my life when I started listening to The Beatles and Bowie, and I realised that was something I wanted to do – write *song* songs."

So after the less than triumphant debut Soil show, the band decided upon a new approach to songwriting, one that would retain the heaviness and quirk factor, but also incorporating a poppier element.

Of course, it was pop music unlike any that had gone before but it was something of an epiphany that would help distance the band from their contemporaries and turn them into an international band. Plus, they were further exploring Armenian music and finding ways to incorporate it into the new songs, which they were writing at an impressive pace.

To mark their new line-up the band decided to re-name themselves. Various monikers were toyed with before they settled on Victims Of A Down, the name of a poem that Daron had recently written. After some debate Shavo reasoned that 'Victims' was too harsh a word so they replaced it with the all-encompassing 'System' to come up with a name that said a little more about the band and their beliefs.

"'System' was chosen as a better, stronger word, and it makes it into a 'whole'," commented Serj. "Instead of people in particular, it's the society." "And now our album will be under the 'S' section," reasoned Malakian. "Next to Slayer!"

System Of A Down. Ambiguous. Cryptic. Anti-establishment. A system of oppression. Negativity. It was also nonsensical and the band would forever find themselves having to repeat themselves or explain the meaning, but they stuck with it. It was as good a name as any. And it was better than Soil.

Besides, there were more important things to think about – like playing shows, something that Shavo as acting manager had set about organising. "We were one out of about five thousand bands and we were the band without a demo because we couldn't afford one," recalls the bassist. "When I was at work I would be making telephone calls to the rock scene but they all punked me around and hung up on me. The first motherfucker to hang up on me ended being our tour manager. He finally got fed up of me calling him fifty times a week and saying 'Hey, give us a show, we'll pack it,', and he caved in and gave us a show."

The first show that Shavo booked them was at The Roxy on Sunset, a popular haunt for up-and-coming as well as established LA bands. A mainstay of the Sunset Strip scene since the early 1970s, The Roxy was the first club to host the opening US run of *The Rocky Horror Picture Show*, was the favoured hang-out of the likes of John Lennon and Keith Moon and had hosted pretty much every up and coming LA rock band in the interim. The venue was located in West Hollywood at the heart of the Strip, with a small club upstairs called On The Rox where bands and their guests could enjoy celebratory drinks afterwards. That the band had already been recommended to the venue's booking agent by another new band on the circuit, Santa Monica-based Snot, certainly helped.

As with most newcomers, System Of A Down were booked to play their debut show on the agreement that they would be allocated tickets to sell themselves and receive a cut of the profits, a standard practice that ensures bands put in some effort to bring a crowd. If they don't, they won't get booked again. Fortunately, thanks to their open house policy at the warehouse, a widespread network of friends keen to support their musical mates and the band's proactive approach to self-publicity – Shavo and Daron plastered posters for their early shows everywhere – they more than exceeded the venue's expectation for a band playing their debut show, despite having no demo tape and appearing on a bill of ska bands on a Sunday night. The date for the band's auspicious debut was May 28, 1995 and System arrived with 175 friends in tow.

"What they didn't know was that we would have friends come over to the rehearsal space and watch us play," remembers Shavo. "So when we first played they all came and the venue owners tripped out. When we went on stage chaos broke out, there were people hanging from the rafters, there was a pit. My Dad was there filming it."

System Of A Down were already an engaging prospect, Shavo and Andy gelling as a rhythmic section, Daron a confident guitarist with an instantly recognisable sound and Serj a compelling and unconventional front man. Plus, they looked *mad as fuck*. For their first show Andy painted himself head-to-toe in white, Serj was sporting a huge beard and wild corkscrew afro, Daron had his hair in braids and was wearing an Adidas tracksuit (which suggested they might have been more influenced by Korn than they later let on) and a shirtless Shavo had the posture and physique of a praying mantis. But one with a well-groomed chin beard and knee-high tube socks, obviously.

The Roxy was rammed – no mean feat for a band who had never actually played before. A complete rarity, in fact. After a sweaty and intense forty minutes, excitable well-wishers poured into the dressing room to hang out with the band and pass on their congratulations. Drinks were drunk and joints smoked. For a new group with a questionable name and a look and sound at odds with the trends of the day, things were going rather swimmingly… "After that it was very easy to get shows," says Shavo. "No one asked us for a demo, no one asked us to sell tickets, they just booked us."

Nevertheless it was during the first half of 1995 that the quartet made their first foray into a recording studio as System Of A Down. With two songs with one word titles that would become characteristic of their first album, their first demo tape was believed to feature two songs, 'Toast' and 'Flake'. As these recordings weren't circulated, little is known of them, and the fact that the band hit the studio again shortly afterwards suggests they were little more than rudimentary efforts from a band finding their feet. The next recording was of a ferocious new song entitled 'Multiply', also dated early 1995. Though the playing was highly promising it was another rough effort let down by relatively poor production and a sub-standard snare drum sound; quite the opposite of the drum sound they have today. The song was good though and it was put aside to be later re-recorded and renamed 'X' and released six years later on the band's breakthrough second album *Toxicity*. Again, beyond their initial circle of friends, few copies of these tapes made it into the public domain. These recordings were as much about putting in the groundwork and documenting the new songs the band were writing rather than sending them out as promotional devices. In fact, a number of the new tracks committed to tape during this fertile early period would resurface in various guises over the years to come – 'Roulette', '36' and live favourite 'P.I.G.' – later re-titled 'Mr. Jack' – would be re-recorded during 2000 and 2001 and finally be available on *Steal This Album!*, some seven years after their creation.

Meanwhile, spurred on by the success of their early shows, System began booking more gigs and expanding on their already formidable following. Anthony Belanger was a booker at hip Hollywood club Dragonfly, who helped launch the career of LA bands such as Sugar and Sublime. As he later told *Kerrang!* writer Josh Sindell, rarely had he been so impressed by an unknown band.

"I got a tape of them from the guys in Snot and everybody was saying 'You gotta book these guys!'" said Belanger. "We were like, 'Okay, we'll give them a try.' As soon as we saw them, we knew. We were just totally blown away."

"The second show we sold the place out – and we kept on selling it out," Serj explained. "But we also played a bunch of gigs with other bands, afternoon slots or whatever, but generally our own shows started selling out pretty quickly, which is pretty rare for a new band. So it was progressive, really – for ten years. We never went straight from the warehouse to the arena – we played the small punk clubs, the theatres, the amphitheatres, the arenas, the big festivals. In that order."

It was round about this time that Shavo relinquished the management reins and the band met someone who would grow to be a fifth member, new manager David Benveniste, known to his friends simply as Beno. Benveniste was a young budding manager in his early twenties with some experience managing bands but who was actively looking around for a new project to be involved in. "I came across them because a good friend of mine had seen them at a show and called me up and said 'You gotta come to this rehearsal space to see this band,'" Benveniste told me during an interview for an article about the early days of System Of A Down. "So I went in there, I was thoroughly dumbfounded by what I saw. I was confused, I was excited, I was blown away. And after that I just started hanging around. After a few rehearsals I went to the next live show and that was it for me…"

What the young manager saw at those early shows in 1995 was the band he was looking for, a unique proposition who looked, sounded and spoke like none of their contemporaries. A band to shake up rock music and change lives. This at a time when the band were still a complete oddity and not an eminently 'sellable' act in the traditional sense.

"There's a strong ethnic energy to the band, which comes out in their music and also the way they speak because they're very educated people," explains Beno. "When I started to hang out with them I was very open and honest with my feelings about how much I loved the band but I was also careful about how I was with them because they had an existing thing that was already really good. What I wanted to do was come in and support what they had started and build on top of what they were building. I wanted to inflate this slow-moving beast of a band and help figure it all out together as we went along."

Finding they had much in common, band and manager hit it off and Beno offered his services through his recently launched company, Velvet Hammer Management. The plan was a relatively simple one: the band would keep developing at their own pace, building their hometown reputation and letting the record labels come to them. Collectively they knew they had something special – too special to risk being messed up by hastily signing the wrong record deal.

With Benveniste handling their affairs, the band concentrated on playing and writing. "When I started working with System everything else just fell by the wayside," he laughs. The band's new manager supplied the support and business clout to spur the band on. He was their number one fan and set about convincing the rest of the world. Early days saw the band congregating at the small house out the back of Beno's father's residence, where the young manager lived at the time. Before shows the band would come over with their girlfriends to kill time and hang-out before hitting whichever club they were booked to play, five individuals against the world. They had nothing to lose. Nothing and everything.

With a management team in place and a growing reputation, System Of A Down entered a studio to record what was their first freely available demo tape – though you'd still be hard pushed to track down a copy today. They recorded four songs, three of which would make it on to their debut album – 'Suite-Pee', 'Sugar' and 'P.L.U.C.K.' A fourth, 'Dam' was described by one website as "a Daron Malakian solo-song, that consists of creepy robotic vocals, muttering 'Everyone is sleeping', over a middle-eastern guitar riff." Though never re-released it remained a mainstay of the band's live set. Compared to the later pristine production of their debut album, that of the band's first proper demo was of poor, garage-y quality, but the songs were getting there. The band-designed cover for this cassette-only release depicted a bespectacled man, mouth bound by gaffer tape and the band's name scrawled across his naked torso; it was sold at club shows throughout 1996.

Meanwhile, the new breed of bands that formed or refined their sound post-Korn were stepping out across California's club circuit, and particularly making a bee-line for the clubs of LA, where bands are more likely to be spotted and signed.

Nu-metal as it would soon be clumsily titled was taking shape. The keys bands of the coming half decade actually had little to do with each other sound-wise, only really united by aesthetics and a desire to do something quite different from the grunge, glam or no-nonsense thrash metal that had defined the previous decade's rock scene.

Aside from the adolescent angst of Korn weighted by its own use of down-tunings to give a deeper, darker sound, leading the pack of the disparate new wave were Limp Bizkit and Deftones. Fronted by sometime tattooist Fred Durst, Limp Bizkit was a lowest common denominator hybrid of rap and rock, blessed with a striking guitarist in Wes Borland and a shameless self-publicist and networker in Durst. Their big break came in 1995 when Durst passed on a demo to Korn bassist Fieldy while tattooing him; the tape reached producer Ross Robinson and they were signed shortly afterwards.

Sacramento quartet Deftones were a far more interesting proposition. Friends from an early age, they were inspired by bands such as Faith No More, Tool and Bad Brains and informed by more catholic (for metal, at least) tastes. Their compelling frontman Chino Moreno, for example, was a big fan of bands such as The Smiths and The Cure, something he tried to reflect in his singing and the band's multi-textured sound. On the strength of one demo tape the quartet – who later added DJ Frank Delgado as a full-time member – were signed to Madonna's Maverick label in 1994 and issued their debut the following year.

Stylistically the new bands had certain things in common, such as appropriating both skate and hip hop cultures (hoodies, baseball caps, long shorts or Dickies work pants) and often sporting much facial hair, tattoos, piercings; a kind of urban tribal look to leave no-one in doubt that the exponent of such a look played in a band. Similarly, for the first time rock and metal bands were featuring DJs within their ranks – something that would have been anathema to the thrash bands of the 1980s.

Throughout 1996/1997, more bands were playing the clubs to varying degrees of success and forging unions with one another that would initially suggest a scene was building, though notably many of the more forward-thinking leading bands would soon be quick to distance themselves from one another. Dozens of them emerged from the woodwork, the rap-metal (or nu-metal) movement seeming to attract its fair share of scenesters and careerists amongst the genuine artists. The hard part was trying to establish who was potentially life-changing or, more likely, irredeemable cack.

"When we started coming up, bands like Korn and Deftones were doing very well in and around LA," Serj told me in 2005. "Korn had their first record and we would listen to it, but we were also listening to a lot of different music at the same time. Journalists lumping us in with them – or with nu-metal – was just their way of defining things; it's just one perspective as opposed to being absolute rule or law. It never bothered me too much to be considered nu-metal, though it did feel like we were being classified without any real investigation into the emotions behind who this band is. It's kind of like running away from doing your job…"

Though time has been the great leveller of the nu-metal scene with only the deserving surviving to reap the awards, in the mid-to-late 1990s in California alone there were LA's Coal Chamber (nu-metal in Goth threads), Huntingdon Beach's (hed) pe (funk and hip-hop-heavy metal), San Fernando Valley's Incubus (funk-rap metal with didgeridoos), Human Waste Project (female-fronted alt-metal, also from Huntingdon Beach), Manhole (later known as Tura Satana and featuring vocalist Tairrie B), Static (industrial nu-metal originally from Chicago, later known as Static-X), Snot (punk-leaning metal)… the list goes on. Each drew on different influences – whether the funk of the Red Hot Chili Peppers, the rap of Cypress Hill, Ice-T and Body Count, Wu-Tang Clan or the electronica thuggery of Minstry, Nine Inch Nails and Fear Factory – to inform their own take on metal. And then there was System Of A Down, sharing stages with many of these bands but already way ahead of them in terms of content and technicality.

"The term nu-metal never actually meant much to us, because metal has been around for a long time in one form or another," sighs Serj. "It just pops up in different ways and displays new characteristics. It's like the word 'alternative'. Twenty years of it being used and I still don't know what that means. The alternative to what?"

Seemingly System were the alternative to *everything*. Though they were part of the new breed of bands, they were also slightly removed from their contemporaries, being as they were the only Armenian-metal band on the scene and their interests and influences stretched way beyond the restrictions of the genre. There was also the fact that they might not have been quite as clued-up as some of the more purely metal-obsessed new bands.

Paul McGuigan was booker at The Troubadour during the band's formative years. "I remember that some of the guys in the band didn't know a lot about heavy music," he told Josh Sindell of *Kerrang!*. "I recall Shavo coming up to me and asking what I knew about Kyuss and Neurosis. He'd never heard of them before. They started to discover heavy music kind of late."

"We were untouched by the scene then," confirmed Shavo. "We came from a different mental place from everybody at the time. But no-one could hate us because we so nice to everybody!" The niceties paid off. 1996 and on into early 1997 was a time of much groundwork for System Of A Down. The time they put in now would reap dividends further down the line during their steady rise to become one of LA's biggest home-grown bands, then America, then the world...

Meanwhile club gigs were packed out as the band continued to enthral and confuse fans. Those who loved them, loved them unconditionally. Those who hated their overtly wacky vibe and crazy time signatures were quite vocal about their disgust. Most importantly, few could ignore them. Their live shows became an increasingly arresting sight, an onslaught of sound, machine gun drumming and four bodies, a blur of war-paint and flesh. For a while the band termed their live show 'The Dark Red Experience' – a term they would use for one of their first national tours.

Offstage, Serj, Daron, Shavo and Andy were consummate gentlemen, engaging and charming, albeit with unconventional interests. Traces of Armenian accents – particularly in Shavo and Serj – gave a lilt to their American speech patterns and their colourful clothes and mixture of mad hairstyles made them stand out, even in a scene full of mad haircuts. They also seemed full of contradictions. One minute their Jesus-like frontman would be gently raising awareness about an injustice which he wanted to highlight, the next their jerky guitarist – Flavor Flav to Serj's Chuck D – would scream something about his cock or pornography or fucking and the band would thunder straight into the next song. Were they politicians? Were they deviants?

Were they really good or really shit?

Two new demos followed in relatively quick succession. With the live reputation growing, the band had yet to match it in the studio. Next up they hit the studio with producer Alex Newport to record a second full demo. Newport was a relatively big name by System's standards – as a teenager in Nottingham he had formed acclaimed sludge-metallers Fudge Tunnel in the late 1980s and released a series of uncompromising records, including an album *Hate Songs in E Minor* that was seized by the authorities due to its depiction of a decapitated corpse on the cover. Along with Sepultura/Soulfly frontman Max Cavalera, Newport then went on to form Nailbomb (who at various times featured other members of Sepultura, Fear Factory, Biohazard and Front Line Assembly) before he became more involved with production. In subsequent years he has produced some of the cream of challenging modern rock music, including At The Drive-In, Will Haven, The Icarus Line, The Mars Volta and The Locust.

But in 1997, Newport was still cutting his production teeth when he recorded three new System songs – 'Honey', 'Temper' and 'Soil', the latter of which would survive to make it onto their first album. With far better production than their first effort, the tape circulated around LA (this time the cover featured a gagged man who may or may not be Shavo with the band name written on his head), but the prolific nature of Daron's songwriting abilities meant they were soon surpassing themselves and in early 1997 they recorded their third – and what would be final – demo. It was by far their strongest yet and featured three storming songs that had already been refined live – 'Know', 'War?' and 'Peephole'. The band saw the demo as a device for getting more shows. "We weren't out to get signed," said Shavo. "We were out to get *fans.*"

The tape certainly broadened the band's appeal as it circulated around the globe amongst metal collectors, finding fans in Europe and, for some reason, New Zealand. It also received a number of reviews, including in a couple of clued-up fanzines and websites (still very much a new medium) in the UK. Not bad for an unknown, unsigned band.

Of the demo, short-lived UK rock fanzine *Attitude* noted "There's a hell of a mix of influences here, from your standard American metal fare to Eastern European and Asian, making for one of the most original sounds you'll have ever heard."

"Three tracks, and not a duff moment in sight," wrote another review on the metal fan site entitled Buried Dreams – just one of many who aided the band at a grass roots level. "They manage to present music which is both exciting and familiar yet different to grab the attention. It's heavy, in the manner that fans of Machine Head, Sepultura or Korn will enjoy, but then suddenly they'll throw in a little more subtlety. This is a band with their own style."

Though already looking and sounding like a unique new musical prospect, System Of A Down had one other factor to distinguish them from the many other metal bands on the LA club scene – their

Armenian genealogy.

Modern America is a country founded upon diversity; without immigration from all corners of the world it would be nothing but a barren-land of badly-organised cowboys having to do their own dirty leg work. Yet America remains a country of strong racial divisions. The government and its supporters, the corporations, the law-makers and the generals of war are predominantly run by white men. Anglo-Saxon men, the descendents of homesteaders and entrepreneurs. The stupid white men that satirist Michael Moore adroitly identified in his book of the same name. I'm generalising, of course, but it's for a valid reason. America welcomes one and all with the promise of success, the country where a peasant can become president. But good luck if you're from one of those far-flung places you only every hear about on the news. Mexico, Cuba, sure? Canadians, if you must. But Armenia? *Where the fuck is that?*

At any given time, the purpose of culture and the arts is to reflect the mood and times of the society that created it – precisely why the scientifically and philosophically enlightened revolution of the Italian Renaissance produced so many works of great beauty and intelligence in the fifteenth century or the drab, economically hard-bitten post-war Britain of the 1960s and 1970s created The Beatles and punk. Because they were needed.

So too System Of A Down were needed. Their Armenian patronage came at a time when American rock – and particularly metal – was just too…American. Whether it was the breakneck riffs of thrash or the appropriation of hip hop rhymes and rhythms into the merging rap-rock, most of the bands were nevertheless formulaic.

Without ever consciously deciding upon the point however, System Of A Down began incorporating the indigenous folk music of the Balkan States and the Middle East – particularly that of Armenia – a type of music from a completely different place to twentieth century rock music. It was a music informed by the time signatures of Eastern European and Russian gypsy music, folk music born out of both oppression and celebration, music to tell tales, to preserve culture, to dance around the fire to. In time some of this traditional music (epitomised by the oboe-like duduk, an instrument described as "best able to convey the emotions of the Armenian people so honestly and eloquently") diversified in all directions – into pop music, jazz and

Christian music. But it had not been successfully incorporated into rock and metal, or least not beyond Armenian's homegrown rock bands, none of whom have taken their language and geography to be part of world-wide successes beyond their own communities. Armenia has produced a number of internationally renowned classical composers but no balls-out rock 'n' roll bands.

So when System arrived on the scene playing music that leaned heavily on the type of Armenian music that Serj had grown up hearing his father sing, they were the first of a musical kind. The proof was in the polka bass lines of 'Suggestions' or the wistful atmospherics of 'Spiders'.

That they spoke of Armenian issues – most notably the genocide – only heightened interest and somehow made them all the more appealing. Here was a band you could mosh to and learn a bit of world history *and* maybe get turned on to a whole other world of sound completely alien to rock 'n' roll yet born out of a similar place – the desire to sing and dance, to laugh and lament, no matter who you are or where you come from. Yet, in the early days, one of the most laughable criticisms levelled at the band by one industry insider was that they would be very hard to sell to a white rock audience, what with them being ethnic and everything. Sometimes the music industry can be a supremely conservative place. Yet, ultimately, their heritage and ethnicity was to be their strength.

"I think it's one of the reasons that we get along so well," said John. "We understand each other. We grew up pretty much the same even though we didn't necessarily grow up together." "Our parents raised us with the same cultural values," agrees Malakian. "Everyone has the same things passed on to them from generation to generation. We can reminisce about the same types of weddings, foods, and we all speak the language."

The curious thing was, being Armenian-born and American-raised wasn't something System Of A Down had planned. They were four friends playing metal. They didn't set out to be an Armenian–American metal band. They also played jazz, prog, classic rock and pop, but couldn't be categorised in any of those genres. Their argument was, why pigeon-hole them by their ethnicity when they were clearly making music that defied obvious categorisation?

"The fact that we're all Armenian and in this band is completely a coincidence," said Daron. "It would be kind of freakish if we lived in Alabama, but there's a pretty big Armenian community in Los Angeles. People have put that gang shit on us before, made us out to be some fucking Armenian militia: that's just pure racism, but the fact we're all Armenian makes us feel like it's us against the world, makes us feel like we belong together. Are we playing Armenian music? No. Are we singing constantly about being Armenian? No. Does it just mean that certain people are so small-minded, so pathetically bigoted that the fact we come from a different racial background means we have fucking 'novelty' value? Yes. Jesus!"

It was something that would go on to follow the band for years to come, but the media can't be blamed for consistently commenting on the band's heritage. In a world of white boy rock bands they provided something else to write about, a handy hook to hang the band on. They were *interesting*.

And besides, culture reflects society. For the four members of the band, that meant being descendents of survivors of a recent genocide, the sons of Armenian artists and musicians, but raised American and loving that music, TV, fashion, and food equally. They appreciated Armenian folk to an extent that it seeped into their music and they spoke of their country of origin because they were repeatedly asked about it, but they loved Sabbath and Slayer too, *dude*. Their music reflected both worlds – bridged them, in fact – in ways politicians or spin doctors could never achieve. And that's where their cultural significance lies.

"We know what being Armenian means to us," said Shavo in a cover feature for *Metal Hammer*. "It means a certain upbringing, it means the fact that three of us went to the same school, it means we have roots we're proud of and our roots will always influence us in a million subtle ways. But to just slap a label on us like that just shows that no-one really knows where to put us."

The final word on the subject can be left to Serj: "If anything, I think coming from where we do, having to fight the battles we've had to fight because of it, has actually made us a lot more able to see things clearly than bands who are more easily assimilated into the music scene."

Not everything was going as smoothly as the band hoped, however. They were still on the bottom rung and had yet to release a record. What little money they made went on equipment, weed and records; all the necessities of modern subsistence. As things got busier and their catalogue of songs began to expand, there was less time for work as the members channelled their energies into the band. Unfortunately they didn't all agree on where System Of A Down were headed – or their roles in the band. Already apparent divisions between Andy and the band became wider and more defined.

"I had something to express more than just sitting behind the drums," Andy told *Kerrang!,* in a rare interview shortly after the release of *Toxicity.* "But I don't think I was frustrated. I enjoyed playing the drums and the type of music System Of A Down plays is so rhythmically driven and rhythm orientated, that the drums did play a significant part. I take pride in saying that I did help them in that way."

When Andy broke an arm shortly before a show, one account of the story has it that Serj, Shavo and Daron made the decisive move of finding a new drummer. System Of A Down Mark 1 was over. "I wasn't 'kicked out' of the band, and that's the truth," Andy writes. "Perhaps people should stop speculating without having the facts. I left System because of an injury as well as creative differences. I wanted to sing. They knew that.

There's a few different reasons. But whatever happened, happened. I think if you ask them, they'll probably tell you that they knew that I wanted to sing or that I wanted to front the band. In that way, there is probably that understanding...There is no ill will between any of us, as far as I am concerned."

After leaving System Of A Down, Andy formed The Apex Theory, playing guitar and singing along with Dave Hagopyan and some other friends in 1999. The Apex Theory had a similarly imaginative musical approach as System, subverting the usual rock formula by incorporating jazz, drum 'n' bass and Mediterranean/Eastern European music, though they were certainly no SOAD doppelgangers.

Echoing the rise of System, they eschewed chasing the record labels to instead build a strong local following and, after one independently-released EP, signed to Dreamworks. Another EP followed before The Apex Theory released their debut album *Topsy-Turvy* in April 2002, reaching Number 157 in the Billboard album charts. A couple of the band's singles received strong TV rotation and they took part in the Warped and Ozzfest festivals and toured the US with Brit band Lost

Prophets. However, The Apex Theory's initial success was relatively short-lived when Andy left the band over "musical differences". As they continued as a three-piece with their Armenian-American guitarist Art Karamian taking over vocal duties, Andy embarked on a solo project (assisted by Alien Ant Farm's Dryden Mitchell and Gavin Hayes of the band Dredg) and in 2003 remerged with new band VOkEE, with whom he continues to work today, now preferring to use the name Ontronik Khachaturian. At the time of writing VOkEE are working on new recordings in LA.

His former band mates in System Of A Down have always remained diplomatically tight-lipped when asked about Khachaturian's departure. "This goes pretty deep," Shavo said. "I think Andy's a good guy, but sometimes good people can't be in a working situation together. It's better for them to just be friends. He's an amazing drummer, and I'll always believe that. And I loved playing with him."

It could so easily have ended there. Another hotly-tipped local band fails to get off the ground – it's hardly an uncommon story, least of all in LA where you can't move for wannabe rock stars. It is they who park your cars, serve your burgers, sell you drugs. But System Of A Down were more than just scenesters killing time until they grew up and got proper jobs; as Daron had said, this was it for them. He had no other options.

Yet System Of A Down was now incomplete. That vital missing component to offer balance and the necessary solid backbone to the band came in the form of drummer John Dolmayan. Not only was he too Armenian-American but he played the drums like the devil himself. System Of A Down first met John when they saw him rehearsing with another band who they knew of through their wider community of budding musicians. The drummer had been involved in various musical projects, most recently playing with a band called Friik (later a System song title) who shared practice space in the Lanksershim Boulevard warehouse, and were awestruck by his drumming ability. He was top of their list as a replacement for Khachaturian. He played the drums so hard and so fast he was impossible to ignore.

Like Serj, Dolmayan was born in Lebanon, on July 15, 1974. It was a year in which recently installed Israeli Prime Minister Yitzak Rabin bombed a number of Palestinian villages in the south of the Lebanon, killing two hundred and rendering ten thousand homeless. The country was in no more a stable time than the seven years earlier when Serj was born into political chaos. The year after John's birth, the Lebanon erupted into a violent and civil war that would last until 1989. "I remember the war vividly," said Dolmayan. "It was horrible. There were bombs going off constantly and bullets flying all over the place."

That the Dolmayans family (it's pronounced 'dole-my-en') were even living in Lebanon and witnessing war there in the first place was as a result of the Ottoman Empire's Armenian genocide and the huge emigration it forced upon the country's citizens. Unlike Serj's grandfather who relocated to the US, both sets of John's grandparents relocated to Lebanon, where they raised their children – John's parents.

Listening to System Of A Down's music today is it a coincidence that both the band's singer and drummer – the voice and the backbeat – were raised to the sound of bombs and bullets, all four members the indirect by-product of genocide?

Even if it would indirectly inspire some ass-kicking musical sounds of the future, Beirut in the 1970s was hardly the safest place to raise children. With the country descending into chaos, a near-death experience prompted Dolmayan's parents to take decisive action when they decided to relocate in 1975.

"I was about three years old, crying in my bed one night, and my parents came and took me to their bed," he explained. "A few minutes later a bullet came through the wall and landed in the bed where I'd slept. My father just said 'I'm not gonna lose my only son to this'. Two weeks later we left the country."

"It's really sad, because it's a beautiful country, but there have been religious struggles there for thousands of years and I don't know if that's going to end any time soon. It's pretty sad what people do in the name of religion."

Once again, the contradictions of organised religion as the genesis of so many wars around the world was something that played heavily on the mind of the young Dolmayan. Like his bandmates, he had his eyes opened at an early age to the lies and hypocrisies perpetuated by religious authorities in the name of their particular god. Sometimes it takes a child to see the casualties of conflict as nothing more than human, rectifiable errors and their multi-national upbringings certainly enlightened the members of System Of A Down in ways that more parochial bands could only imagine.

Music was the outlet for the young John. It was in his genes – his father was a keen saxophone player who had also played the drums as a child, and released three albums of his own music. Ultimately though he chose his family over the pursuit of a potential career in music and all the hardships such a vocation brings.

"He put them out in the Armenian community," John explained to *Rhythm* magazine. "He's an artist and he pursued music in his own way. He had a family to support, so he didn't have the luxury of going for broke, which I have had. But he still found a way to do his music."

Dolmayan traces his interests in drumming almost back to birth, claiming to have first been interested in the expression of rhythm "probably from when I was one or two" – an early discovery of a life's vocation by anyone's standards. "Even when I was a baby, my mother would take me to see my father play live. He'd be onstage and as a one-year-old I would be mimicking the drummer. It was a given for me right from the beginning." After leaving the Lebanon, the Dolmayans moved first to Canada. It was while living there that, at the age of seven, he got his first child-sized drum kit. "It was destroyed on a Sunday morning," he remembers. "My dad had been up until five and I decided I was going to play at six, so it was bye-bye to that drum set. I didn't get another one until I was fifteen."

After living in Canada for three or four years, the family relocated to Los Angeles. They moved into a family home in the San Fernando Valley, that area which also incorporates communities such as Burbank, Glendale, Van Nuys and North Hollywood. Dolmayan's new life in America was as strange or as alien as it was for his fellow band mates, though he too adapted in every which way he could. California certainly had a lot to offer arriving immigrants – the availability of work, the potential for a comfortable lifestyle and the climate, so there were worse places to relocate to when escaping a war zone. John immersed himself in drumming and the allure of comic collecting (an obsession that has expanded into a library of well over 40,000 comics today), but not education. At the age of ten he was already forming opinions that would influence his life and outlook.

"It was fairly rare that I showed up [to school]," he explained. "I couldn't stand it. I've always questioned things as far as I can remember. Religion in particular just didn't make sense to me. Why would one religion be better than another? And why would something that someone said 5000 years ago be true today? What will we know in another 5000 years that we don't know now? I want to discover things. As a species we would never have evolved at all if we hadn't tried to find truths."

This quote comes from an early band interview in which Dolmayan was asked about his school days, his response illustrating that he is not your typical drummer adhering to the drunken, animalistic, sociopathic Keith Moon stereotype. His addition to the band brought a fierce intelligence to make any in-band philosophical discussion even more heated, as well as percussive skills that would define the group's future sound. Serj may be The Voice and Daron the genius professor concocting new varieties of sound in his laboratory, but Dolmayan's drumming was soon to be as recognisable as both. Which isn't to say he didn't display certain drummer characteristics, such as a wilful sense of individualism and a lack of respect for authority. Ultimately they say a band is only as good as their drummer, in which case System suddenly sounded like world-beaters.

"I wouldn't swap drumming for anything, but you don't get a lot of respect," John said. "If you think about it, the first [ever] instrument was vocals and the second was drums. That's the backbone of the band, and if the drummer's off you've got problems. I wish I was more artistic, but I would never trade what I was given as a gift for their gift."

John's induction to rock music came by way of all the expected iconic rock bands, ones tellingly notable for their exemplary drummers. "The first album I heard was *Black Sabbath*," he says. "The first album I ever bought was Rush's *Exit Stage Left*. "Despite heavy metal and prog rock, my influences also mainly stem from classic rock like The Who, Led Zeppelin, bands like that. I also borrowed my dad's large collection of jazz albums. Maynard Ferguson [trumpeter] was one of the biggest influences."

His first show was Pink Floyd at the Los Angeles Coliseum in 1988 – "that night changed my life as I knew I needed to be up on that stage." (Years later John would return to the venue to play there in front of 80,000 people on his birthday.)

By the time John was in his late teens he was an accomplished percussionist, his natural ability allowing him to hone a unique style that was heavy on the snare and hi-hat, and that allowed him to move from free-form jazz to locked-down thrash metal beats with ease – skills, he would later explain, that came from practising for five or six hours every day as much as natural ability. "Feeling is key," he told *Rhythm* magazine. "I may not have technique, but I do have feeling. That's the philosophy I carry."

But drumming only pays the bills if you're in a working band and, with real life beckoning, John enrolled in college before moving on to "the university of life" – dropping out – after a total of two weeks. For a number of years he also worked as a camp counsellor for children – "I love kids and know that someday I'll be a great dad," he says – suggesting a sensitivity that's not normally associated with percussionists.

He was also opinionated and had equally as strong a personality as the others, deadly serious about drumming (something that's reflected in his face every time he takes the drum stool), but a good guy to be around. With his love of comics and cars, a need for order, tidiness and an uncharacteristic habit of rising early, he also had his own thing going on. He was, in short, perfect. Dolmayan was also well suited to System's rhythmically-driven music. They needed a drummer to keep up.

"The band I was in wasn't going in the direction I wanted to take things: they were going towards a more pop, mainstream direction, which is something I was adamantly opposed to. I wanted to keep it heavy. Meanwhile, Serj, Daron and Shavo weren't happy with Andy. We hit if off so well personally, and we admired each other's talents, that it seemed like the right thing to do, so I joined them."

With Dolmayan on board, things stepped up a gear. It didn't take months of rehearsals for him to learn their expanding catalogue of songs; he nailed them quickly, adding new fills and flourishes of his own and just generally tightening everything together. System began gigging again soon afterwards.

Out in Californian clubland, things were getting more competitive and the record company scouts who had been curiously watching from a distance, sifting through demo tapes and trying to separate the wheat from the chaff, were now getting involved. Deftones had already signed a deal and were filling out clubs every time they drove in from Sacramento, their sound and style appealing to metal fans, punks and skaters alike. Other bands on the scene were snapped up soon afterwards – Snot, Human Waste Project, and (hed)pe all signing deals. But as arguably the biggest band of the new breed, System Of A Down were biding their time.

"I like Korn and a lot of the associated bands, but I think that the same is beginning to happen that happens to all scenes," said Serj during an early interview in 1997. "Record labels are simply looking for a 'new Korn'. Bands are being signed, but being dubbed with a label which might discourage some people. It seemed to happen in Britain in the early 1980s, then the thrash scene, then the 'funk metal' thing, then grunge, then the new wave of punk, and now we're at the Korn thing. And somewhere down the line, the bubble bursts, and bands are dropped. The problem is that a lot of good bands, who are individual in their own right, get dragged in and then spat out. So there is a danger that you could get dragged into that scenario."

As the most confusing musical prospect of them all, System Of A Down were rightly not rushing into a deal. There was also the fact that many people just didn't seem to get them. "People from major labels were coming up to me going, 'Don't growl. You'll never get signed by a major label,'" laughs Serj of the more sober reaction from certain quarters of the music business. "The industry doesn't know. Industry people generally don't have their four fingers on the heartbeat of what the kids want. We consider success the ability to play our music for a living. We're obviously not a commercial band, and so we have a lot of conquering to do to get people to 'get' us..." Shavo said, "I don't want to say that we were afraid, but we did have some nervous feelings about the whole record deal thing."

Off the strength of their live show and the demos that had circulated amongst LA's clued-up metal underground, System Of A Down's reputation was growing. Their visibility within the media was still relatively low and had been consigned to the local music press and those fans who had seen the band and cornered them for a chat. With no record label input, any photos of the band had been overseen by Beno and the members and were usually taken by friends.

The arrival of System Of A Down coincided with the unprecedented growth of the internet as a communicative tool, a factor which has certainly had a substantial bearing on the band accruing a massive following, particularly during these hectic early years. Though the internet had been active since 1994, it was not yet the household device we know today.

By 1997 the more computer literate types were installing programmes on their home computers or accessing it via college or work-place computers as the great internet boom – one of the most significant technological developments of the twentieth century – began. The power of the internet could not be underestimated. Here, for the first time, was a widely available medium that could exist largely without policing or censorship. It was the mouthpiece for the global community System had been telling us about, an information exchange that was equivalent to a conference call for thousands, maybe millions of people, simultaneously. For a band like System Of A Down, who were already being pegged as outspoken as they were outlandish, it was perfect.

Through the internet the first snippets of interviews or reviews of the band began to gain a wider audience. Where once such information was confined to the pages of crudely cobbled together fanzines of limited distribution and shelf-life – still the entry point for most underground bands worth their salt – now the spread of information was instantaneous. A snatched interview backstage after a show could be typed that night and available worldwide for interested parties to read over breakfast … if not sooner.

Though System perhaps didn't fully realise it at the time, the internet would prove to be pivotal in the growth of the band; between their early shows and the release of their second album less than half a decade later the growth of the internet would accelerate exponentially in ways few other than a handful of Silicone Valley boffins could have predicted. And the band would feel the force.

On a practical level, for an up-and-coming band things were changing for the better. For starters, flyers were becoming increasingly redundant as a simple website or e-mail out could simultaneously alert thousands of people to the cause within minutes. Likewise, fans didn't need to rely solely on the radio or the mainstream music press – still a pretty conservative place in America – for information or taste-making tips. Slowly but surely the fans themselves were becoming the journalists, the publicists and the opinion-formers and System Of A Down, along with thousands of other bands, were slowly beginning to reap the rewards. Interviews could be conducted with band members via e-mail, fans could trade links and the bands themselves could fire missives direct to their supporters with little external input. The growth of the internet was part and parcel of the accelerated culture we live in. Throughout 1997 the first snippets of band interviews appeared online and System's reputation began to spread – whispers of an exciting new metal band stretching beyond LA. Meanwhile back at home, the clubs were full as System Of A Down played a series of hometown shows that would lead them to their next level, from unsigned underdogs to contenders on the cusp.

Throughout the year they chose to play a number of smaller club shows, the known places where bands could be spotted. They were already a bankable draw, capable of headlining the smaller clubs themselves or acting as the interesting opening act for more established bands passing through. They were perfectly geographically placed to maximise their exposure. After all, Hollywood was the place where dreams were made.

So, they could pack out small venues like The Troubadour on bills which seemed to reflect the burgeoning wave of local bands riding the slipstream of Korn's stratospheric rise, or they could plunder the fan base of established bands. A typical night might see System taking to the stage around midnight after opening sets by bands such as Snot, Suction and Spank (as they did on one bill), some destined to fail, others who would go on to enjoy their fifteen minutes or more of fame or notoriety, all unified by the fact that they were resolutely heavy bands trying to carve a niche within the tried and tested practice of metal.

LA-based photographer Lisa Johnson is a long-term friend and fan of the band and is responsible for taking many photographs of them throughout their career. She was there to witness their rise through the clubs of Los Angeles, while some of her early press shots helped introduce the band to the world for the first time (she is also credited with being the person who later first introduced Serj to her friend, Tom Morello).

"The first real time I remember seeing them play was at the Whisky A Go Go," she remembers. "There was definitely a sense that a highly important band was in our midst. They were headlining and the crowd was intense and knew all the words, and just went nuts. I don't think that anyone – perhaps not even the band at that point – had any idea how much the band would evolve and impact the music scene as they do now."

One show in the August of 1997 saw System back at the Whisky – the same venue that had seen the likes of The Doors, Janis Joplin and Led Zeppelin pass through on the way to immortality – supporting politically-charged Brit metal legends Napalm Death. A band well versed in musical brutality and hard-line activism (anti-animal experimentation and women's abortion rights just two of the long-term causes they have promoted) the two bands were certainly kindred spirits, if only because they were both wilfully non-commercial.

"Though their faces weren't really known to us at that point. I'd actually heard quite a bit about them before we played, and I'd heard they were very politically probing so was keen to have a look," says Napalm Death frontman Barney Greenway today. "They were certainly out there on their own with all the little embellishments they put into the music. There was a lot of anticipation and it was hard to focus on the stage really, as everyone was crowding round. I kind of gave up the ghost and went searching for a veggie burger. A historic event on the cards, and there's me off thinking of stuffing my face. The band were really going for it, though."

Fans were in agreement over these club shows: "Serj, Daron, Shavo and John appeared on stage around 12:20am," wrote one fan in an online chatroom. "The lights were lowered, and some Armenian-style music was playing over the PA. Serj had his arms outstretched, becoming one with the music and suddenly they erupted into demo track and crowd favorite 'Know'. John's thick drumming pummeled the air, Daron pulverized his guitar, and Shavo pounded with booming accuracy on his bass, then Serj screamed the opening words "Cursed earth!" and at that moment I knew that SOAD were real. They are going to explode!"

Off the back of the Napalm Death support, the Whisky show also brought System Of A Down their first proper publicity in Europe by way of a live review in *Kerrang!* magazine that picked up on the potential of their initially baffling sound.

"Bearded singer Serj rattles off his lyrics like a deranged prophet, with the music behind him a brilliant blend of Eastern European gypsy folk and Sepultura bludgeon," noted *Kerrang!*'s LA correspondent and early band champion Josh Sindell, "small wonder they've got one of the most rabid followings among fans and label scouts alike in LA at the moment. You read it hear first."

Chapter 3: A Bullet Called Life

Such secrets can only remain that way for so long and Beno and System soon began to receive calls about the band's long term plans with increased regularity. Such is the way with the competitive music industry. A band can exist for years completely ignored by the larger record labels despite their best efforts and it often isn't until one label shows serious interest that the others come knocking, fearful of letting the latest hot new thing slip through their fingers – or, worse, sign with a rival. And when you're talking about bands who can conceivably sell ten, twenty or thirty million records at $10 a pop over the years to come, it's easy to see how the right bands (and often the wrong ones too) can go from obscurity to the obligatory feeding frenzy in a matter of days. This wasn't quite the case with System, though their strong live following was enough to suggest to all-comers that, in the metal world at least, they were an increasingly bankable bet. Whether they saw and heard a band capable of gate-crashing into number one spots around the world is another matter.

"We didn't sign a deal until a year and a half after me working them," says Beno. "We had offers that came in from Earache and Roadrunner, then the likes of Universal and Columbia came to the party. We knew we had a very specific, special thing and we didn't rush into a record deal. We wanted to make sure it was the right one and that we did it the right way."

The right offer came in the shape of Rick Rubin.

Rubin was already a man of legendary status within the rock and rap worlds, a renowned producer of some the finest records of the day and owner of his own label, American Recordings. Born in Long Island in 1963, as a teen Rubin was a rock fan looking for something new and exciting as a contrast to the Led Zeppelin and AC/DC records his school mates grew up on. He was studying at New York University when he discovered the nascent NY rap scene. Hanging out in clubs – often the only white man in attendance – he heard people rapping over old rock records and saw the correlation between this new form and the traditional rock 'n' roll form; both were outsider's music. Rebel music. He soon began cutting his own hip-hop tracks and met budding rap mogul Russell Simmons shortly afterwards – Simmons' brother played in Run DMC, who Rubin was soon producing.

Though the pair were already making waves, they were on an exponential career ascent, so next up they went into partnership as Def Jam Records in 1984, a label-cum-production house financed by CBS Records (but originally run out of Rubin's college dormitory room).

Rubin also persuaded three young punks called the Beastie Boys to wear tracksuits and turn their hand to a rap-rock hybrid; another huge success, as were his other charges Run DMC. In his early twenties he made his first million producing seventeen-year-old LL Cool J's *Radio* album. It cost a total of $7000 and sold an unprecedented one million copies upon its release.

The Rubin-Simmons partnership didn't last however, and Rubin broke away to form Def American to continue to record and release the latest bands. What followed reads like a guide to some of the key works of modern times, throughout the 1980s and into the 1990s, with Rubin producing seminal albums by Public Enemy and Slayer – two quite different bands, yet both equally as innovative and confrontational in their own way – The Cult, Danzig, Geto Boys, Black Crowes, Red Hot Chili Peppers, Johnny Cash and many more besides. In 1994 Def American dropped their outdated prefix and became American Recordings. Rubin was more than just a producer, he was an advisor too who is widely credited with helping shape bands, as with the Beasties Boys, or in the case of the Chili Peppers saving a band in decline. Most importantly he has tracked down the bands that truly matter, bands that will go down in the history books as some of the most important of their generation.

"When something is revolutionary, it's hard on first listen to accept it," he once said during an interview. "There's a shocking period there where you don't know. A lot of the things that you hear once and you love may fade faster… sometimes it's the stuff that takes a little while to get your head around before you realize how good it is that really stays with you. Because that's the stuff that's different."

Rubin was invited by Maverick Records' Guy Oseary to see System Of A Down play The Viper Room, the small Johnny Depp-owned club at the heart of Sunset Boulevard, to a packed house of System faithful. "I saw him from the stage and he seemed pretty much into it," said Shavo. "Later, he told us he was blown away, which blew *us* away, being

1980s kids who loved all the rap stuff he came out with."

"I remember laughing a lot because they seemed so crazy to me," remembers Rubin. "What I thought was unusual about them was that, first of all, they're very heavy sounding, but original. You hear a lot of bands sounding heavy like Black Sabbath, and you hear a lot of bands sounding heavy like Slayer, but System Of A Down didn't sound like any bands I'd heard before…yet they were heavy."

Rubin was blown away by what he saw and heard and recognised the same potential he had seen in Slayer and Public Enemy: bands that were leaders. Bands going out on a limb because they *didn't give a fuck*. The band met with Rubin shortly afterwards to discuss working together.

Though it seemed like the perfect opportunity to be involved with the man who had produced so many of their favourite records, they nevertheless approached with trepidation. This, after all, was their lives they were dealing with here. Up until now their art had remained pure and free from eternal influence or input. There were no demands other than turning up and playing. Soon things would change, though if all went according to plan, not that much.

"One of our fears before we got signed was that we would get fucked by a major label," said John. "We heard enough stories to scare the shit out of you for life," agreed Shavo. "There were nights we didn't sleep. I'm serious." "The most important thing is to make sure that when the band does a deal with a label, that they're ready to go into the studio, that they've done the work and that they have a real live show," says David Benveniste. "We didn't do a deal with System of a Down for a year and a half. We had labels trying to sign us and we didn't do it. We were fine doing our own little thing. And then, when we were ready, we did it."

Shortly afterwards, at the close of 1997, the band signed to American Records – itself now part of the Columbia Records empire under the watchful eye of Rubin and their A&R man Dino Paredes, a former member of Perry Farrell's pre-Jane's Addiction LA art-rock band Psi Com (he wrote the bass line to Jane's 'Mountain Song' – LA's that kind of place).

As is so often the way when a band from the underground signs up with a major corporation, SOAD's motives were brought into question. Music is about individual taste and taste breeds snobbery. With such a strong and loyal following and an obvious anti-corporate stance, at least philosophically, the band found themselves having to justify the move. It was nothing new though. Rage Against The Machine had faced the same criticisms a half decade earlier, as had Nirvana when they left grungey Sub Pop for the swish corridors of Geffen. As had scores of other bands who had moved up through the clubs and whose music was often deliberately non-commercial. System, with their songs about global domination, corporate-sponsored war and revolution "as the only solution" found themselves deflecting more accusations of 'selling out' perhaps than any other band of their ilk or era. Naturally, the band members have different views on the matter, though all agreed from the outset that – like Rage before them – they wanted to reach as great an audience as possible, otherwise why bother?

"It's a question that I would ask a band like us: since you talk so much anti-corporate shit, why are you with a corporation?" said Shavo. "The answer to that question is that if we weren't with a corporation, you wouldn't be talking to me right now because my label wouldn't have gotten this interview with you. That's very important. You know, like Rage Against The Machine, they're against the machine, well, we're using machines to our advantage. You know what selling out is? It's writing music to cater to other people. That's selling out. Writing music to cater to the radio, to make money."

"I think everybody in the band has different opinions," added John. "I definitely think we need to be more sensitive to the needs of the people and the environment in general, not just the corporations… there's a lot of good people that work at Columbia. Columbia is not just this big machine; there's actual people there, people I correspond with."

"The point is not for them to make money off us or us to make money off them – that's gonna happen anyway," said Serj. "The point is it gets our message across and has a better platform. There are people into it just for the music or the energy, but there are also people who come up to me and have conversations about the lyrics. We reach different people in different ways."

With the band's record deal inked, System Of A Down got busy. Very busy. One of the upsides of holding out for the right deal was that System Of A Down already had an arsenal of songs stockpiled, many of which had been demo'd with Khachaturian.

With Korn leading the way, bands such as Deftones and Coal Chamber were beginning to appear on magazine covers in Europe and many others were gaining attention by being erroneously lumped in as nu-metal, whether they liked it or not. And all the while new bands came crawling out of the woodwork to also sign deals – Orgy, Dope, Powerman 5000, most now consigned to the dustbin of cultural detritus. It was almost like glam rock all over again. For every half-decent band there were ten lame followers – and they would keep coming. Even the Crue's Tommy Lee would soon be getting in on the act with his rap-rock project Methods Of Mayhem!

System Of A Down hunkered down to make a debut album that would stand up against any band, regardless of genre and trends. "We always knew people connected with our music," Serj would later tell one radio station. "From day one, even before we toured or got signed, before 'Sugar', the music seemed to touch people in an honest and raw way." Now they just needed to prove it on record.

In late 1997 they entered Sound City studio in the Van Nuys area of LA and began their recordings with Rick Rubin at the helm. Mixing was done by Dave Sardy and engineering by Sylvia Massey. Both also came with pedigrees. Sardy had been a member of the band Barkmarket and worked with the likes of Oasis, Marilyn Manson and Nine Inch Nails, while Massey got her break producing Tool before going on to work with the likes of REM and Johnny Cash. With much of the music laid down, Serj's vocals were then recorded at Rubin's house in Laurel Canyon. As befitted such a band various techniques were applied to get the best out of the singer.

"We had coloured lights and incense and little antique rugs and just a great vibe going," said Serj. "We actually did some tracks in the Dungeon. The Dungeon was a scary vibe. It's at the bottom of the house, an old storage area. Cement. Real cold. So we just lit some candles and did some recording there and we did some tracks outside. Sylvia even made me record stuff upside down for the hell of it."

Rubin himself was on hand to guide Serj through his first proper recording sessions, coaxing out of him a staggering vocal display that ranged from harmony-laden singing through some bizarre cartoon voices that were fast becoming something of a band trademark to all-out paint-stripping roar.

"He brings a lot to the table," Serj enthused. "He's got an amazing ear for music, in harmony, in what works or what doesn't work. He's got great taste, which is why I think he can produce different genres of music so successfully. He's not a genre producer – he's not known for just producing heavy bands or any certain type of band. He's done so many different artists, let alone the hip-hop stuff he did earlier in his career."

While the record was still being made, System Of A Down received their first international coverage in December when they featured in a *Kerrang!* article as one of a number of US bands tipped for success in 1998. The short introductory piece dryily described them as a "shaven-headed, goatee-bearded group of gentlemen possibly not known for their selection of 'knock, knock' jokes" and noted that though they had only circulated demo tapes they were "creating the biggest buzz on the street since Korn." The accompanying picture was taken from the band's first ever press session and did indeed show four shaven-headed, vaguely menacing and/or exotic looking men. Daron, sporting a pair of braces resembled Russell Crowe's skinhead protagonist in *Romper Stomper.*

The recordings were completed in the new year and the band painstakingly chose the thirteen songs that would make the album – a selection process that would continue throughout their career, given their high rate of productivity. With the album in the bag, work began in earnest to spread the word across the US. Those already in on the secret knew they were a band on the cusp and the few shows they played during this period are still spoken about in hushed, reverential tones. Those who were there could feel this was a band about to blow.

"They did a three-night run in LA at The Roxy, The Whisky and The Troubadour in 1998, which was just crazy," remembers Beno. "The Whisky show in particular was one of the most amazing shows I've ever seen any band play. There was an energy there where they really seemed to click as a touring band. Really, the best way I can describe this band is 'unique specimens'. You can put me on record as saying they are absolutely the best rock band in the world."

"This infectious disease in LA is rapidly infiltrating the minds of many across the globe," wrote one early fan site review of a Roxy show in January 1998. "SOAD has had over ten websites start up within a month's time. The hype is so monstrous that other bands are wondering what the hell they are doing to make this happen..."

While the band's thoughts had been on the making of their debut album and the implications of a major label record deal upon their lives,

Beno was coming into his own as their manager. His hard-sell approach to the people who really mattered – the fans – was beginning to pay, but the record deal was only the beginning. With some money behind them the band had the time and resources to step things up a level, and their manager began to capitalise on System's growing reputation by cleverly using the new medium of the internet to maximise their exposure.

"Before System Of A Down got signed, they were so prolific in LA," he said. "And by the time they got their deal with Columbia, I felt that there was such a big, fat thing happening on a micro level that I wanted to create that on a macro level before the record was released. So I literally started going into chat rooms and typing, 'Has anyone heard of System Of A Down, outside of LA?' and they'd say, 'No.' So I'd give them my home phone number and they'd call and I'd play the demo for them over the phone."

Such a hands-on approach combined tried and tested practices with the new unknown marketing tool that was the internet. It was to pay off for the band. "A bad manager can fuck everything up," Beno explained in an interview with trade magazine *Music Connect*. "The manager is the quarterback. So that means that the manager is responsible for the agent, the business manager, the tour manager, the accountant and everything involved. The manager has to be that nucleus and bring it all together and make sure everything is on point. And if the manager takes his eye off the ball for one split second it can be catastrophic. The manager also has to make sure that there's a constant flow of information and that things are being handled the right way. And most importantly, when I go out and talk about System Of A Down, that people say, 'God, System Of A Down's representation is clean and cool and honest.' Any manager who doesn't represent their band right is doing the band a disservice."

Throughout 1997 and into 1998, Beno pushed the band to anyone who would listen; after all a record deal means nothing without a fan base. Similarly, being big in LA means little in the grand scheme of things. David Benveniste was thinking about investment of both time and money to ensure a lasting career. Many new metal bands were being signed and it was obvious that most would fall by the wayside. He began to put into place a number of marketing practices that would push System Of A Down right to the top of the pile before their first record was even released. Two key factors played a part in the band's organic and rapidly-swelling fan base. The first was the internet, the second was the kids who were being turned onto the band – realising the untapped potential of thousands of adolescents and young adults more than willing to be a part of their favourite band's success. As an offshoot of his management company Velvet Hammer, he launched StreetWise Culture & Concepts, a network of fans whose main purpose was to distribute information about the band. It was, in effect, one of the world's first street teams – a device which is now common practice amongst most labels. StreetWise was instrumental in breaking the band nationally and internationally, and over the intervening years the company has expanded in line with the band's success. System was too awkward-sounding to rely on TV and radio so one of the first things they did was to compile a sampler tape of the band's album and send them out to street teams across the United States. The set-up was simple: volunteers distribute tapes, CDs, stickers and flyers to friends and strangers on the street alike. Their enthusiasm then spread to the internet, ensuring the band's music found an audience before they had even released a record and, most likely, played a budding fan's hometown. It was people-power in full, simplistic effect. Today StreetWise's strap-line is: *"Empowering the youth of America"*

The System tape circulated far and wide and by the time the band played their first proper tours people already knew some of the songs. "We have a very prolific marketing team where I have kids all day saying 'Hey Beno, check this band out,'" Benveniste explains. "I have an A&R scout who I get demos from. I have lawyer relationships and publisher relationships. So it's about creating relationships with people. If you deliver for them, they'll deliver for you."

With the album completed and the street teams mobilized into action, it was time for System Of A Down to announce themselves to the world. Which they did.

Quite vocally.

The days of playing LA club shows or driving to a town a few hours away were coming to an end. Obscurity was fading fast as the major label's publicity machine creaked into action. It's hard to imagine what the ruling executives of Columbia Records must have thought when System Of A Down's debut album landed on their desks, though it's unlikely they saw the future of metal. But they did hear something undeniably unique which could conceivably sell 100,000 copies. Besides, albums aren't cheap to make these days. They, more than anyone, wanted the album to be a success. If it wasn't…well, there are always more bands.

"'Hey, the kids like it,'" laughed Serj at the time. "That's my favorite term. That's what Columbia is saying to themselves right now, 'The kids like it. We don't know what this is, but the kids like it.'"

There was plenty to like – not least their appearance, which made them look like the freakiest gangs of rock deviants since Jane's Addiction had tottered out of LA in the late 1980s. Actually, they looked kind of shit, but it worked. To some they looked like a band to avoid, but to others they looked like a band to hear for the very same reason. The same could be said for every great metal or punk band there has been. Rock 'n' roll is nothing if not the last refuge for the sartorially challenged and System played to their strengths.

"You should never fear what people are going to say about what you're wearing," said Serj. "Dress however you like, screw those who say bad things about what you're wearing. If you wanna wear all black, wear all black; if you wanna wear all pink, wear all pink. That's just part of being a free-thinker and thinking for yourself and not caring what people say, because if you live your life thinking about what people say, you won't be happy. You'll get older, you'll be in your late twenties and you won't be a happy person because you'll be living for other people. Live for yourself." "I've played naked with the word 'smut' written across my chest," shrugged Daron.

Photographer, fan and friend Lisa Johnson was enlisted to take pictures of the band to promote the soon-to-be-released debut *System Of A Down*. "Our first memorable encounter was when I was hired by their label," recalls Johnson. "It was their first professional photo shoot with someone who wasn't a friend of theirs. We all met up at a diner by my place called Astro Family Restaurant. They could barely sit still 'cause I think they were so excited. Serj bombarded me with questions, and eventually we headed towards some locations I'd scouted out in Glendale. We went to this amazing – and scary – abandoned warehouse area, and that's where we took the [famous] shots with the sword. Maybe my opinion is biased, but to this day those are my favourite pictures of System Of A Down. They came out with just the right combination of fun and crazy. They have an incredible sense of humour and irony in their music, and I think because it's so heavy, people often miss the fact that it's also very clever in a humorous way, and I think that session brought all that out. I've shot the band several times since, but those are still my personal favourites."

One manifestation of the band's total disregard for convention during photo-shoots was Serj's often beaming face. Think about it: how many metal frontmen do you see smiling like Cheshire cats in their photos. Not many. Smiling is, like, totally uncool. Yet we know that in the hands of System Of A Down the uncool has a habit of being highly appealing.

"It's a choice," Serj told the *Washington Post.* "I do get a lot of photographers that say, 'Okay, now give me your mean look.' I crack up. What does that mean? Why should our type of music, whatever it is, have some type of mean look associated with it? Why can't heavily charged music be positive and funny? I mean, I pretty much laugh and smile throughout our sets; that's how I get by. That doesn't mean I don't get serious or zone out and go to deep places in a performance. But we can't take this too seriously. It's just music and life."

With a sharp burst of far-from-friendly guitar firing from the speakers, and the thunderous entrance of a locked-down, rhythm section that stabbed with military precision, it took approximately ten seconds into their debut for System Of A Down to throw down the gauntlet with opener 'Suite-Pee'. And that was before the vocals came into play, with Serj bellowing the cryptic lyrics as both confession and declaration before segueing into a clipped, roaring chorus.

As opening songs on debuts go, 'Suite-Pee' was up with there with the best of them, managing to shoehorn so many ideas into one hundred and fifty dizzying seconds of sound: asphyxiating, panic attack guitars tightening like ligatures, an air-punching chorus built on a circle pit slogan, the doomy atmospherics of the mid-song breakdown that name-checked the Messiah, the sandblast of vocals from Serj, then plunging into a breathless, galloping race to a car crash-like conclusion. Confusing, brilliant and slightly ridiculous, in less time than it takes most bands to warm up, System Of A Down had unwittingly forced you to take sides. By grabbing listeners by the lapels and screaming in their face, those who heard the band at this relatively early stage had little choice but to turn away in disgust…or submit, a glazed expression of sheer delight passing across their eyes.

With an opening rattle of tribal drums 'Know' followed with equally blood-pumping intent, Serj's screams painting comic book images of Armageddon as if mutants have just nuked his favourite organic store. Everything seemed to come together perfectly in this kinetic squall that bounced along under its own barely contained energy, Malakian's guitars crisp and crunchy and Dolmayan's metronomic skills sounding like an army of automatons rhythmically striding into battle. Lyrically, Serj upped the surrealist-absurdist ante, adopting a tone that was part-Old Testament biblical and part-timeless tribal that instantly distanced System from their nu-metal contemporaries and created a broader canvas of imagery that sparked the imagination of listeners.

What the countless stream-of-consciousness lyrics actually *meant* is open to interpretation, but it was emotive stuff, heart-felt and heady. Imagery and sounds that melded into one impenetrable wall of sound rattled by at such velocity it was hard to take it all in. Another dramatic slow mid-section within the song allowed just enough time to take stock, Serj switching to full-on vocal preacher-prophet role and offering an argument for the transcendence of the human flesh body as the only true route for emancipation.

The plunging intro of 'Sugar' and rolling, jazzy bass-lines of its verses offered the first chink in the wall of noise, a space filled by the weird polka skank of Daron's playful guitar and lyrics that showed no sign of settling for the literal just yet. Subject-wise, 'Sugar' was a schizophrenic collision of ideas that kicked off with the introduction of the mythical 'Kombucha mushroom' people. Kombucha is a yeast-based tea-like infusion that dates back to pre-AD Chinese dynasties, the salted Japanese variation of which refers to its main components – tea (cha) made from brown kelp (kombu). A sugared version of the drink rose to popularity in both Russia and the West circa 1900 and cordial versions can now be found in certain supermarkets. As for the "Kombucha mushroom people"? Again, who knows. The product of a fertile imagination?

The song then switched into a diatribe about playing Russian roulette and one of the few initially dubious proclamations in an otherwise politically sound body of work, as Serj tells of his girlfriend lashing out at him and him responding by kicking her before she settles down. Cloaked in irony and humour, it's impossible to view the pacifist frontman as an actual 'wifebeater' – as with much of System's work, 'Sugar' saw Serj adopting a purely fictional lyrical voice in character, as detached and identifiably 'other' as his cartoon-inspired wails and squeaks. The middle eight reached another dramatic breakdown, a sordid little scene-setting culminating in the murderous protagonist of the song sitting, chanting in a darkened room.

"That was a song that was one of the first five or six songs that we ever put together," Daron would tell me close to a decade after 'Sugar' was written. "The ending of the song was a left-over riff from the Soil days, when Shavo would come and hang out at the rehearsal studio. He wasn't in the band then, he just used to come by to hang out. I remember one day we were at an amusement park and he told me he'd written a riff on a guitar which he had then attached my riff to – and suddenly the song was born. Shavo came up with the jazzy bassline, Serj did some lyrics and we were there. It's actually quite rare for us to write a song this way and it's also one of the songs – possibly the only one – that we have probably played in every single System Of A Down show to date."

With an acoustic intro and a defiantly non-metal ('nu' or otherwise) quick-step waltzing time signature, 'Suggestions' peeled back a layer of sound to reveal the pan-international flavouring of *System Of A Down* before dropping guitar riffs that hit like newly-forged anvils from the sky. Content-wise it adopted the stance of a lowly light-post watchman scanning the sea's horizon for invaders and infidels. 'Suggestions' continued loose lyrical themes based on old world – or otherworldly – images. The aforementioned cartoon voice was deployed to full effect with Serj's pip-squeaking helium-skewed vocals portraying that of the young look-out warning of approaching legions of ships coming close to shore. What may have appeared nonsensical on first glance was actually a self-contained scene within a song as evocative as a painting.

A flipside to the band's musical bi-polar tendencies, 'Spiders' began as a mood-piece, a nocturnal meditation on the power of dreams and the potential of the sub-conscious (a recurring System theme) with the accompanying Serj-penned sleeve notes offering further explanation.

Where the opening salvos went for the jugular, 'Spiders' went deep into the darkest recesses of the largely untapped human psyche, that space that comes alive during sleep. Paranoia seeped into the song by way of a reference to the V-chip, this being the generic term for the television receiver used by parents to censor their children's viewing habits – television as opiate, another recurring System theme. Yet with no overt message to the song or tangential story as such, instead it successfully depicted the disjointed journey of a human dream; all fragmented images where the feelings invoked are the message rather than what actually *happens*.

Though a scorching sub-two minute song that began with a teasing two-note Shavo bass line and John's skittering snare drum, 'Ddevil' was a little harder to figure out. In fact to decipher it is sheer speculation, though lines collected from a number of Serj's poems carry an unquestionable common sense about them. When the album was reviewed, UK weekly *NME* took such lyrics as "Shake your spear at Shakespeare/Loud and noisy/Strong refrigerators..." as an opportunity to scoff at the notion that System were not so much politico prophets as the latest 'sports metal' (a term briefly used by the paper to define the jock-leaning nu-wave of metal acts) American idiots. They may have had a strong case with some lyrics, but perhaps failed to see the wider picture. When read in isolation a lot of the band's lyrics *are* troublesome and (occasionally) cringeworthy. But then paintings, when viewed from up close often appear to be nothing more than crudely rendered strokes of paint, the sum total usually far more effective than the parts. The reason the song was titled 'Ddevil' may be more prosaic – it was also the name of the publishing company set up by the band, often in name alone as most debuting major bands do. The name 'Devil', you suspect, was already taken.

A throwback to the earliest incarnation of the band, 'Soil' saw a fine vocal display from Serj, warbling and wailing at the sky like a muezzin (the Muslim 'servant' who leads the call to pray from a mosque's minaret) one minute, singing with a muscular tone, then screaming with murderous intent. The song was also given life by Daron's squirming Eastern-influenced guitar sound towards the close, sounding akin to a balalaika played through a Marshall. During live performances of the song, 'Soil' has been introduced by Daron as "a song about death... and friends that die... and life that dies..." Some fans have speculated that it is about the death or suicide of a friend of the band, an idea lent gravitas by some of the lyrics (which included the expletive 'motherfucker', a particular favourite in the band's lexicon throughout their early career – hey, they were still American-raised metal dudes after all).

'War?' was already a long-established live favourite with the fans and certainly one of their most gargantuan-sounding and ferocious moments. A brilliant display of the distillation of an opera's worth of ideas into the context of a rock song, it worked on many levels – mosh-friendly slam-anthem or the soundtrack to the greatest war movie never made. Lyrically the song tackled the idea of history's multifarious perceived heathens – those, as Serj explained in the sleeve notes, who the state or the powers-that-be have fought first in the name of religion, then communism and more recently drugs and terrorism, always in the quest for global domination; the 'heathen' as anti-authoritarian rebel.

"When I say 'we don't talk about war any more', that doesn't mean we don't remember past wars, but that wars are going on today in front of our eyes without them being called wars," explained Serj. "That's why the title of the song ends with a question mark."

With references to the holy land, "partisan brothers of war" and the Selijuks – the Sunni Turks who conquered the Roman empire of Byzantium – 'War?' carried the weight of history from the band's region of origin without ever being too specific. The song's breakdown saw Serj giving an impassioned rant from his invisible pulpit over a squall of guitars and a swirl of atmospherics that was delivered with idol-toppling ferocity. Heard live – as on the B-side to the UK release of 2001's 'Chop Suey!' single – this section encapsulated everything that is great about System Of A Down: turbo-charged riffs, Judgment Day-style reckonings and, in the closing clarion call, a soundbite that is always going to sound good when sung by a legion of hyped-up rock fans.

A study of mind control – particularly that exercised by the post-war CIA as part of their non-lethal weapons programme – 'Mind' provided a stark contrast. A foreboding introduction gives way to a verse of vocals and guitars intertwined before the song gallops away off over the horizon propelled by drum-fills and chugging doom riffs. One of manager David Benveniste's favourite SOAD songs, the key lyric reaffirms the band's position as dissidents, happy to revel in their status as anti-governmental agents using nothing but the medium of electricity to get their messages across.

'Peephole' began with a dark carnival of twisted voices and discordant Wurlitzer before slipping into full-on gypsy-metal rhythms, Serj stomping the dirt under foot to this strange new chapter in Armenian music; it was about as far from Korn as a metal band could get. Daron's Romany-sounding guitar solo was both moving and believable. The accompanying sleeve notes preface the song with a paraphrased quote from *New Scientist* magazine about marijuana being a safer narcotic than either alcohol or tobacco, though you couldn't help but think perhaps System were already preaching to the converted on that front.

Lyrically, the intriguingly-titled 'CUBert' ('Cubert' was an old Atari computer game, though Serj's misspelling may reference the cubed route of a number) wasn't the band's strongest; it seemed to suggest that people are essentially unthinking, passive and ultimately contained; conformity in the face of oppression. This, however, is just one author's interpretation – internet fan sites are awash with alternative takes on the song's meaning. "[It is about] people who don't care to take an extra step in their lives," said Serj, a man never usually keen to explain away the mystique of his lyrics. "It's partially a condemnation and partially a dare to them." Daron's itchy-scratchy guitars and the staccato drum rolls ensured that, musically at least, things were less open to interpretation: it was a metal oddity, pure and simple.

'Darts' was curious, comical and vaguely cosmological . Another song unconventional in sound and structure, with a clunking, time-ticking break, the song concludes with a reference to the gods Ninti and Ishkur, the latter being the name of the storm-God in Sumerian, a language that went out of usage circa 2000BC. In certain modes of thought Ninti is perceived as the first woman – the Eve of *The Bible*. Such gods were part of the Babylonian-Assyrian pantheon of figureheads; a vast field of study in itself. Clearly the band were operating from a completely new lyrical standpoint for their genre, their album containing an abundance of cryptic or obscure references, which even the most educated of specialist historians and theologians would need some time to explain.

"To be able to understand our world and our life as it is, you have to have your eyes open to more than one type of philosophy that's being fed to you," commented Serj. That said – and this is one of few criticisms of such weighty lyrics as epitomized by 'Darts' – Serj's lyrics flirt with many ideas without ever immersing themselves in select topics whole-heartedly. But hell, compared to Limp Bizkit…

System Of A Down's eponymous debut closed with arguably their most angry song, 'P.L.U.C.K', an acronym for 'Politically, Lying, Cowardly, Killers' and their most direct response to the Armenian genocide. It dated right back to their first ever proper demo. Spitting lyrics like bullets from an Uzi, Tankian metaphorically calls his people to arms. 'P.L.U.C.K' was an articulate and heartfelt response the like of which had never before been heard. It was a bold and brave move more valuable than a thousand hours in a stuffy, stifling history class room. Again, the topic is only considered fleetingly – the best you can hope for within the context of a pop song – but by the close System Of A Down had provided more than enough food for thought to those previously ignorant of such subjects. With the feisty "Revolution…" declaration still ringing in the listener's ears by the close of forty-something exhilarating minutes, it was all you could do not load up on Molotovs and run out the door to storm the nearest bedrock of authority.

Though their brute dynamics recalled metal's most hard-hitting bands such as Slayer and Sepultura and their lyrical bite the astuteness of Dead Kennedys, the incisiveness of Rage Against The Machine or the indignant black punk of Public Enemy, the quartet didn't actually sound much like any of these bands. They had achieved the rare feat of sounding and looking unique and singing about subjects hitherto unexplored. With *System Of A Down* these four very different personalities had just effectively reinvented rock music.

The artwork for the album was as loaded with meaning as the music it contained within. Though the image of a sepia-coloured hand reaching out from the darkness of a black background was a simple one, taken in its historical context it represented a whole philosophical standpoint. The image was entitled 'The Hand With Five Fingers' and created by acclaimed artist John Heartfield, a prominent anti-fascist during the rise of Hitler's ruling party. Born Helmut Herzfeld in 1891, he anglicized his name as a response to anti-German sentiment following World War I and devoted much of his art to political dissent. From book covers to postcards to posters, a substantial amount of his work was devoted to promoting Communism and denigrating capitalism and fascism.

One of his most potent images was 'The Hand With Five Fingers', first used as an election poster for the Communist Party of Germany in 1928. Heartfield was exiled when Hitler took power in 1933, but later returned to live in East Berlin where he was celebrated for his contribution to the struggle. He died in 1968. (Incidentally, Siouxsie & The Banshees dedicated their seminal post-punk song 'Metal Postcard (Mittageisen)' to Heartfield.)

"He was anti-Nazi, but he was also anti-West because, and few people know this, Hitler was supported indirectly by the Anglo-American financial institutions during his rise to power," was Serj's explanation for choosing to associate with such a divisive artist for their debut album.

"The fear of Communism was so intense," he continued in *Rock Sound*, "that the Western governments financially supported the fascist regimes throughout the world to create buffer zones – the ultimate shield to Communism. Heartfield criticised all that in the underground press. The reason he did it ['The Hand…'] was to wake up the Germans and to show them they were being taken advantage of."

In addition to the quotes of explanation prefacing a number of the songs, the sleeve also featured a quote-as-manifesto that railed against, amongst other things, neck-ties and "commercial Orwellianism" and concluded "Let us instigate the revolt, down with the System!" – an approach that almost negated the good work within their music by seemingly reducing their ideas to tired slogans. Even the band's 'Thanks' list on the album gave a little insight into each member. As well as name-checking friends and family members, they also gave credit to "Chamomile and throat coat teas" (Serj, naturally) and "porno movies, LA Lakers" (Daron!).

The perfect chance to further spread the message of people power came when System Of A Down were offered a support tour with thrash legends Slayer – the band who had most influenced the musical dynamics and taste for ferocity that drove System.

The eighteen date tour stretched from California, across the mid-West, dipped into Toronto for a Canadian show then continued down the big East coast cities of Boston, New York and Washington DC. System played short sharp sets of seven or so highlights from the forthcoming album. The band were first on followed by grizzly hardcore rockers Clutch.

As the founding fathers of modern thrash metal, Slayer had long since established themselves as the last bastions of brutality. Various extreme, black and death metal splinter genres had emerged in their wake and attempted to push their graphic lyrical topics to new levels but if it was whiplash thrash that true metal fans required it was to Slayer they returned time and time again for a dose of the hard stuff. Since their formation in 1982 they had set the standard and inspired thousands across the globe to form bands – not least the likes of Daron and Shavo. With the increasingly self-important Metallica meandering into more mainstream territories, they seemed ever more uncompromising, an attitude that spilled over into their fans, many notoriously traditional in their tastes. Thankfully Slayer themselves approved and the band were already picking up kudos by association alone.

"If I'm eighty and losing my memory, this is the tour I'll remember," said Shavo. "No radio, no video, no single, none of that crap – just get out there every day and show them what you've got. Everyone knows that opening for Slayer is not an easy task no matter how good you are. Dealing with those crazy Slayer fans is very character building."

"I love Slayer, but you can imagine how unrelenting their audience is," said John. "Slayer fans are there to see Slayer and they couldn't give a fuck. We're wasting their time in their opinion. But we got a really good reaction from them. If they say you're okay, from a Slayer audience you should be jumping up and down. We're just lucky they didn't throw shit at us on stage." "I got a few cassettes and beer thrown at me," laughed Daron. "But a lot of kids came up to us at the end of the shows and said they liked our sound because it was heavy, but original."

System Of A Down was released to relatively little fanfare on June 30, 1998. Critical reaction to the band' s debut was mixed, the majority of reviewers divided into two camps – the minority who recognised the innovative brilliance of a band doing something different within metal, an opinion generally confined to the metal press and the majority who hedged their bets. They had a name which didn't make much sense and an image that was more than a little eccentric with their weird beards, face-pulling and ridiculous make-up (breaking one of the sartorial cardinal rules – beards and make-up don't mix). That was before they had even been heard.

Respected metal publicist Roland Hyams of Work Hard PR was brought in by Columbia Records to help introduce the band to the fickle yet highly enthusiastic British music press for the first six months surrounding the release of the album. "My impressions of the band were they were very intelligent, politically aware and nice guys," remembers Hyams. "I thought the music was astoundingly good, a unique rock hybrid. In my meeting with Sony in July 1998 I wrote notes saying they were like 'Faith No More meets Frank Zappa meets Led Zeppelin' which is something I can thankfully still stand by.

Pushing a great new band is all about getting the music to the right people and trying to get them to listen. Just getting *any* reaction is hard work in the beginning, even a band as unique as System Of A Down so obviously were. As their publicist – any band's publicist – you can only ever take the horse to water. You can't make them drink or like what it drinks..."

Hyams still has copies of the press reaction reports that he compiled for the forthcoming release of System Of A Down's album and a two-track sampler that was sent out – those documents that round-up the verbal reactions of the cream of the press in the country where the band arguably first broke. It makes for telling reading and is typical of the type of reactions they provoked when people heard them for the first time. *NME* hadn't bothered playing the album but would "call back" when they had (which they did – three years later when they would first interview the band); *Metal Hammer* were interested, but concerned that the band might be too similar to Korn; *Melody Maker* liked the record and offered support, as did *Kerrang!* who immediately offered to cover the band over two pages. And a contributor for key monthly magazines *Q* and *Mojo* said "System Of A Down are awful – I could tell by their name they would be noisy and depressing..."

Many struggled to grasp any real comparisons by virtue of the band's unique sound and genealogy. Certain bands' names did keep rearing their heads though, most notably Dead Kennedys and Bad Brains, two of the most important punk bands to emerge from America following The Ramones-inspired first wave of punk. Formed in San Francisco in 1978 and Washington DC in 1979 respectively, the two bands effectively kick-started the hardcore movement of the 1980s with their uncompromising music and live performances that centred around their two singers.

The Dead Kennedys were led by the politically astute prankster frontman Jello Biafra (real name Eric Boucher) who exuded an intelligence and fearlessness in the face of confrontation and censorship and who possessed a voice with a distinctly recognisable warbling, tremulous timbre to it. Such was his commitment to socialism and counter-culture politics, in 1979 Biafra ran for the position of mayor of San Francisco (finishing a creditable fourth) and later became a leading voice for the Green Party.

Bad Brains meanwhile were four young black punks who embraced Rastafarianism early on in their career and were soon melding punk, hardcore, reggae and dub together at a time when hard rock music was still heavily racially divided; not least in DC. Their musical foresight was nothing less than visionary. Their frontman was Paul Hudson, also known as H.R. (short for his childhood nickname of 'Hunting Rod') a volatile force with a galvanised, almost gymnastic live physical presence and in possession of enough ideas and natural charisma to be something of a scene leader. His singing voice was capable of shifting from guttural proto-hardcore snarling to warm harmonising to quasi-operatic scale-bending vocal journeys.

So, on one hand you have a well-read young man with a heavy sense of injustice and the ability to inspire others into action. On the other, a man subverting the musical (and racial) conceits of white, bloated, formulaic rock music. Twenty years later and somewhere in the middle you had Serj Tankian, an accidentally albeit cannily similar heir apparent to those few rock frontmen who have genuinely made a cultural impact.

For the week of the album's release, the band were already on the Ozzfest tour, that travelling metal festival run by Ozzy and Sharon Osbourne. Started in 1996 the festival had quickly established itself as the premier place to see both the biggest and some of the best new bands in the genre. A spot on the tour not only gave new bands the seal of approval from Ozzy but also maximum exposure to fans across America's heartland. Other bands on the bill in 1998 included Motorhead, Tool and Megadeth and newer bands such as Limp Bizkit, Incubus and Coal Chamber.

That month-long tour saw System Of A Down playing to their biggest crowds and seeing some of their idols at close quarters. "There have been moments where we've had to step back and take a reality check," said Daron. "We were sitting in the dressing room with one of Ozzy's band members, and all of a sudden Ozzy himself walks in and starts talking to us."

Plenty of down-time between shows also gave the band a chance to mingle, enjoying the convivial atmosphere, backstage barbecues and drinking sessions that were a daily occurrence on this strange carnival. Long overnight drives were endured for the first time as the band spent more time than ever together. It was perfect training for the months and years of road action that would follow. It was not without incident – at one show Shavo was arrested by police for indulging in his favourite pastime. "After the show some fans came up and asked if I wanted a smoke, so I said 'Yeah, roll it up here,'" he explained. "As they were doing it, some guy approached us and said 'Who's getting arrested here?'. The kids looked really horrified, so I said it was mine. Next thing I know, I'm handcuffed against a wall."

He was not charged with anything.

It was a time of new experiences all-round as System formed friendships with other bands and doing whatever was necessary to make it to that next show. John's fondest recollection of the tour is fairly mechanical, as he told Shoutweb.com: "We were travelling around in this old RV and we were in the middle of Kentucky somewhere and it was about 110 degrees or something when the thing just starts bellowing out smoke. We are in the middle of nowhere with no way of getting to the next show, and on Ozzfest if you don't make the show they will kick you off. Anyway, we all just sat there helpless and Daron starts singing, 'It's A Long Way To The Top If You Want To Rock' by AC/DC, which was so funny. It is something that I will always remember as that was the best fucking time with just the four of us, no bullshit. It's something I will never forget."

With their frantic afternoon performances and well-received debut album reaching the metal masses, the summer on Ozzfest helped introduce System Of A Down as one of the most exciting and respected bands around – what those in LA already knew – and they made plenty of new friends along the way. One such friendship was with Limp Bizkit, whose frontman Fred Durst invited Serj to guest on a track for their forthcoming album.

"The track is called 'Don't Go Off Wandering' and it's amazing," Serj enthused. "They got a whole string section in for it and it's beautiful. Fred invited me down to their studio in LA and said he'd like me to do something. The middle section goes into this whole other feel and I just do my own thing – talking and yelling, coming up with words. I also did some harmonies with Fred for the chorus."

Reading between the lines it says something about the difference between the rather formulaic, relatively conservative musical approach of sometime Universal Records CEO Durst and the confrontational groundbreaking System Of A Down that the Limp Bizkit mainman was a little unsure about the contribution from the most distinctive new singing voice around. "He did a poetic preachy type thing, which was completely awesome," said Durst. "I really like it a lot, but, I don't know. It's very dramatic."

Serj proved to be that little bit too dramatic for Limp Bizkit's testosterone-driven noise. Though 'Don't Go Off Wandering' made it onto their multi-million selling 1999 album, *Significant Other*, Serj was omitted from the final version of the song and appeared on the demo version only, copies of which circulated on the internet. Perhaps history has proven that it was for the best.

The tour stretched across the US and System Of A Down got a true taste of the life of a travelling band with the backing and financial support of a major label, funding them along the way. It was a way of life they would grow increasingly accustomed to over the coming decade, an undeviating formula that all big bands adhere to: travel, press, show, hang out, travel, press, show, on and on ad infinitum, all peppered with liberal doses of weed and beer and political discourse; the winding white lines of the road and the different stages each day the only fixed entities in a changing landscape. They adapted well to the lifestyle, though each in their own ways with their own needs. A crew and a tour manager were employed to take care of the mechanics of the System Of The Down experience, an entourage that would change and grow in the twenty-first century to include techs, personal assistants and various relatives on the pay-roll, a strange and colourful carnival of characters. An Armenian-American peace-loving mafia armed with bongs and books and guitars instead of weapons, spreading a message of celebration, confusion and free-thought above all else. But for now System Of A Down were still the strange and curious sideshow defined by the era of their first album.

By late August they were back in LA at The Roxy, a homecoming of sorts, evident by the number of rising stars of the LA rock community in attendance – members of Spineshank down the front, Fred Durst throwing his arms around Serj midway through the set as the band pleaded for the club's air-conditioning to be turned on, Snot's Lynn Strait climbing a speaker stack to join in on System signature song 'War?'.

"Wide-eyed guitarist Daron Malakian sprays out beefy riffs that swerve into off-kilter folk melodies, while singer Serj chants bizarre slogans as if lost in a trance," noted a *Kerrang!* live review. "Alternating between high-pitched squeals and infernal bellowing, the frontman is one of the most watchable nutters in rock, and even takes the US government to task for the recent [pre-9-11] bombing of Afghanistan."

"The fucking stage is wet, we can't move, our mics are cutting out," announced Serj before an encore of 'Metro' by 1980s new wave LA band Berlin, best known for their *Top Gun*-soundtracking hit 'Take My Breath Away'. "But we're here *motherfuckers!*"

And he was right. In their hometown at least, System Of A Down had well and truly arrived. They had long since amassed an army of Los Angelino fans and were now beginning to make serious in-roads across the US. Now they just had to convince the world. *Just…*

"As the band depart, slipping and sliding across the sweat-covered stage," continued *Kerrang!*, "one listen to the hullabaloo from the audience leaves little doubt that soon the rest of the world will be getting down with the System."

Yes.

It was time to go global.

Chapter 4: We Will Fight The Heathens

System's debut was a sleeper – it sold steadily and quietly, sales increasing with each passing month and newly-converted fans left reeling by shows each night, turned on by the earlier Slayer dates. It peaked at Number 124 in the US *Billboard* charts. With little time off, the band went straight into shows with friends Incubus and unremarkable alt-metallers Ultraspank. Beginning in Texas, they moved on to Louisiana, Florida and the southern states, then up the Eastern seaboard to finish in New Jersey a month later. The shows were in bigger clubs or the smaller theatres, just intimate enough to feel special, but big enough to contain the wild moshpits spinning down on the floor in front of a frantic Serj each night

Six days after the tour ended and the quartet were packing their passports and heading to Europe for the first time, as guests once again of Slayer, with the mighty Amazonians Sepultura in the middle slot. It was something of a dream bill – the year zero thrash of Slayer, the rhythmic tribal metal innovation of Sepultura (though a line-up that no longer featured frontman Max Cavalera, who had departed to form Soulfly) and the plucky newcomers already stealing the thunder from the bigger bands they had played with throughout the summer. It was a big leap – two months earlier they were on stage at The Roxy, yet on October 24 found themselves taking to a stage in Prague, Czechoslovakia, a far cry from the sunshine, scenesters and valet parking of the Strip. System's music was only just beginning to reach the most clued-up of fans, but their reputation preceded them and they picked up more fans on their blitzkrieg visits to Poland, Hungary, Croatia and Greece.

The band were faced with an ethical dilemma when they saw on their tour schedule that they were booked to play a show with Slayer in Turkey, where they already had a burgeoning fanbase. As the country that perpetrated the slaughter of their ancestors in the very recent past and whose actions had directly informed the content of so much of System's work to date, the band were no fans of the Turkish government who still denied that the Armenian genocide had even taken place. This placed them in an awkward position – do you appease the fans whose only crime was to be born into a country decades after a tyrannical government had imposed so much cruelty and play the show regardless, or do you do take an unequivocal stand and boycott the entire country?

Really, the decision was made for them already. Not only does the Turkish government continue to deny such events took place – and with scant international opposition will no doubt continue to do so until otherwise forced to apologise – but it is a crime to protest such matters within the country. The reasoning was, the less protest, the sooner it's all forgotten about. Deny it for long enough and it'll soon be forgotten about. Which is exactly why activists such as System Of A Down are so vital to such a cause: even the casual but consistent mention of such atrocities can steadily help raise awareness amongst millions of fans, not least in the Western world where the knowledge of Eastern European history is typically fairly limited.

Simply put, System Of A Down's safety or freedom wasn't guaranteed if they said in Turkey what they had been saying in other countries – that their former leaders were murderers and their current leaders in supreme denial, and therefore partly culpable too. And as the band pointed out, they were the only known band with a CD out in Turkey that not only openly addressed the genocide but was dedicated to the memory of its victims too.

"Mostly it's a security issue," Serj said shortly after cancelling the show. "We can't play the show without giving vent to our views, because that's part of our music. And if we get up onstage and talk about the Armenian genocide, we've been told we'll get arrested. Prison in Turkey is rather rough. I don't think our record company could have got us out of there. So we decided to cancel the gig. We're against the Turkish government, not their people. To this day their government has denied that the genocide ever took place and the West has contributed to this bullshit. Playing there and not addressing the subject would have been too hypocritical."

"You can't just rewrite history," said Shavo. "It happened and we don't want to blame the population for what happened before most of them were born, but it happened and the authorities should stop denying it."

This stand was taken at a time when System Of A Down were first introducing themselves to the wider world and consequently drew attention to a cause most rock fans knew little about. In turn, the media saw a band saying something in an arena where so few did and were happy to relay the band's message. Rock 'n' roll is about challenging institutions, spreading information, a place where dissidence is positively encouraged. Yet by the close of the 1990s a generation was lacking heroes and rebels – or martyrs. American rock music has produced its fair share of prophets or protestors whose willingness to put their careers – and sometimes even their lives – on the line to fight for their respective causes distanced themselves from the mere 'rebels'.

As the record labels gained greater control over their artists throughout the 1990s (as post-Nirvana, 'alternative' music itself became co-opted from the underground and into more updated and more ruthless business models) and with the socio-political climate in the US placing anti-Americanism on a par with treason, there was little room left for both discourse *and* commercial success. You either spoke out and risked your potential for airplay or you shut up, did what you were told and reaped the financial rewards.

Finally then, here was a band saying the type of things that, when you're American, can bring a whole heap of trouble down on you from the snoop-nosed authorities who like to closely monitor those who have the attention of the nation's youth. The band themselves seemed happy to enjoy their status as a potential threat to the current MTV-led malaise where apathy reigned and acts as diverse yet equally as provocative and thoughtful as Woody Guthrie, Bob Dylan, MC5, The Beatles and John Lennon (whose records, lest we forget, were publicly burned by far-right Christians in the US during the mid-1960s), Sex Pistols or the Dead Kennedys were but distant memories. Even the most confrontational acts of recent times – Public Enemy and Rage Against The Machine – seemed to have had the venom removed from their tails or been overtaken by younger, more anaemic depoliticised versions of themselves. This was the late 1990s and it was a different political, social and economic landscape to the idealistic 1960s or decadent 1970s, though one still ruled by the same few shitehawks, sated with junk food, misled by false media and nullified by tawdry entertainment. Where were the people worth spying on? Where were the revolutionaries?

"We're not afraid to speak our minds," Serj said in one early British interview. "Throughout time, when certain people have spoken their mind they've been silenced in a way that makes it look like an accident. We just want people to be aware if that does happen to us... you'll know why." They were equally unafraid to expand on who this unknown 'they' were, who might offer a threat to the band's well-being. "The intelligence community, whose interests are aligned with global economic interests, have caused a lot of 'accidents' to happen to a lot of people," elaborated the singer to Dave Everley in *Kerrang!*. "They killed JFK, John Lennon too – anyone who had the power to convince millions of people to become true revolutionaries through the transcendence of their own spiritual peace is dead. Psychosis is [also] a weapon these days. There is conclusive evidence that the CIA have experimented with mind-control. They've been doing it since the 1950s. And it's not just technology, it's trained assassins too. Lee Harvey Oswald and Sirhan Sirhan [who killed JFK and brother Robert Kennedy respectively] say that it felt like they woke up from a dream. That's the sort of weaponry they use today. If you accept that, then the possibilities are endless."

Ethical dilemmas and conspiracy theories aside, System Of A Down were seeing Europe for the first time as a band. They were having their eyes opened, seeing the world in new ways, able to compare what was actually going on with what they, as Americans, had been told was going on. And they got to drink and rock the fuck out with two of metal's finest ever bands.

"In Germany I got really drunk with the Sepultura guys," recalls Shavo. "I tried to keep up with them, but I'm not a big drinker and we were drinking Jack Daniel's straight out of the bottle. Then I drank wine, and it was all too much. I ended up throwing up between our buses while Sepultura's people filmed me. That was pretty damn embarrassing…"

The tour rolled on throughout October and November and System got to see the best that Europe had to offer. On through Italy, France, Spain, Belgium, one or two shows in each country – bam! – then onto the next one. Unsurprisingly, given a day off System made a bee-line for Amsterdam, where soft drugs and prostitution are not only legal but practically compulsory for passing tourists

"The bus dropped us off, and we all split up," recalled Shavo in *Metal Hammer* of his induction into European 'culture'. "We didn't know where to go so we went to a reggae shop but there was not one black person in the whole place. I got really, really stoned and there were all these Black Power posters, but only white people there and I was like 'Why are we here?' We went to a few more coffee shops and we smoked and ate way too much – I ate, like, eight brown cookies then I threw up. Also, our district was conveniently located near the red light district, and I found myself there – this is before I puked. When the girls see that you're young and not from there, they try to entice you. There were two girls in one window, and I was flirting a little just for fun, and they got on top of each other and were saying, 'We can have you together.'"

And did he partake?

"It was $25, but I didn't do it," he laughs. "I've never been with a prostitute. Why pay for sex? But think of it this way: you're not paying them to have sex with you, you're paying them to leave…"

The tour continued to London for the first of two shows at the 2500 capacity Astoria theatre. The band's label had already conspired with *Kerrang!* magazine to do a massive giveaway of the same System cassettes that had been so successfully distributed in the US and invited readers to write in for one of the many thousands of samplers they were giving away. Coupled with favourable coverage in a number of other magazines, airplay on the radio rock shows and the fact the band's album had had time to permeate into he UK underground meant the Astoria show was one of the most anticipated metal shows of the year.

Hitting the stage at the un-godly time of 6.45pm covered in body paint and looking like they'd raided Salvador Dali's wardrobe, System Of A Down exploded; a heavy-as-hell carnival in town for all the curious local folk to stare and point at.

Subsequent magazine reviews captured the chaos and absurdity of it all: "As the band prepare themselves to close their set with 'War?', Daron Malakian, doused in silver paint, and duck-walking like a Chuck Berry from an alternate universe, totters over to the microphone and stares out at the audience from those mad, wide, wandering eyes of his.

'We're System Of A Down from LA,' he squeals. 'You'd better make the most of this. You won't be able to see us for much longer, because *they're going to kill us!*'"

System had proved that they were as exhilarating on stage as they were on their record and picked up further positive coverage, as much of the UK's metal press were in attendance. In fact off the back of two twenty-five minute sets over two nights, they had converted enough people to ensure that their first forthcoming headline UK tour would be a success. And this happened in all the countries they went to with Slayer and Sepultura, planting seeds in new soil for the first time.

London was just one more city wondering when these four freaks would return.

On December 11, the band's lives were touched by tragedy when news reached them that their friend Lynn Strait, singer with Snot, with whom they had shared many a stage over the previous four years, had been killed in a car crash near Santa Barbara along with his dog Dobbs, who had been immortalised on the cover of Snot's well-received 1997 debut album *Get Some*. The band and in particular their charismatic frontman had been well liked amongst not just their own fans but the LA music scene at a time when bands tended to be rivals rather than friends. Strait had a reputation as a good guy with a magnetic personality and a mischievous streak – he had served time inside, had been arrested for onstage indecent exposure at an Ozzfest show the summer before his death and had also appeared in Matt Zane's porn film *Backstage Sluts II* – a self-styled 'cockumentary' aimed at the MTV generation – making him one of very few rock stars to have had sex in an adult film.

Though Strait died during the demo stages of Snot's second album, the surviving members took the completed music and invited a number of musician friends, including members of Limp Bizkit, Incubus, Korn, Slipknot and Sugar Ray to the studio to contribute on what would turn into the tribute album *Strait Up*. Shavo joined Soulfly's Max Cavalera on a track entitled 'Catch A Spirit' in which, according to the Brazilian singer, Odadjian "banged the shit out of his bass, making all these spooky songs."

"Lynn died really young, which sucks," commented Shavo. "But he lived his life doing whatever the fuck he wanted to do." Serj meanwhile appeared on another song, album opener 'Starlit Eyes'. "The last time I saw Lynn was two weeks before his death, walking on Sunset Boulevard," he explained. "He looked very peaceful and intense, and he was about to do his vocals on the album. *Strait Up* is a way of communicating back to him and telling him how much he meant to us. Lynn's eyes were so serene. He was a good friend of mine, an amazing person and a beautiful spirit." The album would finally be released in November 2000.

By the close of the year, System Of A Down had notched up a number of milestones in their relatively short career. They'd completed and released a debut album whose influence is still being felt today and which featured in a number of end year polls, toured with Ozzy (Ozzy!) and Slayer (ditto), headlined a string of club shows and covered much of mainland Europe. And all of it had been done with little or no creative compromise on their part – they looked, sounded and said exactly what they wanted to do, a rare position in these times of corporate-sponsored rock 'n' roll. They'd also amassed a small army of fans who dissected every lyric and absorbed every bit of information that filtered through in interviews.

1999 began at is it would continue – with more touring in January, this time as guests of Fear Factory, whose popularity had steadily grown with each industrial cyber-metal album they released and whose guitarist Dino Cazares had been a fan of the band since their demo days. Disaster struck five shows in when System were due to play The Trocadero in Philadelphia, with Nothingface, Spineshank and Earth Crisis also on the bill.

Shavo relates what happened: "All was going amazingly. We were all friends and the bill was great because each band was a little different from the other. Then [in Philadelphia] our techs woke me up screaming, 'Everything's gone, the Ryder truck has been stolen!'. Daron was going crazy because a lot of his guitars were irreplaceable. We weren't a rich band able to say 'Give us more', so we had to cancel. We actually went to the show that night and the kids were outside, pissed off that we weren't playing, so we explained and signed autographs. We had insurance, but we weren't sure if it covered everything. A lot of kids we talked to on the Net were out checking pawn shops and looking for our stuff…"

The theft of all of System's gear from outside their hotel was a major setback, and the management company who looked after Fear Factory and Spineshank offered a reward for the return of their friends' equipment. When it wasn't found, two weeks' worth of shows had to be re-scheduled, the loss clearly more than just material. Though they were not yet a rich band, System Of A Down at least had the backers to re-supply them with new gear and they were soon back in business – with better security guarding their truck and its vital possessions.

After a brief break in early February the rescheduled Fear Factory dates were played with Spinehsank and (hed) pe also on the bill. With other such similar groupings of kindred bands together, nu-metal had turned into a definable genre that was reflected in the styles adopted by fans – lots of piercing, key-chains, baggy jeans, goatees and inventive hair styles. It was metal being dragged into a new millennium, hence the name. The tour continued through to March, culminating with two shows in Philadelphia, where the bands managed to leave with their gear intact this time. It would take a brave man or a fool to fuck with the four bad-ass looking motley bands and their crews a second time around.

So the scene was set for an international invasion.

Though System Of A Down's reputation preceded them, they had yet to play a headline show outside of the US – up until now shows had been confined to those Slayer supports – and that reputation only existed within the rock and metal world. And even then, they were viewed with suspicion or cynicism from certain quarters, if only for their ties to nu-metal and all things pissed-off and Californian. Guilty by association, if you like. Let's not forget nu-metal was one sub-genre of many, the latest new thing, a possible passing fad, a fashion minefield. And it also pays to remember that metal isn't quite the liberal, open-minded world you might expect. Ten years earlier thrash metal was frowned upon by many fans of the founding fathers of modern metal – your Black Sabbath and Judas Priest – because it was new, fresh and more extreme than they were accustomed to and they couldn't quite understand it. Ditto for when Aerosmith and Run DMC joined forces to revamp the former's song 'Walk This Way' and Anthrax and Public Enemy did much the same on 'Bring The Noise'. *Rap and rock…together? It'll never work…*

So as System Of A Down geared themselves up for their first headline dates in the UK – the birthplace of metal, lest we forget – they already had a strong underground following but were hardly hailed as visionaries in the metal world, let alone the mainstream one.

Taking your average Metallica fan in any small dull town in any country as the embodiment of metal's tendency not to always embrace the new and the challenging, System were merely one new group of many. And even though they were already touring buddies with the likes of thrash gods Slayer and one of 1990s metal's most original voices Sepultura, since they didn't all have long hair and wear black they weren't to be trusted; hell, even half the old-school Metallica fans didn't trust Metallica these days. The point being, until proven otherwise most new bands in metal are viewed with cynicism, particularly if they are part of a new scene most associated with Adidas and hair-braids, DJs and excessive levels of down-tuning.

System Of A Down's arrival in the UK as headliners was heralded with a *Kerrang!* cover story, a big step up given the band's relatively low-profile. It came at a time when many already had them down as another bunch of Californian knuckleheads more concerned with style over substance. Naturally, the band seized the opportunity and went for the most flamboyant look for their first international magazine cover, festooning themselves head to toe in gold and silver body paint (Shavo and Daron respectively), strange facial tribal markings and a long robe (Serj) and a touch of powder blue mascara (John – for one time only).

"That was interesting," said Serj. "We always like to do something different visually. For me it comes from the fact that art doesn't belong to artists. Art comes through the universe and we're, at best, skilled presenters, so why put my picture on it? We use regular photos for press shots so people know who the fuck we are. But it's great when the music speaks for itself..."

Painting yourself gold seems a sure-fire way of making sure the music *doesn't* just speak for itself, just the opposite in fact. Thus those who had yet to hear the band were instead greeted by a genuinely bizarre sight – the suggestive stare of a golden Shavo, the all-knowing grin of Serj. The Tin Man from *The Wizard of Oz* on guitar. Weirdness. How could you not check out this band? The tickets for the band's first UK tour sold quickly.

It was at this point that this author fell for System Of A Down, and the indirect inception of this book came about when I was dispatched to Wolverhampton to write a lead live review for the following week's issue of *Kerrang!* Truthfully, at the age of 23, I was already feeling jaded with mainstream metal, disappointed in the conservative streak within the formulaic approach of many bands. I had found Korn ridiculous and one-dimensional, Marilyn Manson thought-provoking and occasionally hilarious, but neither made music I wanted to play. Slipknot looked promising but had yet to make their Roadrunner debut, Metallica were floundering and some of the newly-moneyed nu-metal bands that I was interviewing on a regular basis were genuine morons prone to self-importance; surfers or jocks with obvious sexist streaks or otherwise tedious careerists whose materialistic ambitions were manifested in their willingness to put their name to anything to make a buck. Over the coming months I would sit and listen, bored, as (hed) pe would tell me about "chicks" over and over again, watch as Disturbed's David Draiman got cagey because I didn't love his band unreservedly, evade a scowl from Tura Satana's Tairrie B for much the same reason, grind my teeth as Insane Clown Posse barked some nonsense about being geniuses and offer sympathetic glances to colleagues given the short straw of having to sit through an hour of clinical marketing man speak that comprised a Linkin Park interview. Few things are as depressing as hearing the biggest band in the world talk about demographics and brand development.

All the cool big 1990s rock bands – Rage, Faith No More – were treading water or falling out with one another. There was lots of great music around but not in the American mainstream; the chances of hearing music of any substance on the radio seemed at an all-time low. I wanted extremity and danger, humour and vigour – I wanted to be challenged, assaulted and proved wrong. I wanted a real life subversive rock 'n' roll band, not one you can only discover vicariously through the history books and the bargain bins, like Dylan, MC5 or The Clash. I wanted someone to come along and confirm that I wasn't alone in thinking the world was great but people were shit instead of thanking God, their record company and Pepsi Cola like their president wanted them to.

This wasn't the outsider music whose close approximation to the attitude of punk I was first attracted to, listening to Minor Threat, Guns N' Roses and The Stooges simultaneously. Could *Orgy* really change the life of a fourteen-year-old like those bands had for me?

Of course they couldn't.

I don't mind admitting the first time I saw a picture of System Of A Down I thought they were just one more band at the latest trend-driven gang bang. How wrong a young cynic can be. The debut album grabbed me immediately and I devoured every lyric and sleeve note as it played on rotation. On first play, my blood-pumped quicker around my body as my brain struggled to take it all in at once. What did it all mean exactly – the Kombucha mushroom people and shaking your spear at Shakespeare, and did it really matter anyway? Was this weed just deceptively strong or were System Of A Down really, really fucking good? I suspected I wasn't alone in my thinking. The album reminded

System Of A Down:
'Beards R Us' or alternatively, the best rock band in the world?

System members
Shavo and Daron
have always erred on
the side of caution
with their image.

Despite their high profile, John found the lack of drum sponsorship offers disappointing.

Serj's ceaseless campaigning for Armenian issues has brought recognition from the very top flight of his homeland's government.

System Of A Down: serious as a heart attack about certain issues.

Top: with success comes glamour
Bottom: The band's on-the-road excess spiralled until this low point,
caught out with a double-layered Victoria sponge.

Backstage with Incubus

An Armenian band singing about genocide and raising political
awareness while wearing outrageous beards – it will never work.
SOAD picking up yet another award.

Critical acclaim and public fervour – 25 million albums sold to date.

System's live show has been the strongest weapon in their arsenal.

System Of A Down: a *truly* unique band.

me as much of my favourite punk and hardcore bands like Dead Kennedys and No Means No and cool discoveries like Zappa, Captain Beefheart and PiL as much as they did Slayer.

Wolverhampton is in the Midlands of Britain and remains a stronghold of classic rock and metal. Sabbath and Judas Priest formed down the road and gigs in towns like this are always more fun than in London, where the kids go off at shows but only if they're sure they're looking good while doing it. Elsewhere they don't give a fuck. It seemed an appropriate place for System Of A Down to play their debut headline show in the UK.

The venue had already been upgraded from the Wulfren Hall to the larger Civic due to demand and when I arrived there early there was already a good couple of hundred fans hanging out and drinking excitedly. I sat on a wall and watched a couple of boys casually smashing bottles, enjoying the convivial atmosphere of anticipation. And possibly for the first time ever, I also felt there was a new generation of fans below me, whose fashion tastes I didn't necessarily share but whose enthusiasm and energy I related to. This was a good thing, a reminder that no one can be at the vanguard for long and that there will always be teenagers cooler than you. Because they're teenage and you're not.

Everyone was getting casually rowdier and more pissed – and it was only 6pm. Inside the venue before the doors opened to the public, members of System and support bands Spineshank and Static-X were milling around. Shavo was in his knee-high sports socks chatting to a couple of girls on the stairs who were inviting him to stay at their parents' house that night; Wayne from Static-X was waxing up his spectacular bouffant; Spineshank were hastily re-arranging their set due to a guitarist being refused entry into the country; the usual lull before the storm. The two support bands pass with perfunctory sets and I kill time interviewing fans.

Then, the lights go down, Daron's intro to 'Suite-Pee' rattles out of the PA system then – boom! – showtime. The band are amazing, a relentless, breathless attack of the senses, like the raging charges of Braveheart in an alternative dimension or the offspring of the stylishly sinister gangs of *The Warriors*, everything I hoped for when I first heard the album. It is a rare thing. Serj delivers political between-song diatribes, while Daron counters with his usual demands that everyone should "get naked and fuck". Over to stage right, Shavo ducks and bobs and grins at the front row. Halfway through the show I manage to get onto the closed off balcony where I can look down on the sight below – a sea of bodies bouncing off one another like electrodes and diodes, a sweaty kinetic frisson rising up from the floor. Circle pits form in sections of the seething mass, small spinning whirlpools of bodies and space, before more bodies fill the gaps and the circles disappear, only to resurface seconds later further across the hall. I see a fight break out. I also think I can see some people fucking in there. It feels a little like Armageddon, but not like the one depicted in the bible – *this version is fun*. Presiding over it all, a doe-eyed Serj is looking serene and unflappable, a man whose presence alone gives a quasi-religious feel to proceedings. If this, I think to myself, was a church or a mosque or a synagogue, there would be uproar. Institutions would crumble and new understandings emerge in their wake. The band play the entire debut album and two other songs, 'Honey' and 'XXXX' – later just shortened to 'X'. They finish with album closer 'P.L.U.C.K.' and are gone.

If there's any one reason that System Of A Down have become a success, then it is their ability to convey this type of excitement night after night. This first time I saw them sticks in my mind as one of the greatest shows I've ever witnessed and provided enough food for thought to chew over for some time. They proved that the esoteric and the popular aren't mutually exclusive and that poetry and politics and absurdity can make for compatible bedfellows. They also set a new standard for heaviness – not because they were the heaviest band in the world *per se*, but because their songs were simultaneously melodic, memorable and awkward while being unremittingly intense. Yes, System Of A Down weren't the heaviest, but they were the most *intense*. For a while I found myself unfairly comparing all other bands I saw live to System; few even came close.

Their fleeting debut headlining UK tour continued to Nottingham's Rock City, back to The Astoria in London and finishing in Manchester, all shows sold out in advance. To capitalise on the tour System Of A Down released their debut single. While pop acts and more conventional rock acts tend to adhere to a release campaign that begins with a single, then another, then an album, in breaking the band Columbia Records had done things slightly differently. Recognising a distinctly unconventional-sounding band who were unlikely to get huge amounts of radio airplay early on, they had worked the band from the ground up, filtering the album out with a marketing and advertising campaign to back it up, but letting it breed organically – the only real way a metal band can succeed. Cynical extremists revelling in their outsider status, metal fans aren't easily fooled – which is why they're attracted to the genre in the first place.

However, steps were being taken to introduce System Of A Down to a wider audience. The consensus among fans in the rock media was that this band were quite special, clearly capable of changing the genre as the likes of Slayer or Faith No More or Rage Against The Machine had done before, but beyond that they were never going to be a number one band sounding like *that*. Were they?

Released May 24, 'Sugar' was the single that first introduced a lot of rock fans to the band, the album having slipped out six months earlier without fanfare. In the US, seven-track 'Sugar' samplers had already been sent out to radio programmers in January 1999 in a bid to gain the band more air time, no easy thing with a song littered with guns, violence and 'motherfuckers'. Aside from featuring the album version of the song and a highly necessary yet somehow stunted 'clean' version, the US version 'Sugar EP' also featured both live and 'clean live' versions of 'Sugar' and 'War?' and a short song called 'Storaged'.

The UK single release of 'Sugar' was backed by live versions of 'War?', 'Sugar' and album opener 'Suite-Pee'. The accompanying publicity promised the arrival of a band who were "a red hot bubbling mass of frantic, metallic riffs and body-twitching hardcore grooves that reflect the outrage and chaos of the world today."

A video for 'Sugar' – System's first time in front of a camera – had already been made before the band set off on their European tour by director Nathan Cos, who had recently made videos for Korn and Coal Chamber. Filmed in a cavernous warehouse in Culver City, home to a number of LA's film studios, the band dressed up for the occasion in silver trousers and leopard skin coat (Daron), bare-chested with tribal symbols painted on (Shavo) and a white boiler suit and gas mask (John), and performed in front of a star-spangled banner that had seen better days – "We wanted a kind of defeated-looking flag," said Serj. Projected onto the flag were stark images of riot scenes, burning landscapes and workers marching into factories in robot-like formation – everything the band appeared to sing about. Another scene was shot showing the band being interrogated by CIA-style men in black suits and sunglasses, before, for reasons not fully understood, a bikini-clad blonde stripper made an appearance – possibly as a concession to the titty-friendly MTV programmers. The video also featured the odd subliminal message such as *'Aspartame kills'*, a reference to the controversial artificial sweetener that's used in over five thousand products including soft drinks and which has been linked to a number of diseases.

"It's kind of about what the media does to people," explained Serj on the set of the video. "Showing society at its most monotonous. This is a new experience. It's not a huge budget video but we wanted to give it a shot."

Though 'Sugar' reached Numbers 31 and 28 in the US Modern Rock Chart and US Mainstream Rock charts respectively – positions based solely on radio airplay – it failed to gain a foot-hold in the UK Top 40. It was hardly surprising – few outside of the metal scene heard 'Sugar', or if they did the general reaction was confusion, disgust and a slight souring of the face. I know – I've seen it on the many occasions I have sat people down and said "You *have* to hear this band!" Those who did hear System off the back of this strangest of debut singles certainly wouldn't forget them in a hurry and the many recently-converted fans loved them unreservedly with the type of fervour unseen in metal since Korn had debuted in the mid-1990s. And System Of A Down's debut album was still selling steadily…

Twelve months on from their first major tour and the band were back on Ozzfest, which this year was headlined by an on-form Black Sabbath (people had stopped counting the number of farewell and comeback tours they had done). This time System were given a considerably higher slot than their inaugural trial-by-fire on the second stage the previous summer.

The band were changing, growing, evolving too. Cherry blossom trees (albeit ones made from plywood) adorned the stage on these shows and with their debut-heavy set, crowds were singing their songs right back at them. Further down on the bill were a nine-headed, masked metal beast of a band from Des Moines, Iowa called Slipknot whose brutal self-titled debut for Roadrunner was released in the June. Though not nearly as original sounding as System, the bruisers certainly shared a similarly intense and uncompromising approach to music and the theatrics of a rock show. Their paths would cross again many times long after the summer ended.

1999 seemed to be the zenith of nu-metal – after this point, the new wave of bands appeared to separate into three groups, depending upon the listener's tastes: the good, the bad and the ugly. System had been trying to shake off the tag ever since it appeared, though it would take a second album to prove to the world that their approach was quite different. Elsewhere, bands like Limp Bizkit were outselling their contemporaries yet their fanbase seemed largely confined to white, teenage boys. To critics they represented the worst of the new breed, a mewling, screaming musical hissy fit for suburban jocks flirting with the black culture they didn't understand. It was a view that was arguably corroborated by the infamous riots following the band's slot at that summer's Woodstock show. Their success would be hard to sustain.

"There's always that chance that heavy music could become cheesy again," said Shavo fortuitously during an interview that summer. "It could happen very quickly if enough terrible bands enter the scene. Just look at grunge: there were some great bands when it first started, then it got huge, and the next thing you know, there were all these terrible bands and it just faded away."

A sign that nu-metal was not quite the close-knit scene some of its exponents claimed it to be – or that greed can expose the true personality – came when System found themselves in the middle of a rare disagreement that autumn with Fred Durst. System had been booked to replace new grunge band Staind on the final leg of the 'Family Values' rap-rock tour package alongside Limp Bizkit, Method Man and Redman. At the same time, Durst was competing with David Benveniste's Velvet Hammer to secure the management rights for tipped Chicago quartet Taproot. When the group showcased for Rick Rubin and then consequently decided to sign with Benveniste, Durst reacted by pulling System from the Family Tour – which was organised by his management, The Firm – and famously left a terse voicemail with Taproot frontman Stephen Richards – who, to their credit, immediately made the message available as a download.

"Hey, man, you fucked up," said Durst on the message. "You don't ever bite the hand that feeds in this business bro and your fuckin' manager so-called guy is a fucking idiot... a loser motherfucker goin' nowhere. Don't fuckin' show up at my show, 'cause, if you do, you're gonna get fucked. All right? You and your fuckin' punk ass, man. You call your fuckin' manager, David Manifestease-whatever, ask him what he's done and doin'. You're a fuckin' dumb motherfucker."

When System fans heard that it was Durst that had pulled their favourite band from a tour, they caused a stir via the internet and the ever-contentious Limp Bizkit singer found his popularity plummeting even further.

"Everything is changed," System of a Down commented on their website. "Lots of drama has transpired recently regarding our tours. To make it short and sweet, all of it had nothing to do with the band. Things are now reset in order and justice has prevailed. Advice to people in bands, talk to each other, not through your people." After this minor debacle, System were due to tour with Filter instead, but had to cancel shows when Daron received surgery on a recurring knee injury he sustained onstage during an earlier show in Portland.

The break from touring allowed the band a little time off from playing and to sit back and enjoy a little of the high life that comes with being a rock star. In August they were invited to the annual *Kerrang!* Awards in London, traditionally a hedonistic excuse for a party with some of rock and metal's finest in attendance. The band were nominated for the 'Best International Live Act' award, up against bands such as Marilyn Manson and The Offspring. John and Shavo – dressed in a brand new Versace jacket and brothel creeper shoes for the occasion – flew into the country to represent the band. Guest presenters of the category were Coal Chamber who were briefly reunited with their fellow Los Angelinos when System Of A Down won the coveted award voted for by readers of the magazine.

"I can guarantee you that table number 14 is going to be the drunkest tonight," slurred John as he received the award before yelping Daron-style: "C'mon everyone – let's get drunk and naked!" "We had no clue, this was a total mystery to us," Shavo told me afterwards with the all bonhomie and enthusiasm of a seasoned Oscar winner. "Now we're going to get drunk and fucked up."

Highlight of the night though was not the band winning their first music award but meeting Led Zeppelin guitarist and bona fide rock legend Jimmy Page, who Shavo was photographed with alongside Stereophonics frontman Kelly Jones, for the cover of the magazine.

By the close of 1999, System Of A Down were capable of selling out venues like LA's 4,500-capacity Hollywood Palladium, but instead opted to close the year by playing three consecutive shows (rescheduled from September during the confusion of cancelled shows) at their old haunts, The Whisky, The Troubadour and The Roxy by way of a homecoming thank you to those fans who had stuck with them since the early club shows.

The Troubadour gig saw one of their most unconventional shows to date when Serj caught a nasty bout of flu that meant he was unable to perform. Rather than cancel and disappoint the many friends and family members in attendance, they decided to play the show anyway by enlisting the help of various singers and scenesters in attendance, including (hed) pe's frontman Jahred (aka MCUD), who joined the band for 'Suite-Pee', former Kyuss vocalist John Garcia, whose new band Unida were supporting, and a rare reunion with Andy Khachaturian, who sang his vocals direct from a copy of the band's debut album. It was a memorable, if somewhat surreal evening. But then it was System Of A Down and people had grown to expect the unexpected. No one asked for a refund on the way out.

In the meantime, another single from System's debut was released. 'Spiders' was the chosen song and the band made another video. Aside from being sent out to TV and radio, 'Spiders' was also being included on the soundtrack to *Scream III*, the latest film in Wes Craven's post-modern slasher film resurgence. Recognising the huge crossover between horror and metal fans, the executive producers of the sound-track – another poor post-grunge band, Creed – also included choice metal acts such as Slipknot and a roll-call of mainstream rock and nu-metal mediocrity that System Of A Down clearly had little in common with musically: Sevendust, Orgy, Godsmack and Staind. Still, sometimes you just have to keep quiet and go with it.

The video was a little more elaborate than that of the promo for 'Sugar' and involved the band members being suspended in the air by harnesses for hours on end – while being watched by Dave Grohl who had stopped by to say hello – a set-up that brought a whole new meaning to the term 'cock rock'.

"It was very embarrassing to do," confided Serj. "I was fastened to this rig up in the air and I couldn't get out of the harness. After about three hours I really needed to piss and I was told that it would take an hour to get me down. Because it was during a big shoot with a stage set and a lot of cameras, they cut a slit for me to piss through."

His discomfort didn't end there however, as he all too happily explained. "I was sitting on a bicycle seat, so my balls were strapped in and there was no way that the urine could pass through my urinary tract and into my penis. In the end they took me out of there anyway, while fifteen people waited for me. It was fun though."

Sounds it.

While Shavo contributed visual ideas and would later direct band videos and Serj did what was needed to be done for the sake of spreading their message, John was a little less enthusiastic towards matters concerning the aesthetic side of the band.

"If it was up to me, I wouldn't even be in the videos," he shrugged. "I only feel comfortable behind my drum kit. In the first video, I'm wearing a mask; in the second, I'm in it for two seconds – by choice." The song reached the Top 30 of the US Mainstream Rock chart.

System Of A Down's final shows of the Millennium were on a bill they could only have dreamed about playing a half decade earlier – main support to the original Black Sabbath line-up in the metal godfathers' hometown of Birmingham. Afterwards System did a signing session at a local nightclub, partying long into the night at the close of what had been another productive year. Sooner or later though they would need to start thinking about writing and recording that difficult second album...

★

December 1999 and System Of A Down, perhaps more than any other band encapsulated the strange feelings permeating the collective human psyche as the end of one millennium crept into the beginning of another. 'Millennium tension', the press called it. Amid post-9-11 rumours of impending Armageddon, a technological meltdown due to an unseen 'millennium bug' and natural disasters of Biblical proportions – humans have such wonderful imaginations – System's music seemed to perfectly reflect the paranoia of the times, a position that would be affirmed over the next couple of politically turbulent years. But theirs wasn't music about numerology or the alignment of the planets or plague, pestilence or paranoia for the sake of it, but rather a frantic indictment and interpretation of the chaos of the modern world.

As the decade, century and millennium drew to a close, the band took a well-earned rest, opting to spend the beginning of the third millennium since the birth of Christ at home with family and friends. Which isn't to say they didn't take the preceding month or two as an opportunity to espouse their opinions about the rotten state of the world.

"What's another year compared to the billions of years that this planet's been around," said Daron, in response to another magazine questionnaire about 'the millennium'. "I'll probably go down to the post office and take out a bunch of people…"

"I think it would be pleasant to welcome in the New Year with a good spirit of joy and friendship," said Serj. "This last century will be remembered for genocide and death. There have been more people killed by the hand of man this century than any other. There has been an uplift recently, an awakening in certain people, which is really interesting to watch. That might be a last-ditch way of dying, but it might also be rebirth. We're now living in a society of complete technological advancement that takes away the human spirit and heart. We've created loneliness in its worst form, and it's that loneliness that has caused people to go beyond what we call human."

The dawning of the new millennium was heralded in with little more than worldwide firework displays, then, alas, it was back to work for everyone. Though the songs on their debut dated back nearly five years, System Of A Down's album had only been out six months and was still selling. More road work beckoned in January when the band headlined 'Sno Core', a tour package aimed at 'snow communities' in the US that was co-founded by Californian ska punks Sublime. They were joined by Incubus and kindred spirits Mr Bungle, whose musical approach perhaps came closest to System than possibly any other band and whose frontman Mike Patton had influenced them in the first place. Still sporting the body paint look, System stole many of the shows playing to crowds that were there to see them for the first time, despite the fact they'd been on tour since they finished recording the first album. How long was it now anyway? No-one could quite remember; all that remained in their wake was a trail of empty hotel and dressing rooms, smoked out weed pipes in the back lounges of tour buses and a mass outbreak of tinnitus.

"The edge of burn-out that permeates the show adds another

dimension to it all," wrote journalist Don Kaye who noted that they had now been playing shows most nights of the week for twenty months by the time the Sno Core tour hit New York in February. "Even though it might be time for SOAD to get themselves off the road and start writing a new record, their uniquely eccentric sounds and irresistible presence is always welcome around these parts."

The band's profile was certainly on the rise, predominantly through that tried and tested rock 'n' roll method of relentless touring and finding themselves on big festival bills – in July they played alongside Metallica, Korn and Kid Rock to 50,000 at the Los Angeles Memorial Coliseum. It was a performance that saw Serj dressed in the regalia of a South American dictator, simultaneously denouncing the US government and announcing that it was John's birthday – "so give him a blow-job if you see him", added Daron, getting the biggest cheer of the day. They also played a cover version of Pink Floyd's 'Pink Blue Sky'.

But other marketing forces were at play too. Despite their rhetoric, System Of A Down were still part of the hard-sell of corporate capitalism, evident in their appearances on a number of other projects. All were worthy, though did detract slightly from the myth the band were creating for themselves; up until now they had been outsiders and their inclusion on the occasional film soundtrack, with a bunch of the latest nu-metal no-hopers that the labels were pushing, didn't always sit easy.

Throughout 2000 the twisted System vibe proliferated. The offers kept coming in as their label people set to work, capitalising on the quartet's growing reputation as one of metal's sure-fire bets by licensing out their songs. Their rousing version of Berlin's 'Metro' (later also cover by Blink 182) complete with a great staccato solo from Daron, appeared on the soundtrack to Wes Craven's forgettable movie *Dracula 2000* alongside all their old mates – Static-X, (hed)pe, Slayer – as well as newer acts surfing the nu-metal wave such as Taproot and Linkin Park. They also contributed 'Marmalade' to the metal-heavy soundtrack for *Strangeland*, the screenwriting and production debut of Dee Snider, a throwback from the Sunset Strip days when he fronted Twisted Sister (an even more ludicrous looking band than the young System Of A Down).

They then furthered their good relations with Ozzy and Black Sabbath by contributing a version of the metal god's paean to cocaine,

'Snowblind' for a Sabbath tribute album, *Nativity In Black II*. First heard on 1974's *Volume 4*, a cornerstone album for metal, System's version of the track joined a line-up of some of the strongest metal bands of the day playing choice cuts from the Sabbath back-catalogue, including Pantera, Machine Head and Ozzy himself, who teamed up with Primus.

Another appearance was on *Chef Aid: The South Park Album*, the tie-in compilation to the popular TV show. If System Of A Down were going to lend their music to such a project, then *South Park* was a worthy cause. Matt Stone and Trey Parker's colourful creation was a scathing and scatological satire of modern America that deployed irony, sarcasm and surrealism to critique the institutions that the populace is taught to accept without question – the police, education, the military, morality, the media (we could deconstruct the image of Cartman's anal probe by aliens in Episode 1 as being representative of the US's fear of all things intrusively non-American and the national preoccupation with self-analysis, a form of anal retention – but we won't...)

Plus, *South Park* was a cartoon and so, in some ways, were System Of A Down, the influence of old Warner Brothers characters evident in the voices employed by Serj on their first album, their musical world one of bright colours and reality, twisted and tweaked into new shapes. Though the best songs on the album were the ones sung by the cast themselves, the line-up was strong, drawing everyone from the pairing of Ozzy and Wu-Tang's Ol' Dirty Bastard to Rancid and Joe Strummer through to Meatloaf and Elton John.

System Of A Down's collaborative contribution 'Will They Die 4 You' was recorded with hip-hop's big hitters Mase, Puff Daddy (soon to abbreviate himself to P Diddy, then Diddy) and Li'l Kim when the band were still a relatively unknown entity – it was released only five months after their debut dropped. It was also recorded by post – that is, parts were laid down at separate times in separate places. Not a good way to rock. Never a great rapper, Puffy's vocals are sluggish against the backdrop of Daron's clunking, squeaking guitar. It was all part of the learning curve and the song remains one of the band's least favourite musical moments.

"I don't really like the thing we did with Puff Daddy," Daron later said. "That was just a comedy CD and it's definitely not one of the more powerful System songs. In fact, it's not even a System song. Other than that, I'm proud of every song we've done." Shavo agreed: "It was just something we did for fun; it wasn't something that should represent our band. Personally, I don't like it."

A much-discussed interesting musical collaboration came to fruition in September 2000 when System Of A Down were invited to work on a song with members of hip-hop collective Wu-Tang Clan. The band had been approached by Loud, a label showcasing a number of their rap acts by pairing them with some of the big names in rock and metal for an album entitled *Loud Rocks*. Though the album was heavily influenced by the soundtrack to the 1993 movie *Judgement Night* which successfully paired together a number of rock-rap collaborations (Faith No More and Boo Yaa Tribe, Cypress Hill and Sonic Youth, Slayer and Ice-T) and was a major influence on the rock-rap genre that emerged in the mid/late-1990s, the *Loud Rocks* musical summit did produce some decent stand-alone tunes and was a fair reflection of the state of this music in the hands of the major labels. In fact, the album had been inspired by a double bill of Rage Against The Machine and Wu-Tang Clan that the CEO of Loud, Steve Rifkind, had seen when the two bands had undertaken a controversial tour together in the mid-1990s.

While the likes of Sugar Ray and Tha Alkaholiks or Incubus and Big Pun produced nothing more than you would expect from distinctly average bands, it was the big players who saved *Loud Rocks* from sounding like little more than a cash-in on nu-metal – most notably Rage Against The Machine's Tom Morello and Red Hot Chili Pepper's Chad Smith work with Wu-Tang on the slamming 'Wu-Tang Clan Ain't Nothing Ta Fuck Wit' and System's version of the Staten Islands nutters' 'Shame On A Nigga' – in this instance shortened to 'Shame' for obvious reasons.

Taken from the Wu-Tang's 1993 genre-defying RZA-produced debut *Enter The Wu-Tang (36 Chambers)*, the song was already huge enough before System Of A Down set to work giving it a makeover. Recorded and mixed by Rick Rubin and Rich Costey, it featured Wu-Tang members The RZA, Ghost Face Killah and U-God spitting lyrics over System's now-trademark sound of snappy snare drums and Daron's squeaky and fluid guitar while doing lyrical battle with Serj. The result was a slamming, under-rated rap-rock classic where the gruff and ready vocals of Ghost Face Killah and Co. perfectly complemented Serj's demented bark – the sparse, dark heaviness of Wu-Tang's original was retained by System's inherent understanding of musical intensity.

The two bands shared some common ground – they were both outspoken innovators whose debut albums had blown apart their increasingly formulaic respective genres, and both were outspoken groups who said and did what they liked. Unsurprisingly the two parties got on well together, Odadjian and the RZA particularly hitting it off. It was the start of a friendship that would spawn another creative collaboration some years down the line when stories circulated in 2005 about a side project between the two and fellow Wu-Tang member GZA.

The *Loud Rocks* album was released in September and few could disagree that SOAD and Wu-Tang stole the show with their forceful opener. A harder reinterpretation of Wu's raw original, 'Shame' painted a picture of violence, bravado (based around the hook *"I'll fuck yo' ass up!"*) and thug life, including an encounter with *"20 white boys in the back of a pick-up truck/With hockey pucks and skateboards/On their way to Woodstock"* before Serj stepped in to 'System-ise' Ol' Dirty Bastard's already-surreal closing section (*"Burn me, I get into shit, I let it out like diarrhoea/Got burnt once, but that was only gonorrhoea"*). The rhythmic delivery of Serj's vocals alone on this song are quite special.

"People who don't know the original will think this is a completely new song," said Shavo. "RZA added a new verse ... we added an ending that the original didn't have. We turned it into 'Shame 2000.' It was an amazingly creative experience."

In amongst the proliferation of new material came a final radio single from *System Of A Down*. With its anthemic hook-lines, atmospheric middle section and slamming race to the finish. 'War?' was a rousing and highly dramatic long-established live favourite. The accompanying video was raw and basic, depicting the band in their element in a sweaty club with Serj sporting bleached hair and Daron shorn save for an antenna-like tuft.

Another sign that System Of A Down were well and truly on the radar of mainstream culture came when they received the obligatory threat of legal action. Given that lawyers practically run the two worlds of politics and entertainment, the only thing that was surprising was that they hadn't been threatened before. In October 2003 the band received a threat of legal action from lawyers representing former boxing compere-turned-WWF master of ceremonies Michael Buffer. Apparently on July 4 at a show in Baltimore, Daron had shouted "Let's get ready to rumble!" as the band returned to the stage to encore with 'Sugar'. The show was broadcast on MTV and seen by a source close to Buffer who owned the copyright of the phrase "Let's get ready to rumble" and immediately threatened to sue as the band had not sought his personal permission. Luckily the band got off with a warning – Buffer had already previously taken action against Lieutenant Colonel Oliver North (famous for selling weapons to Iran during the Reagan administration) and shock jock Don Imus for uttering his phrase in public. Whether he ever went after UK pop stars turned TV presenters, Ant & Dec, is unknown.

America: land of the free.

Chapter 5: Battalions Of Riot Police

Finally the tour ended. After a rigourous schedule that had now taken up close to two years, the System crew departed with bulging pay packets and the band finally returned to LA. While it might be an exaggeration to say they came back different men, they had changed. Expanded. They had fulfilled hometown expectations by proving that they were more than just destined to be one of the biggest new bands in LA – their debut had sold 850,000 copies, though they still had some way to go before they were household names. Bands such as Korn and Limp Bizkit were easily outselling them (though not for much longer), albeit without the wider kudos that would soon be sent their way.

They used their spare time wisely. Daron took the opportunity to hole himself up at home in order to write new material and make sense of the many ideas he had recorded on the road; Serj took the opportunity to use his new platform to further engage himself in the political activism he had been pursuing since his teenage years.

The cause at the top of the list was promotion of the passing of House Resolution 596 – better known as the Armenian Genocide Resolution. System's contribution to raising awareness about this cataclysmic yet still under-acknowledged tragedy was already huge – as we have seen, through their music and interviews the band had brought millions of people's attention to what had happened in Armenia in 1915. Now Serj stepped it up a level by putting pressure on the government to officially recognise the atrocity for it was – a mass genocide.

The efforts of Serj and many more like him in the Armenian National Committee of America (ANCA) initially appeared to be working. In August 2000, US House Speaker Dennis Hastert made a statement to the Armenian community that he would allow the House to vote on the resolution, thereby making it highly likely that it would be properly acknowledged and at last finally recorded in the history books. Up until now the events had still been denied and covered up by the Turkish Government, the US State Department, the US Administration and Turkey's allies in the defence and oil industries.

At the last minute however President Bill Clinton stepped in and told Hastert to withdraw the bill from the vote and raised "grave national security measures" over a resolution whose mere discussion could seemingly pose a threat to American lives.

"How can Clinton let Turkey threaten him with the 'danger of the lives of American soldiers' stationed on U.S. bases in Turkey?" raged Serj on NYRock.com, upon hearing of the setback. "And with Turkey ostensibly threatening the United States, what kind of an ally does that make them?" The frontman also then went on to call Clinton's dismissal of the resolution due to instability in the Middle East as "a sham. The only fear is that we'll be pissing off the oil industry.

At the Holocaust Museum was a quote on the wall from Hitler, talking about the Jews, and at the end of his speech, he said, 'Who remembers the Armenians?' It's obvious he knew he could get away with it, so he went ahead. And the idea of this impact…that alone has so many implications."

Frustratingly for the worldwide Armenian community, Hastert admitted that had it reached the voting stage, the resolution would almost certainly have enjoyed majority support in the House.

The band's commitment to the cause was only strengthened by this setback and they spearheaded an ANCA fundraising concert for the following month called 'Souls: A Benefit for Recognition Of The Armenian Genocide to Stop Crimes Against Humanity'.

It was something that they had been talking of doing since their earliest interviews, but had held off in case, as Daron eloquently put it, they "shot their load too quickly". From some members of the band though, especially Serj, it was merely the latest in a long line of awareness-raising events in which he was involved. As he explained, their struggle for historical recognition was at the core of the band and its individual members' very existence – but not necessarily the sole point by which they should be defined.

The show took place at The Palace in LA in early November and drew a capacity crowd of 1300, each of whom paid $20 to get in. Further financial contributions came from a variety of organisations, including their management and record labels and other benevolent companies such as Vans shoes.

"It's like the other news," Shavo told one reporter on the night. "The media revolves around what's happening with our nation only. It's not really concerned about the world and how the world reacts to other nations; it's all about how America reacts to other nations and how people react to America. Serj talks about what's happening in East Timor, Indonesia, he talks about a lot of things that the media doesn't have here. I know if I wasn't in this band and I heard this band, I would be a fan."

It was an interesting and emotive evening, the band taking to the stage after a moving, short documentary about the genocide by ABC reporter Peter Jennings was aired. In the crowd were a selection of fans, industry people and the likes of Guns N' Roses' reclusive frontman Axl Rose who stirred himself from exile to join the throng. System gave the club crowd their money's worth by playing a hefty set that included the highlights of their album, ten new songs from their next one and some choice songs that would later surface on their *Steal This Album!* collection. They also played an Armenian language ballad entitled 'Im Nazelis' (which translates as "my love" or "my dear", though Nazeli is also an Armenian female name). System raised a total of $20,000.

"System of a Down continues to educate countless thousands about the Armenian genocide, reaching out through their concerts, television appearances, interviews, website to new audiences – both inside the Armenian community and within their growing base of fans around the world," said ANCA Director Aram Hamparian. "Serj and the entire band deserve a tremendous amount of credit for all they have done to educate a new generation about the Armenian cause."

Whoever says politics and rock 'n' roll don't mix might want to reconsider their opinion.

Daron had been busy too. Intentional or not, System Of a Down are a band who tend to loosely exercise a division of labour that echoes Marx's ideal of each citizen playing to his strengths and therefore maximising the potential of the society as a whole – *"from each according to his abilities, to each according to his needs."*

"The thing with our band is we try to do everything ourselves," asserted Shavo. "We're a team; whoever's strong in whatever they do, they do it so we can get everything from the band's point of view. Like the music, the production, the vibe of the shows and everything from the album packaging to the minuscule layering of every track, I want it to be a band. We all give each other space to do whatever we like doing and are good at doing so it'll come out the way we want it to come out. That's our band's motto: 'we do it our way.'"

If Serj was asserting himself as the leading political conscience of the band and Shavo increasingly involved in their presentation then Daron was busy doing what he does best: writing songs. During this period the guitarist was increasingly living within his own self-created world. A nervy and often shy character offstage, Daron cared little for the social scene that LA had to offer and when not on tour preferred to spend every spare minute working on new music. He liked to watch sit-coms such *Three's Company* and *All In The Family* or ice hockey games on TV – his ice hockey shirts would be ever present in photo shoots over the next year or two – and maybe take in the odd baseball game, but mainly it was all about writing while surrounded by home comforts such as a steady supply of weed and his favoured food of McDonald's (which he admitted to living off on a daily basis when in Europe).

He was becoming a prolific and increasingly inventive songwriter, a misanthrope seemingly compelled to write stronger songs than ever before – and many of them. As System's star rose, so too the guitarist's productivity increased as he quickly accrued an arsenal of new songs, most of them first recorded and played back on the same boom-box he'd had since his early teens. There were way too many for one album but most were good enough to be recorded. Some older ideas dating back to 1995-1996 were re-written and re-worked and others had already been played live for some time, but mainly Malakian was writing song after song running the gamut from comedic thrash to punk-polka to epic classic rock. It was an impressive creative outpouring untainted by outside musical influence. Anyone can write a song, but few in the world can do it with such originality and consistency.

"I went home and did nothing else but concentrate on writing the record," Daron said in July 2001. "I didn't fuck around in any clubs, I didn't go out drinking at night or anything. I was in the back of my room, pretty much locked up writing the record, and it's not very healthy. The approach is different because now you're writing an album, before we used to write live songs and think of them in that context. This time around mentally it was more like writing an album."

In a sign of things to come, Daron had already written thirty-odd songs ready to record by the time System Of A Down hit the studio. After a period of rehearsal and demo-ing the band went into Cello Studios to begin work on their second album. One of the best studios in the city, Cello was perfect. It was located in the heart of Hollywood and had a rich recording history. When I visited the studio the previous year to see Green Day at work there, it was hard not to be impressed by the roll-call of artists who had recorded there – everyone from Frank Sinatra to Motley Crue to REM. Scattered with rugs, incense and candles burnt out into strange new shapes, there was also a discernible vibe tailored towards creativity. Film footage of System's time there that later surfaced on the extra disc of the finished album showed the band in their element, each member with his own little creative corner decorated with little trinkets and symbols of their own personality (Daron decorating his booth with pictures of Charles Manson – more of who later). Hanging-out was confined to the studio's lounge and all the band's sustenance needs were taken care of by the various local take-aways; many tofu corndogs were eaten during the recording of the album that was soon to be entitled *Toxicity*.

The approach was also more expansive this time, incorporating sitars, banjos, pianos, a string section, mandolins "and instruments we don't know the name of." Daron even used a metallic vibrator on new song 'Psycho' (a technique that Jane's Addiction's Dave Navarro had also previously employed). The members worked at different paces – John laid down all his drums in six days, Shavo played his bass parts over three weeks, while Daron and Serj spent longer piling on layer after layer of guitar and tweaking and refining vocals.

Though it was a time of high concentration, various friends and crew members did stop by the studio, including the likes of Mike Patton ("I felt stupid not asking him to guest on a track after he dropped by the studio to visit us," Serj later lamented) and a passing Tom Morello who, upon hearing the band in rehearsal, noted "That's crazy-person music!"

Another friend welcomed into the System circle was fellow Armenian-American musician Arto Tunçboyaciyan (pronounced 'tunk-boy-a-jian') who Serj had met recently at the 3rd Armenian Music Awards in 2000, held on System's home turf of Glendale, where Tunçboyaciyan was performing. The multi-instrumentalist was already well known within Armenian music and had an impressively colourful CV.

Born in Galateria, Turkey in 1957, Tunçboyaciyan began playing traditional Armenian music at the age of eleven on the encouragement of his brother Onno. As with the members of System Of A Down,

Tunçboyaciyan relocated to the US in 1981 "to escape from the subtle restrictions on identity" he had to face as part of the Armenian minority in Turkey. He released his first solo album in 1985 and over the years which followed he established himself as an inventive musician doing credible work spreading the word about Armenian folk music, a genre with a limited audience beyond its indigenous population and far-flung ex-patriot communities. By the time he came into contact with Serj, Arto had already fronted and toured heavily with the Armenian Navy band, collaborated with numerous musicians, scored soundtracks and guested on the work of others, including renowned jazz man Chet Baker. In 1998 he released 'Onno', a poignant tribute to his musical mentor brother who had tragically died in a plane crash two years earlier.

"At the Armenian music awards I was watching him play a little bottle of water," remembers Serj. "It was a Coke bottle that he had just filled with water," Serj told Tim Cashmere for undercover.com, "and he was playing it like an old world flute and he had a tambourine that he was doing some jungle beats with. I was like, I can't believe that guy is making that sound from those two instruments – if you can even call them instruments – and I was just intrigued by his presence in artistry and how it worked."

"I barely said 'Hi' to him when I first saw him and met him. But I had him in mind because I was so into what he was doing. I picked up a few of his records and then just saw what he was all about. I showed a small video clip of him to the guys from System when we were doing *Toxicity* and they were like, 'Yeah, we'd totally want to have him here.' So I invited him to come and do some sessions with us."

Tunçboyaciyan consequently visited the studio and recorded a piece of music that the band named 'Arto', included as an extra song on the album, and added some percussion on other tracks – including some of his trademark Coke bottle-playing. It gave Serj in particular a chance to watch this famed Armenian musician at work from close quarters.

"He rendered his little interpretation of the album on the outro after 'Aerials' and he did some other percussion work and we became friends," said Serj. "When the appropriate time arose that we both had a week free we got into the studio and just went mad." The result was a collaboration that would see the light of day in 2002 – again, more of that later.

It wasn't all plain sailing and inter-band harmony during the creative period that would spawn their second album, *Toxicity*. Far from it, in fact. After years on the road together and months in the studio things came to a head – somewhat literally – when Daron and John came to blows, an incident that the band didn't mention to the press until 2005.

Arguably the two polar opposites in a band full of strong personalities, Daron, the creative, eccentric ideas man, took offence at something that John, the stoic, no bullshit backbone of the band, had said. Suddenly any grievances that had previously lain dormant were aired and all notions of pacifism and non-aggression were forgotten as the dispute was settled in that time honoured male tradition: fisticuffs.

"It wasn't a matter of punching – we used weapons!" Daron revealed of this previously secret incident. "Something happened that had nothing to do with the music. It was just something he said and I was in a bad mood and I swung my guitar at him, aiming for his head. I kind of missed and he was trying to grab the guitar, but instead his elbow hit my face and cut my mouth open.

"I realised I was bleeding so I grabbed the microphone stand from the bottom metal end and just whacked it on the top of his head, so he had about eighteen stitches on his head and I had about fifteen in my mouth. We took each other to the hospital and we were laughing about it. And we have pictures! It was one of the most memorable days in the band's history."

That the pair were able to flare up so extremely then settle their differences straight afterwards says something about the strength of the band and the union of its members. That this rather nasty incident was kept secret says something else: System Of a Down are human beings, perfectly flawed like the rest of the species and, despite the politically-driven rhetoric of their songs and interviews, nevertheless remain a heavy metal band, complete with all the drama that goes with it.

"I think a lot of things that have happened between us might have broken up other bands," said Daron. "That's where being Armenian comes into play, because it makes us feel like a family. We see that we're in a unique situation. No other Armenians have ever done this. That Armenian pride will never go away, even if we wake up one day and hate each other. Which isn't the case."

"When you've got any group of people confined to each other's company for three years on tour, you really do find out about those people, maybe shit you don't want to know, maybe shit that casts them in a whole new light," said John. "We all know that there's nothing we can hide from each other any more, cos we've all seen how low and high we can go."

What is surprising is that a band of such strong personalities had remained harmonious for so long, not least the songwriting core of Daron and Serj, two vastly different characters, each wantonly eccentric in his own way. But then like Lennon and McCartney, Page and Plant or The Clash's Strummer and Jones, great songwriting partnerships are often founded on discordance, light and shade, opposites. Daron lives off Big Macs, Serj off veggie food. Often one chats about poetry, the other about porn.

One is a sea of calm, the other a bag of nervous energy. Over the years however, such opposites have made for a stronger creative output that would be considerably weakened without the other.

"I can't say we don't get into arguments," said Daron of Serj at the close of the *Toxicity* sessions. "I get pissed sometimes, he gets pissed sometimes. Giving birth is not the most simple thing to do, so it's got to be painful sometimes. I've had a few episodes, but at the end of it now, we're close to done. As long as it's great, and me and him are still sitting together, and I don't hate him and he doesn't hate me, then everything is right, everything happens for a reason."

Creative minds don't remain inactive for long and while the band were recording *Toxicity*, Serj was working on other projects of his own, including a record label and the publication of a collection of poetry and the beginnings of the project with Arto Tunçboyaciyan. Flushed with the financial success of their debut, Serj launched a website-cum-record label Serjical Strike as an outlet to "introduce words and music that have been otherwise unavailable in stores."

"It was really a very simple idea," he explained. "I've always wanted to write a book and release some words, so I decided to do that. And then I thought the best way to put it out would be on a website, so that people can actually look it up, sample it and get directly involved. And then I thought, 'Well, if I'm going to set up a web page, I've got friends' bands that I really want people to hear.' It just started that way, on a very simple note."

"The aim is can get some original music out there and so we can do what the music industry is supposed to do – artist development, getting music from its raw stages to an interesting end product," explained Serj in a short promotional film about the label. "I started with an idea of having different types of music, different artists that have not been able to get heard in this glacial pop climate that we have at the moment. None of the bands sound remotely the same ... the niche we're looking for is creative originality within art."

The first bands he sought to promote were all suitably outlandish: 1980s-inspired art-rockers Kittens For Christian, dreamy Beatles-ish quartet Slow Motion Reign and, the best of the bunch, twisted chaos-core thrashers Bad Acid Trip, whose name perhaps best described their sound. Though none of the band have yet to have broken through commercially, Serj did achieve his goal in bringing wider attention to otherwise largely ignored acts.

Serj had been writing poetry for years predating his lyrics for Soil and System. Rock stars and poetry have enjoyed a strange relationship over the years to varying degrees of compatibility. Bob Dylan was arguably a more naturally gifted poet than he was a singer, while Jim Morrison's work suggested he was generally better at swaggering around in his leathers. Tom Waits – of whom Serj is a big fan – is one of few artists to draw together poetry and music in near-perfect symbiosis. Elsewhere people such as Patti Smith and Leonard Cohen dragged poetry into the musical form to great success, Henry Rollins mixed poetry, polemic and comedy. Charles Bukowksi meanwhile was one of the twentieth century's greatest rock stars without so much as looking at a guitar (he hated rock music).

Poetry in metal however was another matter altogether and generally associated with the realms of indulgent fantasy, so Serj's publication was a relatively brave move, though Deftones' bassist Chi Cheng had done something very similar the previous year with his eloquent spoken word album *The Bamboo Parachute*.

In April 2001, Serj self-published his debut collection, *Cool Gardens*. As debuts go, it was a colourful and diverse collection. Serj once told me that one of the masters of modern American letters, TS Eliot, was an influence, and they certainly shared the same fragmented, image-heavy approach and disregard for literary convention. Whether Serj's poems will resonate as powerfully as Eliot's *The Wasteland* continues to do today however remains to be seen.

"Serj's words, like his voice, have a distinct aesthetic sensibility connected to an unyielding, visceral roar of passion," said poet, singer and activist Saul Williams, on a quote used on the book's cover. Those already familiar with Serj's lyrics will have noticed certain recurring themes in his bite-sized meditation on life – man's inhumanity, ego, greed, philosophy – with plenty of provocative, absurdist and dubious scatological humour finding meaning in the unlikeliest of places.

"Sometimes it's the same process and sometimes it's a little more based on the music," Serj told website www.suicidegirls.com, when asked of the difference in approach to writing lyrics and poetry. "For that [lyrics] you need to manipulate the phonetics and the rhythm in a way that makes sense. Whereas with prose poetry you can just flow. I really enjoyed the stream of consciousness with words a lot. I put it down and generally I have no idea of what I am saying then I read and I try to make sense of it. It's more fun than trying to write something down."

Given that poetry collections usually sell in the hundreds, *Cool Gardens* was a resolute success, though, as with most poets, it's unlikely Serj published the book to make money. The book featured artwork by Serj's friend Sako Shahinian – his striking, politically-charged images can be viewed in full on his website www.sakoshahinian.com. Initially sold via Serj's site, the limited print-run of signed copies quickly sold out and, in October 2002, was bought by MTV Books, a subsidiary of Simon & Schuster, and published in a new format with a different cover.

"I like to try everything at least once," Serj told me in 2005. "I have thousands of poems from over the years but I'm not sure whether I want to publish another book just yet. Maybe I will further down the line..."

Meanwhile work on *Toxicity* continued throughout the summer of 2001 and by April the band had relocated to Burbank's Enterprise Studios to mix down the record with Andy Wallace. They had recorded a staggering thirty-two songs in a relatively short period, many of which still had working titles – songs such as 'Suicide', 'KITT' and 'Chic N' Stu'.

Approximately half an hour north of the seedy glamour of Hollywood and the Strip, Burbank is a wholly suburban area centred around the thriving television industry which is based there. Anonymous TV studios and production company offices litter the area, amongst the usual real estate agents, restaurants and houses of the reasonably well-off.

The mixing process is a long and laborious one that can make or break a record. If it's mixed badly, all the hours spent laying down the sound will be to no avail. Fortunately the band had the best in the business at the controls. New York-born Andy Wallace had first moved to LA in 1974 to open his own studio, a venture which enjoyed little major success and later saw him move back East. His return to New York coincided with the first wave of hip-hop and the engineer found himself working with a number of these visionary groups, which lead to remix work with two of America's biggest stars, Prince and Bruce Springsteen. But it wasn't until his work on Run DMC's collaboration with Aerosmith on the old album track 'Walk This Way' – the first known song to mix traditional white rock with black rap music, effectively spawning the rap-rock movement of the 1990s – that his true worth became known. Run DMC were, of course, the charges of Rick Rubin, and the union of Wallace and Rubin sparked a fruitful working relationship. Wallace's output reads likes a roll-call of the best alternative records of modern times: Slayer's *South Of Heaven*, Rage Against The Machine's self-titled debut, Jeff Buckley's *Grace*, Faith No More's *King For A Day*, Soulfly's *Soulfly*, Rocket From The Crypt's *Scream Dracula, Scream*, Rancid's *...And Out Come The Wolves*, At The Drive-In's *Relationship Of Command*, not to mention various tracks for Nirvana, Jane's Addiction, Tricky and Guns N' Roses, amongst others.

It wasn't so much that he was one of many potential mixers for what everyone hoped was going to be System Of A Down's true breakthrough record, but rather he was the *only* one. The band ensconced themselves in Enterprise, overseeing the mix and gradually winding down from a furious few months of creation. Quietly confident of their abilities, the only real dilemma was which songs to put on the album, there were that many. It was a decision that would provoke much discussion.

It was also a time to relax and begin to let the world at large know that after three years' recording absence – lengthy by a new band's standards – System Of A Down were about to drop an aural bomb, which they did by letting the odd journalist or photographer into the studio to report on the closing sessions of an album which they confirmed was to be entitled *Toxicity*.

"When we were throwing around words for an album title, Shavo had already come up with the 'Hollywood' sign for the cover art," explained

John during one such interview. "So it was like, well, what represents Hollywood, and Daron pointed out the lyric in the song 'Toxicity' and we were like, wow, *that* represents Hollywood. It's kind of glamorous looking from above, but when you look inside it's poisonous. It's full of venom, which represents Hollywood."

Perhaps for the first time, because of *Toxicity*, critics and fans alike were about to see the full extent of Daron's contribution to the band. As the album would show over the coming months, he was more than just the mad-eyed guitarist prone to Tourette's style outbursts on the mic. He was the major songwriter, the maker of melody and, collaborating with Serj, contributed a lot of the lyrics. And while footage filmed around the making of *Toxicity* – some of which made it onto the finished album as a bonus DVD – showed that it was very much a group creation, it was Daron who effectively acted as midwife, titles such as 'Prison', 'Suicide', 'Needles' particularly giving an insight into the state of the guitarist's creative mind during the writing of the record.

"I've been going through a tough time," he said during the mixing stages. "It was difficult to adapt to home life after being on tour for two-and-a-half years. It was a rollercoaster ride for me to write this record, but even if we sell only two copies, I feel a lot more attached to the lyrics of this album because I feel I had more to do with them. They touch me because I *lived* them."

By the time *Toxicity* was completed, it's fair to say the album had casually drifted into the category of 'long-awaited'; it had been over three years since System Of A Down's debut had been released and though the band were already established as a wholly unique musical entity, they nonetheless remained a niche band unknown beyond the world's far-reaching metal scene.

All of that was soon to change when the first fruits of these intensive labours was released, a single by the name of 'Suicide'. At the last minute – or certainly between promotional copies of the album being sent out and finished copies reaching the shops – the title changed to the totally unrelated 'Chop Suey!', presumably with the reasoning that suicide doesn't sell (whereas, erm, chop suey does). Listen closely and you can still hear a voice say "We're rolling 'Suicide'..." at the start. There was no hidden meaning to the new title, though given that chop suey is a dish cooked with disparate leftover ingredients, it made some sort of sense.

The title mattered little once the song was heard. Despite it being one of the oddest rock singles in recent memory, the song received a highly positive reaction from the influential radio and TV schedulers, who put it on heavy rotation. It was a multi-layered song with a deceptively soothing acoustic intro that lulled listeners into a berserk, staccato verse and a dramatic chorus; 'schizophrenic' was the word used most to describe it.

Lyrically the song was believed to be inspired in part by a poet named Father Armeni, who in writing about the Armenian genocide asked God "why have you forsaken me in your eyes?" He also wrote that a "self righteous suicide" had taken place. Little is known about Father Armeni and, indeed, he could merely be a fictional name used to present a wider Armenian voice.

The evocative lyrical finale also harked back to the bible, echoing almost word for word Jesus's final plea to his Almighty Father when he was crucified on the cross of Mount Calvary, though Christianity being what it is – a series of myths – no-one can seem to agree on the exact words. And, System Of A Down being who they are, have never fully explained the sentiment of the song; everything is open to interpretation.

"I remember writing that song in the back of the RV van, in the days of the first record, which is a rare thing for us because I hardly ever write songs on tour," Daron told me. "I wrote all the music and the lyrics for the chorus first, then Serj added lyrics to the melody. It's a song with lots of different meanings, but to me it's about how people view death. For example, if I died of a drug overdose everyone would say I deserved to die because I took drugs. Or if I died in a car accident, people might say I deserved it too, hence the line 'angels deserve to die'. It's not a song that's *anti* or *for* anything, but more of an observation or an attempt to capture these strange feelings people have." "My mom cried when she heard 'Suicide'," said Shavo. "She's a converted System head, and our harshest critic."

A video for 'Chop Suey!' was filmed over two days in the courtyard of a seedy motel called Oak Tree (the same motel, incidentally, where a young Shavo had seen a lady of the night *in flagrante*). Days before the shoot the band posted a message calling for fans to take part and received an overwhelming response when many travelled from far-flung towns across America to be there.

The video was their slickest, most MTV-friendly yet. Ostensibly capturing the band rocking out while surrounded by their black-clad fans, it was enlivened with visual flourishes such as Serj, Daron and Shavo being morphed into one Shiva-like figure and the use of digital cameras creating a wired, kinetic effect befitting the song.

Released as a single in August 2001, 'Chop Suey!' was an immediate worldwide hit, reaching the likes of Number 7 on the US Modern Rock chart and Number 17 in the UK Top 40. But its appeal seemed to be broader than mere chart positions – this Biblical rock oddity earned the band their first Grammy nomination and brought in thousands of curious new listeners keen to hear more by the band. It was also soon covered by Jack Black's Tenacious D, tongue-in-cheek lounge singer Richard Cheese and, much to the chagrin of many of the band's fans, Avril Lavigne.

In the UK, 'Chop Suey!' was released over two limited edition CDs, the first backed by live recordings of 'Sugar', 'War?' and the song's video, while the second single featured storming live versions of 'Chop Suey!' and 'Know' and an odd, jazzy song called 'Johnny' which saw Serj utilising his talent for mimicry and cartoon voices to great effect.

In that strange limbo between the completion of a hit record and it actually being released – and the combination of quiet confidence and self-doubt that goes with it – System Of A Down flew to England, where they played on the main stages at the Reading festival, which had now expanded to also include a site in Leeds on the same weekend. The band found themselves in good company, playing on the same festival bills as big live draws such as Green Day, Marilyn Manson and Eminem. Taking to the Reading stage in the mid-afternoon between their old mates Fear Factory and Rick Rubin's reformed ex-charges The Cult, they trounced all-comers with a show-stealing, lunatic performance – "SOAD continue to be so far ahead of the pack it must be a bit embarrassing for them…" noted *Kerrang!* reviewer Paul Travers.

Job done, they left the country.

To mark the release of this album – one which those close to the band recognised as a potential landmark record of the coming decade – System Of A Down decided to launch their new cycle of activity with a free show for the good people of their hometown, the Toxic City that inspired it.

The plan was simple enough: a vacant lot was secured opposite the Vynyl nightclub just off Hollywood Boulevard for an outdoor show on Labour Day, Monday September 3, 2001, as advertised by LA's premier alternative station KROQ. Some people would come, the band would play an evening set at 5pm; everyone would leave happy.

Only it didn't quite work out that way.

The fans arrived early – and kept arriving. Soon a mass of bodies gathered, estimated by police to number 3500, with several thousand more outside the perimeter of the makeshift arena pushing up against the barriers separating the crowd from the stage. A high police presence added an air of tension and officers began to attempt to turn fans away from the already over-subscribed inner city space. Backstage the band were nervously viewing proceedings, not least because they had a stage full of brand new equipment they were breaking in before their forthcoming US tour.

"I had Tama make me a new kit," John proudly told a passing reporter. "I explained to them about seven or eight months ago that I wanted a kit that was reminiscent of the old 1970s look. It's a beautiful kit, and I'm really happy to be playing on it. This is really the first show that I'll be playing with it."

Or was it…

Minutes later behind the scenes, word reached the band that the situation was bordering on the potentially dangerous and that they should consider cancelling.

"Have you seen what's going on out there?" John said minutes later, all thoughts of his shiny new drum kit forgotten. "It's pandemonium. I'm trying to make sure that my friends and family are okay, and I'm more worried about that than being excited to play right now."

As Serj and David Benveniste reasoned with the authorities that it would be more dangerous *not* to play, mounted police and riot squads positioned themselves at key points around the now not-so-vacant lot. The LAPD didn't want a bunch of noisy, weird-looking fuck-ups taking up their valuable time when they could be out doing something more important than containing heavy metal idiots, while the fans didn't want a bunch of artless, gun-packing doughnut-eaters spoiling *their* fun. The tension was palpable as the crowd swelled and swayed, impatiently awaiting the arrival of a band due to showcase the culmination of two years of writing and recording.

Only moments later an announcement rang out over the PA: "for safety reasons the show is being cancelled. Fire marshals have declared the area as hazardous. Please leave quickly and quietly."

All good and well, but the menacing police presence and reasons for cancellation just didn't seem to ring true for the fans who had waited patiently for hours to see America's most exciting and provocative rock 'n' roll band. Their only crime was turning out *en masse*, but this was after all a rock show so what did the authorities expect when they granted permission for it in the first place? As the band's backdrop was removed – a sign that the show was definitely off – the fans reacted angrily by breaking the barriers, storming the stage and toppling the towers of speakers into the crowd.

The police reacted even more forcefully as they sprayed tear gas into the crowd and attempted to disperse those shirtless stone-throwing, bottle-toting teens currently destroying every piece of equipment in sight; a strange reaction given that it all belonged to the band. But then riots aren't always based on reason, but rather that destructive streak that is normally dormant within humans.

It was the usual chicken-or-egg scenario. Who instigated the antagonism: the hyped-up fans or the pissed-off police? It mattered little. With a notoriously heavy-handed and historically racist police force and an immense division between the wealthy and the poor in the city, Los Angeles is no stranger to riots – whether the 'Zoot suit riots' of 1942, the six day riots in the Watts projects in 1965, the insurrection witnessed after the Rodney King beatings of 1992, or the plain old punk rock melées that surrounded local bands like Black Flag, The Germs and Suicidal Tendencies.

Thankfully this one was fatality-free and over just as soon as it started. According to the *LA Times*, a total of 160 officers were deployed to disperse the crowd "with less than lethal" methods, resulting in six arrests and a number of minor injuries.

In the fall out of the 'mini riot', the band cancelled a scheduled instore appearance at a nearby record store for the following day. They had lost all of their touring gear, including guitars, basses and amps – and John's new custom-built kit, which surely had broken some new record for the shortest life span of a musical instrument. Months in the making, it lasted mere minutes before being immolated, unplayed. Property damages to the location and surrounding area were estimated to total around $30,000. Those who had heard advance copies of the album recognised the wry, life-imitating-art irony of certain lyrics, like those of 'Deer Dance' which predicted battalions of riot police and showers of rubber bullets.

As the dust settled, the band reviewed the situation and saw it for it was: a potentially great day spoiled by over-zealous local officials and authority figures threatened by the idea of fun. In a lengthy message posted on the band's official site, Serj laid the blame at the feet of the police, many of them on horseback and their "ancient feudal tactics", which only inflamed an already intense situation on what was meant to be nothing more than "a beautiful day." It was, he declared, "one more blow to our freedom to convene."

"We believe that all of this could and should have been avoided had the band been allowed on stage," he continued. "We also believe that there is lack of understanding and communication dealing with such events between promoters and the LAPD. We strongly suggest the creation of a communications forum and an officer-training program between the LAPD and KROQ, as well as other promoters/radio stations." (see www.SOAD.com) The police were less understanding, blaming the promoter for underestimating the turnout. "It was a poorly planned event," one LAPD commander told the *Los Angeles Times*. One thing was certain: System Of A Down had arrived. They would never need the keys to the city when the door could be kicked down any time they liked.

The next day, the *Toxicity* album hit the streets – like a mortar attack.

Beginning with a strangulated thud of guitar, bass and drums, just short enough to make you wonder whether you'd actually heard it, the album opened with the hard-hitting staccato thrash of 'Prison Song'. Indebted in some small way to Rage Against The Machine, it was their most overtly political song to date, one which named and shamed their government over its prison system and unrealistic drug laws.

The facts were unavoidable: at the time of the song's inception in the US the prison population was approaching the two million mark for the first time – a staggering one in every 142 citizens incarcerated, including one in twelve of every black male between the age of 20 and 40. Such a worryingly high figure can partially be attributed to the strict drug laws that fail to differentiate between the types of drugs and the amount that perpetrators have been caught in the possession of, and also fails to recognise the difference between drug use and drug *addiction* – something quite different. So someone arrested for possession of, say, an ounce of weed for their own use might find themselves alongside rapists and murderers. In short, an every day, otherwise law-abiding citizen who likes to unwind with a joint is suddenly institutionalised and exposed to crime in ways they would have otherwise avoided had they not been given a custodial sentence. Such laws also failed to recognise that drug addiction can be a social problem, not so much the cause of crime but a by-product of poverty and/or desperate circumstances and a knock-on effect was that it was the poorest and most marginalised people who suffered the most – more, in effect, than those with money. Another reason for the doubling of the US prison's population since 1995 was the introduction of the 'three strikes and you're out' law that indiscriminately asserted that any felon convicted for a third time – of any crime – should face a minimum of 25 years. So, again, someone convicted of, for example, minor drug possession and a couple of shoplifting charges could conceivably get the same treatment as a multiple murderer.

'Prison Song' also drew a link between drugs and the funding of wars, laying blame on the influx of drugs into society as a means of governmental control. "We are the biggest drug-using nation, and if we can't stop it from coming into our borders, we have no right to go and mess with other people's countries and crops and set up puppet regimes to give us what we want," explained Serj to livedaily.com. "You've got to think of when the drug problem started in the first place. It started in the 1960s, not because of the freedom movement or the rights movements. It started in the 1960s in the ghettos as a form of oppression, when the police were going and shooting around the Black Panthers' offices, when they needed something like drugs to make people ... numb. So I think the administration has been very complicit in the drug problem. In my opinion, they partially created it."

From their most politically agitated moment to one of their most ludicrous, 'Needles' was notable for the immortal sing-along line about pulling a tapeworm out of your ass! The song was about being consumed from the inside, its protagonist the victim host of an unwarranted parasite. Though largely a heads-down whiplash metal track it did swerve off into a moody meditative section sung by Daron as the central character toys with a needle in his darkened room, possibly an escape route from the life-sapping succubus. 'Deer Dance' sounded like it had been written with LA riots in mind. High on images such as the depiction of LA landmark and home of the LA Lakers, the Staples Center, it read like a pretty accurate indictment of life in a heavily policed capitalist state.

The 'Deer Dance' of the title most likely referred to that practice of the Navajo Indians, in which masterful practitioners were said to be able to attract deer simply by standing immovable and singing a particular chant, imaging the human and the deer to be at one. It was a shamanic ritual that has been used by various indigenous populations and in the context of the song could be seen as a metaphor for the luring or the manipulation of the proletariat – the hunted deer – by the hunter, the state. For a song essentially about police brutality and bully-boy tactics (and something of a companion to 'Prison Song') the track was appropriately hard-hitting and featured some quite beautiful melodic Eastern European-sounding strings.

'Jet Pilot' meanwhile was outright *ferocious*. A song seemingly written from the point of view of a jet pilot tilting his way over a bay, it was two minutes of unrelenting fury, cinematic in scope yet fashioned from one simple fleeting image. For a song about not much it managed to evoke images of Pearl Harbour, of man versus machine, of the futility of war. Coupled with 'X', the two songs made for an awesome pairing of the band furiously firing on all cylinders. Based on an invigorating down-tuned guitar riff and with the same few lyrics in repetition, it *sounded* like the call of a long lost tribe fighting for the survival its own civilization. Lead single 'Chop Suey!' came next and acted as a brief moment of calm within the aural chaos – for about a minute anyway, until the vocals kicked in. Compared to most other hit singles of the day, 'Chop Suey!' was way out there, but was about as mainstream and musically accessible as the band ever were. You suspect in years to come it will still be viewed as one of the great rock singles of the 2000s.

Just to remind you that while SOAD are as serious as a heart attack over some subjects, ultimately the sense of humour and their surreal Dali-esque tendencies never lie dormant for long no matter how hard they try, 'Bounce' was about – and I quote their singer here – "a sex orgy on pogo sticks". It could also be interpreted as a protest against the Third World totalitarian dictatorship seizing land from its workers for their own means but that would just be ... stupid. It sounded exactly like an Armenian-American punk-metal band should sound when singing a song that namechecks 'fun for all the family' game Twister. Let's not get carried away here.

'Forest' was a more serious proposition, a well-structured big rock song with increasingly cryptic lyrics. "How can I put this?" Serj said in one interview with *Kerrang!*, by way of explanation. "You know how a paedophile looks at a young boy? Well, the way that a paedophile looks at a young child is the way that ... someone is looking at their own mind. People can define it for themselves." Quite.

The plaintive sounding 'A.T.W.A' was inspired by Charles Manson's philosophy of 'Air, Trees, Water, Animals' that was essentially a plea for increased ecological awareness – a worthy cause from a dubious man. The song was one of *Toxicity*'s more tempered moments with Daron and Serj's harmonies carried along by a folk-ish cadence before slowly growing into a monstrously large rock song with a roaring vocal display. 'Science' was pure musical vim and vigour and tackled notions of science versus spirituality; the death of God and/or religion in light of scientific advancements – something which Tankian identifies as 'faith'. Not for the first time the band juxtaposed facets of the modern technological world (such as science) with more timeless deep-rooted concepts from both East and West and similarly combined the heaviness of unambiguous metal with another unexpected and moving musical passage drawn from their Armenian heritage. Another sub-two minute song written by Serj, 'Shimmy' upped the nonsense quota further, but with its slam-happy rhythms, wailing vocals and "indoctrination of a nation" pay-off, provided one of the most direct songs in a truly diverse selection.

The album's title track 'Toxicity' – originally entitled 'Version 7.0' was an abstract portrait of the band's hometown – or, indeed any big city of industry that spits out fumes and where everyone is a stranger, an anonymous disenfranchised ant in the vast capitalist colony. Urban versus rural. The city which is the centre of System Of A Down's chaotic world, warts and all. The Toxic City. Post-apocalyptic in tone it eased from down beat melody to a crescendo climax . A centre point to the album, it was also one of the strongest tracks, revealing as it did a flipside to more straight-forward songs such as 'X' or 'Jet Pilot'.

The stop-start 'Psycho' tackled the subject of groupies. The song adopted an uncharacteristically (for American rock music, at least) almost feminist approach, the message being: don't be subjugated, don't let yourself be used by someone just because they're up there on a stage and you're not. It was an attitude born out of experience.

"Let's say you live in Iowa and you have a band coming on once month, and you're impressionable," explained John. "You haven't seen a lot of the world and here's someone that you've listened to for a year. They're on stage, the girls get starstruck, even though we're not stars and, yes, sometimes they want to do things that they normally wouldn't want to do because they feel it's the only opportunity they'll have to be with someone like that. It's the image that they want."

"That's a nice way of saying it," added Shavo, talking to Jeanne Fury in *NY Rock*. "There are a lot of stupid girls who are ho's. Period. The world is full of them. There are a lot of guys that are ho's, a lot of band members too. They go hand-in-hand. You go around the world, and girls are available on tour. They're there. It's actually the guy's choice to do it or not. This is our ode to groupies – saying that these psychos exist. Most of them have psychological problems. We're weird because we've actually talked girls out of doing what they do. We're like, 'Why are you here? Why are you on our bus?'... I've laughed at them to the point where they understand, like, 'I'm stupid. I shouldn't offer my body to meet a band.'"

Album closer 'Aerials' was a moving piece and one of the most obviously 'spiritual' songs, lyrically at least. Downbeat and epic-sounding it was the calm after the storm that preceded it. "Lyrically, 'Aerials' is another observation," Daron explained to me. "I write a lot of songs with pictures in my head and for this one I had a picture of a disabled or retarded child – I'm not sure that's the politically correct term – at a circus, and seeing how the child is amazed by a trapeze act. I've never seen this in person, these are just visions in my head, you understand. And I see people around the child just talking amongst themselves and not appreciating the trapeze artist. So it just goes to show how we've lost touch with the simple things in life. It's about how someone who is perceived to have a more simple way of thinking than the rest of us can be amazed by something we take for granted. It's about losing touch with the simple things in life and how in some cases, a disabled kid is in a better position of taking something in than we are."

Some copies of *Toxicity* also featured the aforementioned extra bonus track 'Arto', a short instrumental song recorded with Arto Tunçboyaciyan (included on an extra disc alongside the footage of the band recording the album). Based around an Armenian flute the piece was believed to be inspired by a traditional piece called 'Der Voghormia' that is sung in the Armenian Orthodox Church as a funeral song for the dead.

In a little over forty minutes, System Of A Down had created an album expansive in its world vision, a characteristically schizophrenic and epic beast that somehow avoided indulgence and managed to contain its ideas within the regimented structures of the pop song. Here was a record with the flab trimmed away and a collective musical vision realised – crucially it also expanded the band's oeuvre of their debut into wider territories without ever compromising any of the ideas or strange sounds. In fact, they had just gone ever weirder, more confrontational and more focused. A rare achievement, by any band's standards. Reviewing the album for a magazine, I noted that System Of A Down were carving their own unique niche within the modern American rock genre: "The Los Angelino quartet have little in common with their contemporaries – which is precisely why they sound like the most vital band in the world right now. There are no fronts here – no samples, no lame rapping, no convoluted notions of rebellion and no claims to be anything other than a band with something to say." For the record, at the time of writing it's probably the album that I've listened to most in the past decade. And I'm a fussy bastard.

The majority of critics seemed to share similar sentiments and as advance reviews of *Toxicity* began to run in the world's music press, System Of A Down looked set to breakthrough on to the world's stage.

Chapter 6: War? / Boom!

It seemed fitting and somewhat ironic that the first thing people know about *Toxicity* was that it had caused a 'riot' in LA. Ironic because *Toxicity* was nothing less than a portrait of a city, an open love-hate letter to a place that is both heaven and hell, a city of riddles and secrets, success and unrest and a glitter-gilded history. Though the band's depiction of the modern world is one that draws on the disconnection, turmoil and chaos of it all, the influence of LA was unavoidable. It was part of the fabric of the band. That System Of A Down was so heavily inspired by the city that was its adoptive home – pretty much all they had known, in fact – went some way to revealing their thoughts on the place. They clearly loved it, fed off it and, at times, were completely exasperated by it.

"System Of A Down have been shaped and informed by LA as a city," says band friend and photographer Lisa Johnson. "Entirely. Completely. Though a quite different band, they were hugely influenced by the impact of Rage Against The Machine. Both bands probably wouldn't have evolved had they come from cities like San Diego or Denver. You can add a band like Downset to the list – while not at all as commercially successful in retrospect, they played the same circuit and shared common goals.

Los Angeles is a city of contradictions, injustice, decadence, wealth, poverty, insanity, squalor – and all within a city block," continues Lisa. "The unrest that exists in Los Angeles fuels the band's anger and their politically-motivated lyrical content. The need to unveil these injustices is one of the characteristics that these bands share. And System of A Down also have their cultural heritage to cull from – for example, their annual 'Souls' benefit concert on April 24 as a day of remembrance marking the Armenian genocide. Los Angeles is also much more open to art and expression than cities that might exist in the red [Republican-run] states. So having a voice, protesting, rallying … all of this is allowed – as long as you don't throw rocks at the riot police."

One of LA's most infamous sons who proved to be of particular interest to Daron while making the record was Charles Manson, who inspired the song 'A.T.W.A.' and whose pictures decorated Daron's corner of the studio as he recorded his guitar parts for *Toxicity*. A career con during his formative years – up until his mid-thirties he had spent half of his life in institutions for crimes of varying severity including forgery, theft, assault, pimping and while in reform school, male rape – Manson gained notoriety when he set up a commune at Death Valley's Spahn ranch in the late 1960s. From this remote outpost Manson presided over a 'family' of disaffected young men and women drawn to his articulate, if jumbled, anti-establishment rhetoric, while Manson himself simultaneously harboured ambitions as a singer–songwriter and developed outlandish plans to start a race war by committing a number of random murders and then blaming them on the black community. Manson was a racist, yet he was also a keen environmentalist. He had a violent past, yet, on the surface, was living the peace-and-love Californian hippy existence of his time. He also drew inspiration from The Beatles, particularly *The White Album*, which he believed contained a hidden blueprint for impending race and nuclear wars and a social upheaval of biblical proportions. He was in short, a riddle of contradictions with a dangerous messiah complex.

Ultimately though the Manson family – many of whom had come from relatively privileged backgrounds – were nothing more than a rag-tag bunch of lost young adults, living in poverty, eating out of dustbins and hanging on every word of their leader, himself bitter with Hollywood over the failure of his stalled musical career. With his followers in tow Manson went on 'creepy crawly' missions breaking into the houses of the rich. When the horrific murders of Sharon Tate, wife of acclaimed film director Roman Polanski, wealthy supermarket executive Leno and wife Rosemary LaBianca, were traced back to Manson and his followers, he became an overnight international figure, to many the personification of evil, as epitomised by an iconic *Time* magazine cover that captured him with a swastika carved into his forehead and deeply penetrating eyes.

Though Manson wasn't proven to have committed the murders, he was seen as the instigator and sentenced to death, later changed to life imprisonment (in 1972 all California death sentences were commuted retrospectively) following one of the trials of the decade. His followers stuck by him, a number of the women shaving their heads as a sign of support and merely adding to the myth of a group of LSD-eating, permissive outlaws.

The impact Manson had on LA was considerable, the city's white wealthy citizens temporarily under siege. That the perpetrators turned out to be hippies effectively killed off any naïve notions of peace, love and communal living as a means of achieving a more harmonious society and instead signalled more malevolent forces at work.

Though irrefutably guilty, Manson always maintained that he was merely a product of modern America, abandoned as a child, alienated as an adolescent, marginalised as an adult: "Your society is so distorted that a sane man would appear like a mad man," was just one of many highly-quotable Manson philosophies to be grounded in certain truths – albeit *his* truth. This outsider status gained him favour and in the intervening years his legend within pop culture grew, not least for symbolically seeing off the naïve 1960s and harbouring in the darker 1970s.

Over the intervening years Manson's legacy grew, particularly within pop culture and he remains the prisoner who gets the most mail within the US prison system – an estimated *60,000* letters per year. Punk bands such as Black Flag and The Germs referenced Manson's nihilism as an inspiration of sorts, Sonic Youth's song 'Death Valley' 1969 was inspired by the Manson family, Guns N' Roses covered the Manson song 'Look At Your Game Girl' and, most notably, Brian Warner from Canton, Ohio flambuoyantly reinvented himself as Marilyn Manson – his name a combination of the polar opposites of two totems of good and evil in recent American history. He was even the star of a *South Park* episode entitled 'Merry Christmas Charlie Manson'.

Scores of other bands have either covered or referenced the Manson murders – from Iggy Pop to Neil Young, The Ramones to Philip Glass – while Manson memorabilia continues to do a brisk trade. His sceptre still symbolically casts a shadow over LA.

Daron Malakian's interest in Manson was not unusual, intrigued as he was (like so many before him) by the contradictions of a man interested in ecology but perfectly happy to instigate the killing of humans. Manson was also someone who was misrepresented in the media as inherently evil when in fact evil generally only exists in contrast to goodness – proof that morality is rarely black and white, but rather a grey area to be interpreted depending on individual beliefs, and that the media consistently editorialise to suit their own means. Then there was also the fact that Manson has theoretically served his life sentence, yet all parole hearings dismiss the possibility of release. During interviews for *Toxicity*, Daron was keen to discuss the man who had inspired 'A.T.W.A.'

"I collect a lot of Charles Manson's stuff and I have all his parole hearings," explained Daron. "When they only show a few seconds of what Manson is saying on television, like him saying 'If I was going to kill, I'd kill everybody', they don't show you what he said for the hour leading up to that statement. There is a whole other side of Manson that isn't so evil, but is actually very just and very right.

Manson talks about how humans are killing the world for quick-fix money. Later on, you're going to have to buy the air. If you don't have money for that, then you ain't breathing. It's going to be like water is today. I remember a time when you didn't have to buy your water for a dollar a bottle from the 7-Eleven. There are things that I agree with Manson on. There are others that I don't. He's got some racial views that aren't exactly mine…"

Released on September 4, *Toxicity* debuted at Number 2 in the *Billboard* 200, behind Alicia Keyes' *Songs In A Minor*, which had sold 192,000 copies. Also in the Top 10 that week were Staind's *Break The Cycle* and fellow LA rockers Linkin Park's debut *Hybrid Theory*. Slipknot's recently-released metal opus *Iowa* dropped to Number 12.

Or that's what the trade newspapers initially reported. But in a strange and unprecedented twist, the sales figures were reconsidered and *Toxicity* was deemed to have sold an extra 52,000 copies of an enhanced CD version whose sales had gone unregistered, pushing the total first week domestic sales up to 222,000 copies and roundly trouncing Alicia Keyes before she'd had time to pop open the champagne.

"The overwhelming popular success of *Toxicity* goes a long way to restoring your faith in the eminent good taste of the public at large," said rock magazine *Metal Hammer*. "It makes up for all those Nickelback albums that the fuckers bought."

But for once – arguably since the invention of the charts in the first place – few people cared about the trivialities of sales figures, the one-upmanship of the record companies or critical respect. Something else happened that week. Something that turned America upside down. Something that made *Toxicity* seem like a chilling prophesy.

On the morning of September 11, 2001, terrorists connected to the well-known Al-Qaeda cell headed up by Saudi Arabian multi-millionaire Osama bin Laden attacked America through a series of devastating plane hi-jackings. Their attack on the Twin Towers in New York killed close to three thousand innocent people and plunged America – and the Western world – into a state of paranoia and panic. The statistics for the tragic event were staggering – three thousand children lost a parent and nearly twenty thousand 'body parts' were found in the wreckage. A landmark event in modern history, the details of 9-11 – arguably the first man-made tragedy of the digital camera age – are well-documented.

On the day of the events, System were actually scattered far and wide – either on vacation or at home, preparing for a year's worth of touring *Toxicity*. "I was stuck in Upper Wisconsin the day it happened," remembers John. "It was a very rural town, about 2000 people. I was vacationing there before we started our tour and I figured it would be a good place to get away where no-one could bother me. I woke up and my girlfriend was like, 'You've got to check this out'."

The repercussions of the events were equally as worrying. The US had never before suffered an attack of terrorism from a foreign organisation and were shocked into retaliation, the implications of which are still unravelling as I write, years later. George W. Bush embarked on a war against terror – "You're either with us, or you're with the terrorist," he declared, leaving little room for impartiality. The Bush administration first attempted to bring Osama bin Laden to justice but with the search going nowhere they diverted attention to those they believed were connected to the terrorist network, and rendered thousands of suspects in secretive foreign prisons. Then, Bush began to talk about going after Saddam Hussein, despotic leader of Iraq.

With a strong interest in politics and a spirituality-based humanitarian streak running right through their music, System Of A Down were naturally hugely affected by the events. How could they not be? Their music was a clash of East and West that spoke of man's many injustices fuelled by greed, religion and dead-end leaders – and now *it was happening*. The ruthless American foreign policy that Serj had been discussing since his first interviews in 1997 was coming back with terrible consequences – and it was only going to get worst. Any long-standing divisions between America and the oil-rich Middle East were only going to get wider. The mad visions of Armageddon on

System Of A Down's first two albums now seemed less like prophesies and more like a bloody truth. As great as some of the songs were, no one actually wanted to *live* them…

"Kids were dissecting our songs on the internet," Serj told *NME* six months later. "Some of those songs were written three years before, but they were saying 'they must have known!' Kids out there were frantic, they were just insane and they were trying to find people to blame. It was like the only people they could look to protect them were the government. And so anybody who was criticising the government – including our band – was frowned on because that's not what people wanted to hear. They don't want to hear the truth – like what does our government do that we don't know about that causes this stuff? They want to hear things that are going to calm them down and make them feel better. That's sort of why we got bashed for a little while."

The 'bashing' was due in part to *Toxicity's* depiction of a chaotic world ruled by corporate sharks, a war-mongering president and mad fundamentalist mullahs alike, but also more likely because of an essay entitled 'Understanding Oil' that Serj published two days after the events of 9-11.

In an essay which read as an informed manifesto for peace, Serj outlined recent historical political events that placed the attacks in their necessary context – that of decades of American-sponsored oil and arms deals with various Middle Eastern counter-insurgent groups now considered the enemy – the arming of both sides in the Iran–Iraq conflict, the CIA's support of the Afghan Taliban in their conflict with the former Soviet during the 1980s, the close-ties with Iraq's leader Saddam Hussein and so forth.

"What scares me more than what has occurred is what our reactions to these occurrences may cause," wrote Serj. "President Bush belongs to a long generation of Republican Presidents who love war economies… What everyone fails to realise is that the bombings are a reaction to existing injustices around the world, generally unseen to most Americans. My belief is that the terror will multiply if concrete steps are no taken to sponsor peace in the Middle East *now*."

The singer then outlined some simple solutions to prevent senseless deaths in America and the Middle East, from working with UN Peacekeeping troops to the stopping of the bombing of Iraq to the increased use of alternative fuels to decrease the dependence on oil. The ultimate message was one of attaining peace as a means to rendering all extremist activity irrelevant and unnecessary.

Naturally, not everyone in the community shared the same opinions nor had the intelligence to see beyond a media smokescreen that suggested America was an innocent party and had never itself killed innocent people. Written the day after the attacks on New York and published on the band's official website on September 13, 2001, Serj's manifesto was promptly withdrawn. With national emotions running high, seemingly it was still too raw a subject to warrant intelligent debate. The band had also received a number of death threats. In its place came a simple statement from Serj to illustrate that he was not anti-American: "I would not be alive if it were not for the American orphanages that raised my grandfather after the Armenian Genocide of 1915, so I have a lot of love and respect for the good things that America has and can continue to achieve."

However it was too late for the more conservative elements of America. As if to illustrate the blindness of some American patriotism, the obliviousness of much of their own foreign policy, along came critics like Billy Milano of old-hat thrash bands S.O.D (Stormtroopers Of Death) and M.O.D. who published an anti-Serj rant on popular website Blabbermouth.net in reaction to 'Understanding Oil'.

"People know more about politics than the actual politicians," Milano wrote. "I would just like to remind that anti-American piece of shit Serj and that liberal Berkeley twat Tom [Morello] that I don't see them living in Europe or Armenia. These guys complain like they have never had an opportunity, but live comfortably in *California*… Enough with these fucking clown musician cry baby cunts talking shit. Get the fuck out and show your integrity. Serj, go fuck yourself, you anti-American asshole." Milano concluded his piece with "America rules!!!"

It certainly seemed that in the weeks and months that followed the heinous attack on the US, people were forced to take sides, philosophically, if not physically. The problem was – and still is – beyond what they read in the morning paper (if they read one at all) or see on the news, most people don't generally know what is going on. They're happy in their torpor. If the President tells them terrorists are trying to destroy their way of life for no other reason than they are evil, then that's good enough for most people.

Which is where the role of the artist comes into play. Whether a rock singer, sports star, writer or actor, people with a platform and the eyes and ears of the world should use the responsibility wisely. The famous artist (I shall refrain from resorting to using the word 'celebrity') may be unqualified or censored, but they do nevertheless have an opinion as valid as anyone and can use their powers to spread information accordingly. Which is what System Of A Down and, particularly, Serj Tankian chose to do. With the passing of time, the ideas discussed by Serj and other counter-culturalists like him have been shown to be more or less true. A few years on from the terrorist attacks and many deaths of American and Iraqi citizens and the world is a far more unstable place than ever. It doesn't take a rocket scientist to work that out.

For the most part, the rock, metal and punk worlds were united in their defiance against terrorists *and* their own incumbent President's talk of taking on these Afghani and Saudi terrorists by invading... Iraq.

These conflicting feelings of being both anti-terror and anti-Imperialism needed consolidation and it was in the arts that such feelings could be manifested in accessible ways, most notably in film and music. To his credit, not long after his essay was removed, Serj appeared as a phone-in guest on Howard Stern's radio show to explain his position and defend himself against knee-jerk accusations ("That really offends me big time," he told one interviewer who wondered whether their fans would consider him unpatriotic.) Still scared by recent events and fuelled by the aggressive take-no-prisoners tone of the mass American media, many listeners – and indeed the crew on the show – were unwilling to consider anything other than war as a necessary retaliatory reaction and repeatedly interrupted the ever Zen-like singer, failing to see the wider argument: terror breeds terror, war breeds war.

Toxicity certainly seemed to take on new meaning post-9-11 where previously the ideas may have been dismissed as the paranoid or conspiratorial ramblings of a rock band. Again, lyrics such as those of 'Deer Dance' noted the dichotomy between the actions of the elected leaders and those who elected them. Elsewhere *Toxicity's* key-line *"How do you own disorder?"* merely reflected on the chaos of a world that no individual can fully understand.

"The words 'System Of A Down' were almost too close to the mood that everyone was feeling that week," said Serj. "There was a whole sense of 'What the fuck?' in the air. The words almost seemed *too* appropriate, and it was too scary. It scared me to think about what it all means."

Despite their tag as a political band in the vein of agit-pop acts that had gone before, the lyrics on *Toxicity* were actually non-specific to the political arena, and instead painted a broader picture of a country – an empire – teetering dangerously on its axis. But myopic critics chose to brand them un-American nonetheless.

With guitars that sounded like an air strike and melodies that rumbled as if this mortal coil might crack wide open at any given moment, *Toxicity* was a powerful album and history will surely mark it as perhaps the rock album that best defined the turmoil of the early twenty-first century. But let's not forget, for all their political insight and vehement sense of injustice, System Of A Down were also singing songs about psycho groupies whacked on coke and pulling tapeworms out of your ass. Which perhaps is the beauty of rock 'n' roll: it is one of the few popular art forms where social commentary and an unhinged sense of humour can still co-exist, where drinking and dancing are as much a priority as discourse.

"When people just talk about politics, it becomes one-dimensional," Serj reflected in an interview with Matt Ashare of *The Boston Phoenix* in 2005. "But when people talk about politics as part of the larger picture, it's fine. It's a tough road, not because of the reactions or condemnations or program directors dropping our single, which happened when *Toxicity* came out and I made that 'Understanding Oil' statement, but because things like that can just blow up in your face. I mean, I was just trying to make sense of the 9/11 situation. I was like, 'What the fuck, you can't even say what you think.'

I want people to know us not just as a political band. You know, The Beatles spoke out against the Vietnam War. But no one remembers them as just a political band, because they had love songs and quirky songs. And if you look at our albums, there are probably only two or three political songs out of fourteen – the rest are either socially-inclined, personal stories, theoretical excursions, or quirky shit. For example, I was doing another interview and the person said, 'What separates you from Rage Against The Machine?' I said, 'Our song 'Bounce' is about a pogo-stick orgy.' That's what makes us different."

Along with many other rock and pop bands, in the days following September 11, they announced that they were to postpone their forthcoming European dates until 2002 due to "political unrest".

Ironically it was outside of America that System were able to speak more freely on the subject, where accusations of anti-Americanism were less forthcoming and where there was a greater degree of sympathy for those who wished to instigate debate rather than react with extreme, blind prejudice.

"When you say 'America' what the hell are you talking about?" Serj pondered in *NME*, elaborating on notions of patriotism. "The American people have a huge heart. The American people spend so much on non-profit organisations – billions and billions of dollars. My grandfather was raised in an American orphanage, OK? I might not have been around if it wasn't for the heart of the American people. But the American government, utilising our voice, our blind consent, has done so many things for the rights of corporations – for the 5 per cent that control the 95 per cent – around the world and fucked things up, and now the world's looking at us to blame. I'm an American and I didn't do it. But I know that these guys did and I want the right to say this to people."

One knock-on effect of System Of A Down's increased exposure and defiant ethical stance was the very type of censorship that came to light when 'Chop Suey!' was brought under close scrutiny by the powers that be. For reasons not fully understood, it was one of many that made it into a recommended black list of songs that should not be played on the radio in the wake of 9-11. It wasn't the first time the authorities had clamped down on music in such a way. During the first US invasion of Iraq in the early 1990s similar lists had circulated, provoking comical reactions due to the sheer absurdity of some of the choices.

While the death of thousands of innocent people is an inherently sensitive subject, the authorities' new agenda of restricting musical listening choices was a vulgar and opportunistic display of power and disrespect to the memories of those who died.

"I think it's sad that we got to go back to Nazi Germany for our influence on how to take care of the situation," Serj reflected on *Music Channel*. "The radio stations that pull any song off the air, in my opinion, are big fans of Adolf Hitler. They may not know it, but they are fans of Hitler. Censorship is un-American. They also put 'Lucy In The Sky With Diamonds' by The Beatles [on the list] too for having the word 'sky' – same reason we were on there. 'What A Wonderful World' too!"

As it turned out, the ban didn't matter too much – in light of recent events it was hard to complain and besides, the song had already been released and received heavy advance TV and radio coverage pre-9-11 and had served its purpose in drawing attention to the attendant album. Nevertheless such a blanket banning of a song lent gravitas to System's argument that the media controls our tastes and that our opinions and options are being policed by outside forces, whether we even know it or not. The old 'Big Brother is watching you' argument in full malevolent effect.

"They probably didn't even pick the songs themselves," shrugged Serj. "They probably did a search utilizing words, you know: 'sky', 'plane', 'pilot', 'tower' and probably took off every song having to do with that. Welcome to the 21st Century."

They may have cancelled their proposed international dates, but System Of A Down still had a US tour of duty to do in what was one of *the* metal live packages of the year. A joint headline tour with Slipknot, the poignantly-named 'Pledge Of Allegiance' tour also included more original metal bands such as Teutonic industrialists Rammstein and conceptual metallers Mudvayne, with newcomers No One and American Head Charge opening up the shows.

Though quite a different band, both musically and aesthetically, Slipknot's rise had run in parallel to that of System Of A Down and, as something of outsiders erroneously dismissed as nu-metal, the two groups shared much common ground. Slipknot had formed in Des Moines in 1995 and spent their early years struggling to get noticed by the industry while building up a strong following and a reputation for danger and unhinged live performances. Though one of the leading exponents of nu-metal – in the eyes of the media at least – Slipknot were inspired by glam rock, death and black metal, as well as techno and drum 'n' bass and the aesthetics of horror films, an interest manifested in their masks and stage gear. Like System, Slipknot were also a band of conflicting personalities – whether the barking mania of front man Corey Taylor, the twisted, nihilistic philosophies of founder member Shawn Crahan or the unnerving silence of enigmatic 'samples, FX and digital media' man Craig Jones. The two bands had known each for some time and for most, the pairing was a ferocious prospect.

"We were in Des Moines a long time ago, when we were touring with Snot," remembered Shavo of their first meeting. "We were playing a little hole in the wall there, and some dude came up to me and said 'Hey, I'm in Slipknot, do you want a copy of our demo?' That turned out to be Shawn. He knew of us and was into our band. I didn't think all that much of their demo at the time, I didn't know what they were all about, to be honest. But I probably didn't give it the attention it deserved.

Both Slipknot and our ourselves are definitely into doing our own thing. We respect that about Slipknot, and although I can't speak for them, I think that they respect that about us. Since we're both doing something that's completely different from what other bands are doing, it made sense that we should tour together some day."

In light of recent events the 'Pledge Of Allegiance' double-header was postponed for a week, as much to ensure people still came to the shows as out of a fear of terrorist attack (you suspect Slipknot and System Of A Down wouldn't have been top of a hardline terrorist cell's list). Though it was something of a dream bill for young fans of the genre, the line-up also reminded how far System Of A Down had come, and how little they had in common with their contemporaries. Kicking off on September 21 in Denver, the tour took in 27 dates across the US during the most paranoid and fraught time in recent American history, maybe ever. And contrary to certain stories that circulated at the time, the tour was not named in honour of the victims of the attacks of New York; the name had already been chosen long beforehand.

"It was about heading back to school!" laughed John Dolmayan. "It had nothing to do with patriotism or anything, we just wanted to have a vibe of going back to the classroom, that whole feeling of buying new notebooks and pens and pencils. Now, it's like it has all this unintentional significance. Whatever humour it had has gone now…"

Six shows into the tour and System were back in Los Angeles to play a hometown show at The Forum, their first since the riot three weeks earlier. Though long since sold out, Daron seized the opportunity to offer a big 'fuck you' to those who had smashed and stolen their brand new gear on that fateful day. The LA show also saw a gathering of celebrities, here to see the two biggest bands in metal. Milling about backstage at the hottest ticket in town were producer Ross Robinson, Tom Morello, Dave Grohl, Josh Homme, Casey Chaos, Limp Bizkit's Wes Borland and members of Deftones, Static-X, Spineshank, Powerman 5000 and The Apex Theory.

The tour wound up on Halloween with a show at East Rutherford,

New Jersey where fittingly, given the show's location, all proceeds from the night were donated to the American Red Cross Liberty fund set up in aid of victims of the attack

"All of us in the band were very shaken by the events of September 11," Serj said in a statement. "We know that there are so many victims of this tragedy who need help, and we felt that since were going to be performing in the New York area, it was a perfect opportunity for us to do something that would make a difference. The donation is from our hearts."

Some light relief from righting the wrongs of the world came when System made their first foray into the Hollywood world that had surrounded them growing up when Shavo made a fleeting, blink-and-you'll-miss-it appearance in the Ben Stiller/Owen Wilson comedy *Zoolander* in September 2001. In a movie that was full of cameo appearances, the bassist appeared in a non-speaking part in an audience scene playing one of Hansel's (Owen Wilson) 'Posse Members'. Just look out for that recognisable beard.

Can't miss it.

By the close of 2001, System Of A Down had established themselves as the most exciting rock band on the planet with sales figures to match. But if they wanted to avoid being dismissed as empty pop stars preaching from a pulpit or pogo-obsessed jokers, they had to at least attempt to make changes themselves. Leading by example, Serj joined forces with the aforementioned guitarist Tom Morello of Rage Against The Machine.

Morello was the perfect foil for Serj and System's plans. If anyone commanded respect and was capable of making things happen, it was him. A Political Science graduate from Harvard and the son of activists, unlike most rock stars who dabble in politics Morello was qualified and informed enough to speak on a wide range of subjects. "People will ask me, 'How did you become political?'" says Morello. "And I always say, 'Uh, I grew up black in America. How are you not political?'"

After graduating he worked in Washington DC for two years in the office of liberal-leaning Democrat senator Alan Cranston before moving back to LA and joining funk-metal band Lock-Up, who released one album on Geffen. Then in 1991 he formed a new band with bassist Tim Commerford and drummer Brad Wilk. Though singer

Maynard James Keenan was touted as their first frontman, he was forming a band of his own – that would become Tool – so Morello enlisted the services of twenty-year-old former hardcore singer Zack de la Rocha and Rage Against The Machine was born. Their aim was to mix militant politics with the power of Led Zeppelin and the lyrical bite of Public Enemy. In a similar pattern echoed by System Of A Down later in the decade, Rage quickly became one of the hottest unsigned bands in LA off the strength of a self-released, cassette-only album. In 1992 they released their self-titled debut album on Sony (again, like System, many questions were raised about such an anti-corporate band signing to one of the world's biggest labels) and became one of the biggest bands on the planet, a whole sub-genre of bands mixing rap and rock following in their wake. Their riotous live shows were unrivalled by any band of their time and de la Rocha and Morello were widely considered two of the best lyricists and guitarists of their time.

Rage suffered for their own political convictions though and by the close of the 1990s were descending into disagreement over their direction. "There were few moments of pure, unadulterated joy," Morello told me in 2005. "A dark cloud followed us everywhere and for nearly a decade we had nearly been about to break-up *any day*. It was nothing new to us; that was the life we were leading: one of heroic music and great personal tension. We'd sold twelve million records but we had also demolished our personal relationships along the way."

Naturally, before they had even met, there was kinship between Rage and System Of A Down. With Rage on the slide, System Of A Down were the only rock band doing anything with as much meaning and potential for change as Morello and Co. had done in the 1990s. When the guitarist met Serj it was a meeting of minds that would spawn something quite special.

"I met Tom on New Year's Eve a few years ago, when I was invited to his house by my friend Lisa [Johnson]," remembers Serj. "We were hanging out in Hollywood with a bunch of other friends and she said that I should come along as she was sure Tom would love to see me. Actually, I'm not sure that was the very first time we met, but it was certainly the first time that we spent some time together."

"I was overwhelmed by what a kind and gentle soul Serj is," Tom Morello told me. "You listen to a System Of A Down record and it's so crazy and aggressive, yet I've never met a more peaceful soul in all of rock 'n' roll. He's a great friend, one of the good guys."

At the time, Morello was putting together a new band with Commerford and Wilk, tentatively called Civilian. A number of names had been suggested as a singer – Cypress Hill's B-Real, Downset's Rey Oropeza and Orange 9mm's Chaka Malik being three of them – but it was former Soundgarden frontman, Chris Cornell, who was top of the list. In May 2001 he joined the band, who changed their name to Audioslave shortly afterwards. A less overtly political band than Rage, but with a right-wing president in power and more to protest about in America than ever before, Morello needed an outlet for his beliefs, an alternative way to put his influence to positive use. It was round about the same time that Serj and Tom considered the possibility of the two politically compatible bands touring together, before instead deciding to combine forces to create change beyond the music they played. The collaboration was to be called Axis Of Justice.

"[That] came together when Tom was putting together his new band, but back when they had another name. Or different names, as they went through a bunch of them," Serj told me. "They were meant to play Ozzfest in 2002 and so were we, but something happened and they didn't end up doing it, but Tom had set up this whole idea of having a booth with lots of organisations participating to give out non-commercial information – organisations with something to offer besides commercial goods. I knew that Tom had this concept so we talked about it and I encouraged him and told him that we would back him up on this. Then they said they weren't going to do the tour. So I went back in, we re-started it and that's when Axis Of Justice properly began."

When the Axis Of Justice booth first appeared at Ozzfest 2002, it was with the support of a number of organisations, including high visibility ones such as Amnesty International and Greenpeace, but it soon expanded to include many smaller, but equally important educational and charity groups involved in various racial, political and social justices.

The first time the pair spent any time together was, appropriately, on a demonstration in LA. "They had placed an injunction in Santa Monica, California against feeding the homeless," remembers Tom. "So the fledgling Axis Of Justice organisation went down there in defiance of the injunction and did exactly that – passed out food to the homeless, just daring the authorities to arrest us."

As word spread about their new organisation, Tom and Serj began to pre-record a series of radio shows for broadcast on the LA network 90.6PFK in which they interviewed figures such as documentary-maker and satirist Michael Moore and a number of activists, in between playing "politically or socially viable music of many different genres." Soon Axis Of Justice had grown into a vast and disparate self-supportive network of resources and charity groups that used music as an entry point to raise awareness about various issues. Their approach was non-dogmatic and placed emphasis on the sharing of information and galvanizing people into taking action.

"Axis works two ways," explains Serj. "It's music engagement in politics, but it's also direct political engagement. It's straight out activism. We use the music as a way of bringing attention to certain just causes or injustices. We have an LA chapter that is very active, we have the website, we have bi-monthly radio shows that we prepare – it's a lot of work and it's good. It's about bringing actual positive change and it's not just about the music."

Axis Of Justice grew quickly and, away from party politics, remains an important self-facilitating grass roots organisation. High profile press coverage ensured that the organisation remained at the forefront of counter-cultural resistance. In November 2004 Tom and Serj would stage an Axis Of Justice benefit concert at The Avalon in LA that brought together a number of artists to perform, including Serj and Tom (in his guise as acoustic protest singer The Nightwatchman), Red Hot Chili Peppers bassist Flea, Pete Yorn, Jurassic 5 and MC5's Wayne Kramer. The show was subsequently released as an album and DVD.

The most tumultuous year in living memory had, conversely, been kind to System Of A Down. 2001 saw them go from metal oddities to mainstream rock stars. It's usually at this point in a band's career that their original fanbase begins to drop off. Some rock fans are snobs who like their bands to be obscure, elusive or off the mainstream radar – nothing wrong with that – but System had given their fans no reason to question their integrity or artistic direction. Everything they had achieved had been done with minimal musical compromise; in fact, *Toxicity* suggested the band were only getting weirder. Miraculously they had broadened their fanbase considerably, bringing in people who knew little of metal and couldn't care less about politics, much less this strange niche the band had carved for themselves. *Toxicity* featured highly in numerous music magazines' 'Albums Of The Year' lists the world over, including *Rolling Stone, Time, Spin,* and *Alternative Press.*

The band's appearance was ever-changing too. Gone was the body paint, shaved heads and plastic trousers of three years earlier. Now they were a strange mix of sportswear (Daron's ever-present hockey shirt, Shavo's trademark long shorts and socks combo), metal chic and couldn't-give-a-shit hairstyles, each reflecting just a little of their colourful personalities.

"Daron Malakian's catfish whiskers droop down on either side of his mouth in lugubrious tribute to Fu Manchu," noted *The Daily Telegraph* in a piece circa *Toxicity.* "Singer Tankian has a luxuriant, yet somehow disciplined, chin eruption, reminiscent of an Afghan mullah. Odadjian has braided his own impressive beard into a strangely intimidating plait, and drummer Dolmayan has a kind of hair halo, ruffled about his head like the fur on the spine of a Rhodesian Ridgeback." As manager David Benveniste described them to me in 2005: "Serj is The Prophet. Daron is the Mad Scientist Genius. Shavo is the glue. John is the rock. He's the pillar of strength."

The next single from System was the moving title track from the album. It gave Shavo, a budding film-maker since his days as a teenager cobbling together short skateboarding films, a chance to flex his directorial muscles for the first time. Having assisted director Marcos Siega in the making of 'Chop Suey!' and having received encouragement from his band-mates, the bass player immersed himself in the new project whole-heartedly.

"You should have seen me on the set," he said. "At first I was really timid, but then I felt this passion coming through me. It's cool to know that I can do it and I'd rather someone from my band represented the band in that way because then it's the band's eye instead of someone else's vision."

Shot in December, the video for 'Toxicity' was a simple concept that captured the band clad in black juxtaposed playing against either white or black screen back-drops, with added flourishes such as film footage of images of the city played onto their torsos. The battle-cry denouement of the song saw the band playing to a violent mosh-pit. A special hydraulic stage was used to lower and raise the band into the pit.

When it was released the following May, this moving single reached Number 2 in the US Modern Rock Chart – their highest position yet

– and Number 25 in the UK. Any chart placing still felt like victory given the content of the music. Commercially the band – or certainly their label – now found themselves in competition with the likes of Coldplay, Queens Of The Stone Age, Foo Fighters and The Strokes for album sales, though they blatantly had little in common with any of them. They were doing good.

By the time *Toxicity* was released the band were already on tour. In January they flew to Australia to play the country's biggest rock festival, Big Day Out. A sign of their swelling popularity, their set was cut short when barriers down the front collapsed. The previous year a fan had died after being trampled at the same festival during a Limp Bizkit performance, and no-one wanted that to happen again. The band left the stage, but returned later to finish their set after a performance from popular New Zealanders Shihad.

February saw the band back in the US to start more tour dates in Las Vegas – where John had recently bought a condo for himself with his share of the band's spoils of musical warfare – with Clutch supporting again. Two weeks later and it was on to Europe for an extensive tour beginning in Portugal and taking in Germany, Italy, France and Holland.

At the band's request, for these dates they were joined by New York hardcore quintet Dillinger Escape Plan. An inspired choice of opening act, Dillinger were one of the most brutal bands around, their music an assault of guitars and apoplectic vocals delivered with mathematical and hateful precision. They sounded like free jazz played on angle-grinders; naturally, utterly brilliant.

"I remember hearing SOAD's early stuff and thinking, 'Woah, dude, that's intense!'" says Dillinger frontman Greg Puciato on www.suicide-girls.com, who only joined the band months earlier and that summer would seal his reputation in the UK by taking a shit onstage at the Reading festival. Then throwing it in the crowd. "I think their early stuff sounded to the mainstream what our stuff probably sounds like to the mainstream now. We feel a strong kinship with them."

"We pick bands that we like to watch everyday," said John at the start of the tour. "We don't want to have a band up there that disgusts our taste in music that we have to sit there everyday and put up with. I enjoy watching Dillinger Escape Plan and maybe they aren't the biggest band in the world and don't have a huge draw, but we are introducing something a little different to our audience and I think we have an audience that understands a little bit more about different kinds of music and being open to music whether you like it or not. We don't want to let them down by bringing the newest rap metal band whose label would pay fifty grand to have us take them out on tour."

Though they came endorsed by the band – Daron in particular was a fan – large sections of System Of A Down's new fans were less open-minded to Dillinger and swiftly disproved the drummer's claims. When the tour reached the UK, I was in the crowd to see two of my favourite bands together at London's historic Brixton Academy. I was disappointed then to see Dillinger Escape Plan met by a sea of middle fingers, agitated boos and the odd missile. Not that it hindered their performance, but if fans of a band such as System Of A Down were expressing an intolerance for such challenging music then either rock music was in a bad state, or System's popularity had brought in thousands of narrow-minded fans – an inevitability when you're selling millions of records. I think perhaps it was a bit of both. The members of Dillinger Escape Plan would later tell me with a wry chuckle that they lost thousands of dollars of their own money to be booed at or met with looks of boredom most nights across Europe – and still be called sell-outs by their own fans for touring with a band as 'commercial' as System.

While in the UK, a *Pledge Of Allegiance* compilation live album was released featuring the bands who had toured together the previous October. Recorded at a date in Rosemont, Illinois, System Of A Down contributed three of the new album's strongest tracks, 'Chop Suey!', 'Toxicity' and 'Bounce'.

A final single from *Toxicity* was released as a CD in the UK and a radio single/video in the US. One of the album's most poignant moments, 'Aerials' had a suitably thought-provoking video to match. Directed by Shavo and Marcos Siega and picking up on Daron's original explanation for the song as being about seeing things from different perspectives – about a disabled child being mesmerised by that which able-bodied people take for granted, about the inordinately simple to one person being complex to another – it depicted an unconventional-looking child in a role normally occupied by someone more conventional look-ing. In this case it subverted the norm and showed the protagonist, cavorting with women, cruising in flash cars and so forth. All the staple signifiers of the modern pop video. So though it was clearly designed with MTV and its ilk in mind, it also subverted traditional concepts of beauty and subtly suggested that the parameters that define normality in society are narrow and discriminatory. The slick video and stirring song had a great impact, rising straight to Number 1 in the US Modern Rock and Mainstream Rock charts – their highest radio airplay-generated placing yet – and Number 34 in the UK singles chart.

Throughout the band's career, but particularly since their profile had widened considerably after the release of *Toxicity*, a number of the band's songs had begun to appear on the internet for download with increased regularity. The laws about musical ownership and the buying and selling of it on the internet were still being decided upon, the internet itself having only been in use for less than a decade and the music itself no longer easily identifiable as a tangible physical 'product' So there were still many grey areas, though Metallica had already famously launched lawsuits against download site Napster, even suing a number of their own fans and setting something of a legal precedent which thankfully hasn't yet become common practice in the rock world. But System songs were being leaked and were appearing on the internet to be traded amongst fans, songs which hadn't been released for a reason – many of them were incomplete.

"It's not about the money, really, it's that the songs being downloaded weren't finished," said Daron. "It was so frustrating; we had lost control of our own songs. On some of them my vocals or guitar overdubs hadn't been added or the best version of Serj's vocals hadn't been used or the drum and bass tracks weren't all there, so we had to do something to get the right versions to our fans. Does it bother me that some people are burning their own System CDs and taking money out of my pocket? Not really. This has always been about putting the best possible version of the songs in the fans' hands. It was like selling an artist's painting before he had finished it."

How a number of the band's songs from their own archives were making it into the public domain was unknown, but a variety dating back to the warehouse of 1995 were already out there, culled from the band's own CDR copies. So they decided to do something about it. Rather than go after the teenagers who had put them where they were today, they decided to collate the bulk of their unreleased material in its finished state and release it as an album to render the bootlegs irrelevant and sub-standard.

"Some of the songs were recorded for *Toxicity,* but some go back way further than that," explained Daron when I caught up with him at the close of 2002, on the eve of the record's relatively low-key release. "It's drawn from right across the board, but to us it's still a brand new album. A song such as 'Mr. Jack' goes back to 1995, before we'd even played our first gig I guess. 'Roulette' was written for the first album, but we didn't really feel like it fitted in at the time. In fact, as a song it still sticks out but it kinda fits in more with what we're doing now. In putting the record together I've actually gone through about fifteen different possible versions of the track-listings so I can't even remember what goes where."

Though billed by some as a stop-gap release, the band insisted that the album was a collection in its own right and that the songs would stand up against anything else they had released. "We don't consider any of these songs B-sides or outtakes," they said in a band statement. "The songs that didn't make it onto *Toxicity* are as good as, if not better than, the songs that did."

The record was called *Steal This Album!,* the title inspired by the counter-cultural manual *Steal This Book* by 1960s counter-culture radical icon Abbie Hoffman. A founding member of the Youth International Movement – the Yippies – in 1968 Hoffman was a highly visible anti-war protester and prankster who wrote *Steal This Book* as a 'survival guide' for fellow radicals or those living on the margins of society – hippies, drug fiends, musicians, artists, dissidents; anyone likely to receive heat from the authorities. Though quite dated in style and tone today, the book nevertheless offers an insight into the political climate of the day and has certain close parallels with the early 2000s – Vietnam was raging, overt racism was rife, rock 'n' roll was still considered an evil force and alternative or anti-government existences were viewed with suspicion. America was white, clean-cut and tolerated no subversive behaviour and *Steal This Book* was packed with facts, advice and information for would-be agitators, victims of persecution from the government or those who fall foul of the law for anything from drug possession to shoplifting; a necessary reaction to conservative times. It was rejected by thirty publishers before finally being self-published in 1970 and quickly became a cult success. The actual title of the book referred to the anarchist belief that "all property is theft", therefore money is meaningless and everyone is equally entitled to anything they want.

The link between Hoffman and his ilk with System was obvious – both were freedom fighting pacifists inspiring the young to question their own corrupt, untrustworthy and untouchable governments.

"I don't actually read that many books so I've not actually read it," admitted Daron, laughing, "But I'm sure Serj has. I saw the movie [*Steal This Movie*, the 2000 adaptation of Hoffman's life] instead and I know what it's about. I just felt like that title fitted with what we're about. Originally a lot of these songs were released on the internet, so really a lot of people stole them. So it was like, OK, steal *this* then."

The title and context alone of *Steal This Album!* reaffirmed System Of A Down's position as a political band, even if their politics were surreal, absurd and non-dogmatic. Strangely it was an image the band – or Daron especially – often played down, either denying they were a political band or preferring to see themselves as a people's band – four individuals interested in the world and everything in it.

"So what if we sing a few songs about politics," said Daron. "Why wouldn't we? We are living in turbulent times. This is what it must have been like for musicians in the 1960s. The big issues then were war and racism. Forty years later, nothing has changed. So Bush is about to take us to war with Iraq and I'm just supposed to write love songs? Hell no. I won't stand for that."

Though System Of A Down were keen to stress that *Steal This Album!* should be viewed as an *album*, nevertheless it was the least impressive of their three records to date. Not weak, just more disjointed than either *System Of A Down* or *Toxicity* – understandable given it was compiled from material recorded over seven years – and, at sixteen tracks, arguably too long. But in a music industry that deploys techniques such as multi-formatting and releasing/repackaging to maximise profits by playing on the hardcore fan's desire to have everything by a band, it was value for money – an unspoken allegiance between the band and the fans that they may have hit the big time but they were no sell-outs. And in amongst the collection were some great stand-alone tracks. A song that had been touted for some time during interviews, album opener 'Chic N' Stu' sounded like it would be at home on any System album. A rant about consumerism and ruthless advertising techniques that used the idea of the smorgasbord of pizza toppings as some sort of a metaphor for the choices buyers are bombarded with, it was also one of their daftest. Next week: System Of A Down tackle the moral dilemma of sandwich fillings.

Another song that had been played live for some time was the rock lament 'Innervision', previously dropped from the final cut of *Toxicity*. Though favourite tracks on *Steal This Album!* vary from fan to fan, 'Boom!' was certainly one of *Steal This Album's* most instant musical moments. Mixing spoken word verses with a simplistic chorus, it saw Serj flex the muscle of his mind in a protest song that effectively condensed the band's politics into one song by depicting a world where (once again) over-bearing advertisers force people to relent – consumption as the new religion, TV as the great desensitizer – but yet four thousand children die of starvation per day. It was sharp and straight to the point as such subjects should be. 'ADD' was equally as incensed. Preceding the US invasion of Iraq by six months it read like a critique of foreign policy – "an unjustifiable, egotistical, power struggle" – that sends young men and women out to fight the battles of their leaders, only to have them sent back in body parts. Daron's guitars created an almost symphonic wall of sound as Serj whispered thoughts on the deceit of the American Dream. 'I-E-A-I-A-I-O' was a true oddity, even by System's standards. Who else could combine the lyrics of "Peter Piper picked a peck of pickled pepper" with some maudlin tribal chants, name-check Lois Lane and Jimmy Carter and drop in the riff of the theme tune from 1980s TV show *Knight Rider*? Such an eccentric approach only works best in short bursts and *Steal This Album!* may have suffered from an abundance of – for want of a more appropriate word – wackiness.

Elsewhere, other songs included 'Streamline' (which originally appeared on *The Scorpion King* soundtrack album, of all things), 'Ego Brain', which featured a rare appearance by Theremin and, referencing Abbie Hoffman again, 'Fuck The System', a song whose message just somehow seemed that little too obvious. As a whole though the band managed not to overstay their welcome. And *Steal This Album!* was still better than most other rock records released in 2002.

The packaging for the album was interesting. Completely at odds with the stylised album covers synonymous with today's rock and pop music, *Steal This Album!* came in nothing but a simple one-sheet replica CDR cover with the title handwritten in black on white – a sly dig at those who had stolen their songs perhaps, or maybe just a subtle acknowledgement that the contents *were* a compilation of archive material rather than the latest new studio effort. All sleeve notes were included on the band's website. Continuing the mock-bootleg feel of the album, the on-body print on the CD came in four different DIY-drawn versions, each designed by a band member. It was pot-luck as to which one fans received. Released in November during the pre-Christmas deluge, *Steal This Album!* charted at Number 15 in the US (eventually going platinum) and Number 56 in the UK. Though the album wasn't anywhere as near to being as commercially successful as *Toxicity*, it was released in addition to their planned forthcoming records so with little promotion it's hard to see how their label could have been disappointed.

"When I saw that we put out three singles [from *Toxicity*] and all of a sudden everybody in the mall knows who the fuck I am, I realized that we had to go away," said Daron at the close of 2002. "Yeah, we put out *Steal this Album!* but we didn't tour and we put out one single. And the reason we put out the single 'Boom!' was because we felt we had to because the war was coming out and we had an opportunity to say something. It was more of an integrity thing."

Maybe the band did need a break from the limelight. Though their huge success had been many years in the making and fully deserved, it was nevertheless unprecedented. If the band's first couple of albums had sold 100,000 copies each they would have been deemed a success, such was the awkwardness of their music and subject matter. Instead they were selling millions and enduring the added pressures that come with living life through a lens, yet remained as much hated as they were loved. There were simply many who just did not get this band. And rightly so. For any important artist is going to divide opinion, whether Elvis Presley, John Lennon or Chuck D, all of whom have been vilified in America at various points in their career. It's when everyone is in agreement about their safe little rock or pop stars that we're truly fucked; just watch an episode of the reality TV music talent shows for a nightmare vision of a homogenised artistic future. Plus, there was the danger of burn-out and overkill, the downfall of most bands.

If System Of A Down's music sounded like the end was nigh – like a musical panic attack – then that's because they were products of their time: modern America and all its foibles.

"I've suffered from panic attacks over the year," Daron told me. "I've stopped getting them so much, thank God. There are a lot of kids who suffer from panic attacks – and not just kids. It's interesting to see how many teenagers suffer from them, which is freaky, because it's all really based on stress. Do teenagers have that much to be stressed about? Well, yes. It's says something about modern life. Then of course, some of the methods of treatment are more fucked up than the thing itself – Prozac and all this shit. I went on that for a couple of months and it was definitely a rollercoaster ride. I got nothing positive out of it. I basically got through it all through transcendental meditations. At the end of the day there are all sorts of things you can do and things you can take to make yourself feel good but there's nothing you can't spark within your body with a little concentration, you can take all these medicines, but you can do it with your mind too. Oh, and pot helps too."

The band's next release couldn't have been timelier. Though 'Innervision' had been released as a promotional-only CD ostensibly to promote *Steal This Album!* in late 2002, 'Boom!' became the album's lead track when it was released as a radio single, complete with video.

Given the current political climate, the band pulled out all the stops and invited controversial film-maker Michael Moore to direct the promo. "Michael Moore seemed like the only real choice for directing," Serj Tankian told MTV.com. "He's an amazing storyteller and he's not egotistical about his work because he approaches it from the angle of the truth and leaves himself out of it. He lets the camera reveal whatever happens, and he's a very courageous person. He can actually tell the truth very bluntly in a way people understand and eventually politicize people that would not be politicized otherwise. It's pretty impressive. To me, it was a no-brainer."

Perhaps more than anyone in the US, through a series of documentaries, books and the TV show *The Awful Truth,* Moore represented the voice of righteous dissent of the disenfranchised everyman, a persona he was happy to play up to in his casual appearance and accessible works – most notably his study of US gun control, *Bowling For Columbine* and a film he was then currently working on, *Fahrenheit 9-11.*

Moore's work is packed with the type of information that is often buried or suppressed lest it provokes the general population into thinking too hard about corporate America's wrongdoings.

Consequently as a liberal and mischief-maker Moore was already hated by many, including many leading Republicans, industrialists and capitalists.

He had also directed two videos for Rage Against The Machine, 'Testify' and their controversial promo 'Sleep Now In The Fire'. During the filming on Wall Street of the latter, Moore narrowly missed arrest after the band failed to gain permission from the City of New York to shoot there. An ideal collaborator for System Of A Down then on this most incendiary and direct of songs.

"I had seen *Bowling For Columbine* three times," added Daron. "It's such a great movie and I knew that he would be the perfect person to put together the 'Boom!' video for us. It turns out he knew our stuff – he's a System fan – so we all got along great."

The concept for the video was simple but highly effective and followed a similar editorial pattern to Moore's longer documentary works. The director shot the band members taking part in anti-war demonstrations that took place in LA on February 15 2002 and cut it with footage of the many protests the world over, including statistics of the people who took part internationally. The overall effect was of a world at odds with itself showing millions actively taking time out of their lives to protest.

"The majority of people in these peace marches are your average families with kids," said Serj. "We didn't think that the media has really portrayed the enormous aspect and the beauty of people on the street voicing their opinion. And that's what it is to be American. To me, 'Boom!' is kind of like building a little pyramid of what may or may not lead us to bomb someone or be at war. It's about human life, and there's a lot of civilians that die when bombs fall, and that's the problem. Taking out Saddam Hussein isn't a matter of making an incision and going in and taking one person and taking them to jail. It's the death of many innocent people who just happen to be living there, and it's a travesty."

Chapter 7: Bring Your Own Bombs

Despite widespread international opposition, in March 2003 the terrorist attacks on the US of eighteen months earlier reached their (il)logical conclusion − with a major retaliation on an unrelated country, Iraq. George W. Bush's ruling Republican party had unfinished business with Iraq − or rather, its despotic leader, Saddam Hussein − dating back to the early 1980s when his father was vice president to Ronald Reagan. Amid much fanfare and controversy, George Bush Jr, backed up by UK Prime Minister Tony Blair, broke international UN laws and launched a series of ferocious attacks on Iraq. The Republicans cleverly used national feelings of fear of terrorists to justify the attack on a country that itself had been living in fear of its own leader; the fact that the perpetrators of the 9-11 attacks had been Al Qaeda members of Saudi and Afghan descent was neither here nor there. They weren't American, and that's all that mattered.

"The political climate here is very split right now, it reminds me of the 1960s, only without people being involved," Daron had told me four months earlier during a discussion about the relationship between music and politics − and the impending war. "You have people who want war, and those who don't. Those that do just blindly follow the flag. But those who don't, don't always stand up to be noticed. That's the sad thing − people are getting smacked in the face, and they're just taking it. Whether they want war or not, they're going to live with it. This is supposed to be a government that we are in control of.

None of it makes sense and I'm frustrated. Frustrated with songwriters, frustrated with bands, with artists. I feel like we need people with guts, people who aren't afraid to be called whatever the hell they're going to be called. We need someone to tell the new generation what's going on, instead of showing them tits and ass, or the wonderful new cars they can buy, twenty-four hours a day. At least in the 1960s you had bands who actually sang about topics which brought awareness to people. Where are these people right now? The only reason we stick out is because we're one of the only bands speaking out. Do people have no guts now? The kids want it. The kids would like to hear the truth. Who's inspiring these kids? There's a whole generation who have no-one to look up to, to hear the truth – their icons are show-off rock stars and rap stars with plenty of tits and ass and pussy. Hey, these things are important – I love to fuck – but there is so much going on in the world and no-one is singing about it. But people are scared they won't get a record deal or that the government will point them out as communists. It's McCarthy-ism all over again. People don't like it when you get heavy … but these are heavy times, man!"

On April 3, 2003, Baghdad fell and the following month the ruling Ba'ath party was overthrown and Hussein removed from office. Bush announced the end of major combat during a carefully orchestrated, overly theatrical homecoming rally and was viewed as a hero by many, even though it had only ever been a one-sided conflict in which, at the time of writing, an estimated 30,000 Iraqi's lost their lives. In December 2003, Saddam Hussein was finally captured and rightly put on trial for various hideous crimes.

Naturally such a turn of events confirmed much of what System Of A Down had been singing about for the past five years – that the world is ruled by power-hungry warmongers, the people have little or no say and we're slowly sliding towards Armageddon. The band had a greater reason to protest than many in the West – Daron had many family members in Iraq.

"They work in the city," said Daron during the initial invasion "One's a school teacher, a couple of my cousins take the bus to work…it's scary. Having family there makes me feel closer to the soldiers and their families. To have loved ones in danger, basically. I'm not this American-hating guy though. I mean, I was born in Hollywood. But I'm not one of those crazy Americans who think that America is the only place on earth … I visited Iraq when I was a teenager, and I can tell you first-hand that the people who I met there are really nice, ordinary people who don't want war with us or with anyone.

The last two or three months or whenever that happened was probably the toughest time of my whole life," he continued. "Because it was like not knowing what's going on until we got a phone call. And when we get a phone call and they're OK we can breathe a little bit. For one month I didn't know if a bomb had dropped on my grandmother's house …"

Daron also revealed that Iraqi relatives of his had asked passing US troops if they had ever heard of a rock 'n' roll band called System Of A

Down, to which they replied: "How the fuck do you know who they are?", little realising they were bombing relatives of the very band they liked.

"People see citizens who are anti-war as anti-American or anti-patriotic and that's so wrong," added Shavo. "There's nothing anti-patriotic about wanting peace. There really isn't. There is a fine line and I guess that people don't know how to separate it. I don't know how to tell which one it is. It's not unpatriotic to have feelings and beliefs that don't go with the President. There's a lot of facets to this war. I'm no politician and I'm not going to only be talking about the war, but there's so many other reasons he's doing this other than what he tells us."

Only the absurdity of war can produce such bitter-sweet ironies as an anti-war band soundtracking attacks by their adopted country on one of the very countries that they had come from. As such topics as American foreign policy were placed under great scrutiny and ideological and philosophical debates concerning the definition of such notions as terrorism and freedom raged, the band naturally drew inspiration from what they saw on the news or read in the newspaper – or not, as the case often was.

Either way it was during this period that many of the songs and ideas for the band's next releases began to take shape – songs such as 'Solder Side', 'BYOB' and 'Attack'. But that was all still yet to come. "It brought out a lot of good material," said Daron. "Not necessarily political music, just emotional music, you know?"

In May 2003, Serj's friendship with Arto came to fruition with the release of their collaboration. In down-time from the band following the *Toxicity* cycle of activity, he had been collaborating with Tunçboyaciyan for a release on Serjical Strike, under the name Serart. The duo's impromptu recordings took place over a mere six days of concentrated activity some six months after the recording of *Toxicity*. Various friends dropped by to contribute, including singer Jenna Ross (of LA band Rue) on 'Narina' and 'Devil's Wedding', Serj's friend Vahé added a guitar solo and sometime turn-tablist Shavo contributed some scratching to a couple of songs.

"Serart to me is like a compelling collaboration between two artists and it represents a moment in time," says Serj. "It was a spontaneous work in the studio. I guess it could be seen as a side project but it's not a side band or anything like that. Arto was so compelling as an artist and I was so intrigued by his work and what he did that I just wanted to go into the studio and jam with him you know? It was as simple as that! Those six days of working together in the studio is what Serart is."

The chosen name for this project was self-explanatory, an amalgamation of the name of its two creators and also, as Serj later explained "'Ser' means love in Armenian, while 'Art' is art in English ... so maybe it's like the love of art, or the art of loving?"

The duo's description of Serart's music in their own biography was an accurate précis of the album's contents: "Sessions for the album took a spontaneous approach in a free form atmosphere akin to expressionistic painting on a sonic canvas. The cross-pollination of rhythms and alternating tones and scales in the album present a diversity that reflects our own globe."

Serart offered a wider insight into the System frontman's tastes and interests beyond such notions as rock or metal and into the realms of what is loosely and erroneously termed 'world music' – a handy tag for pretty much anything that is not indigenously Western-based such as pop or blues-born rock music.

"I listen to all sorts of music," said Serj. "I do like world music to a certain degree. It depends if I like the song or not. It's the same with rock or hip-hop. If I like the song and the artist is compelling and original then I like it, but yeah I listen to jazz as well, I listen to all sorts of music." For the frontman Serart also offered a different approach to songwriting techniques. "It was mostly improvisation," he said of the collaboration. "When we went to the studio I did take a lot of songs that I had pre-constructed with beats and guitars and some other stuff that I brought in that did make the transition a little smoother and we added different instruments and vocals but for nine out of sixteen tracks, we just improvised right on the spot. I didn't know what he was going to do next let alone what I was going to do next. It was fun. It was really challenging just to trust in the moment and let it go without judgment and see what comes out and we actually used everything that we worked on, we didn't throw anything away, we didn't leave anything on the side so it was interesting."

Over the course of sixteen songs – 'pieces' might be a better description – Serj and Arto traversed the globe like musical voyagers with unlimited round-trip air tickets. The music of *Serart* was more than world music tourism though, the pair drawing on a wide range of styles that they were already *au fait* with. Arto had a wealth of experience and credibility (in 2006, his Armenian Navy Band would be nominated for a BBC World Music Award), plus, Serj's knowledge of Middle Eastern politics, religious faiths, philosophy and his deeper spiritual persuasions gave a certain credence to the multi-national mélange. 'Cinema' for example was based on a simple drum 'n' bass beat, was sprinkled with some of Tunçboyaciyan's recognizable percussion and coloured with Serj's instantly-recognizable voice that mixed mock-falsetto and wordless wailing before dropping in some jazzy sax, Japanese-sounding kabuki music, Chinese wind chimes, then swerving towards a foreboding rhythmic climax, an electron-tinged mantra about personal faith. Yeah, it was that kind of approach throughout. Eclectic didn't really come close.

Serart certainly wasn't for everyone but it worked as a record in its own right. Open-minded System fans could get off on the rhythms that permeate throughout and recognize the unique personality and voice of Serj, while the new age Peter Gabriel-loving post-WOMAD world music fans could revel in a record made by *genuine Armenians* and not fail to be impressed by the neat production and wealth of ideas. I even got to write about the album in *Kerrang!,* in whose pages of punk, hardcore, metal and emo bands the album stuck out like a big sore thumb. But with a beard.

Not content with a new association-by-proxy with world music, System Of A Down were also the subject of a weird and wonderful tribute album of their music played by a string quartet. Part of a series of albums where metal bands were given a chamber music makeover, *String Quartet Tribute to System Of A Down* featured various artists' string renditions of most of their big 'hits'. Actually, the project wasn't that odd. Compared to most of their contemporaries System's music fitted well as classical instrumentals – after all, music of their music already had a symphonic feel to it that was as dramatic and powerful as Wagner or Mahler were in their day, composers who wrote controversial, emotive music about war and triumph and tragedy to be blasted out to vast auditoriums. Not that much different at all then.

The success of *Toxicity* and the momentum gained with the quick release of *Steal This Album!* opened new doors for the band. In the coldest sense, they were now a bankable band. They were in the big league, a commercial success. They were exactly what a record label wants from its rock bands – a touch of danger, a legion of young fans, but a work ethic and productivity that ensured it wasn't just a heroic sense of glory that they were achieving. Now their opinions would be listened to and, yes, their projects bankrolled. Plus, of course, they were now millionaires from record sales and publishing deals alone. Factor in merchandise, large performance deals and any other sponsorships deals they had on the go and System Of A Down enterprises was a flourishing, highly lucrative entity; the equivalent of the latest blue-chip high flyers. Materially their lives had certainly become more comfortable; a financial status best represented by a trip Shavo took to Armenia.

"I went back and I took my family there – my mom, dad, brother, gramps – just everyone who hadn't been back since we moved to America," he said. "I was like, I'm going to get my family a gift and have them see their family again, because we have family there we hadn't seen for thirty years."

Another by-product of the freedom offered by their success was their non-System interests, each an extension of their personality. Shavo got deeper into video direction (working with Taproot), John enjoyed the benefits of a bachelor life and worked on his comic and car collections and Daron announced plans to also set up his own record label, EatUrMusic, which he launched in 2003 with the modest claim that rock music needed saving and he was just the man to do it.

"When rock and roll started, it wasn't a bunch of people pretending to be somebody else – Pete Townshend was Pete Townshend, right? And Keith Richards was Keith Richards, and The Beatles were The Beatles," Daron argued. "When those people came out, they were originals, but now most rock bands just seem to follow formulas. Well, my band didn't follow any of those formulas! And that's why my band's successful. The Chili Peppers? Original. Tool? Original. You've gotta look for true characters, true artists, the people who don't give a shit what people think of them. That's why rap is so popular right now – there's nothing in rock and roll that the rebellious kid can really grab onto. I wanted to produce records, and starting a label gives me an outlet to release stuff that I want to produce ... because I don't really like what everyone else is signing, you know? I do have my opinions about rock and roll, about how it's suffering and how I can help."

EarUrMusic was established as a subsidiary of Sony as an outlet for Daron's ideas and production skills. "Serj is not into rock music, so I don't see him signing rock bands," said Daron in response to the question of his and Serj's differing tastes and lifestyles. "If he listens to rock, he listens to shit that's out there. His is more of a progressive-style label – I can't say it has more of an artsy twist, because my stuff will have that, too. I'm more into songs, though. I'd say you could probably take some of my shit to radio, but that's not because I'm looking for the next radio hit. It's just that songs turn me on. They always have."

The first band Daron signed were LA-based punk-metal – or neo-metal, possibly – crossover band Amen; essentially Casey Chaos and a number of changing musicians (one early member included former Snot bassist John 'Tumor' Fahnestock, who in 2006 resurfaced in a band called KCUF whose album featured an appearance from Shavo – LA's smalltown syndrome in full effect once again). Chaos, a former pro skateboarder and graduate of the hardcore/punk scene and fleetingly a member of LA goth-punks Christian Death, was a driven individual who had put together Amen. Former Sex Pistol Steve Jones once famously said that Amen were "far more pissed off than the Pistols ever were."

When nu-metal happened, these far-from-shy grubby Americans found themselves lumped in with a breed of bands and prospered, particularly in the UK and around Europe, and gained tonnes of press thanks to Casey's volatile onstage behaviour (in which self-harm regularly featured) and his natural charm and charisma offstage. Though 2000's *We Have Come For Your Parents* was an agreeable explosion of metal riffs, slogans and barely contained angst, their records never quite matched their live show – or the songs never quite justified the energy put into them – and Amen failed to step up to the next level. Many musicians came and went, as did a number of record deals. So they seemed like a slightly odd choice to launch a label, yet Casey was an obvious kindred spirit with Daron. "I'm proud that Amen is my first signing," he said. "Casey is the Iggy Pop of my generation, he's creating his art and his music on his own terms, and I'm very happy that I have an outlet to support that."

The guitarist produced the band's next album *Death Before Musick*, released in 2004. Though a strong record with plenty of acclaim from critics and fans alike, interest in the band had waned somewhat and the record essentially under-achieved. Another EatUrMusic release followed soon afterwards though with the US release of *Volcano* by Norwegian black metal legends Satyricon. Daron had been a fan of the band for many years and worked out a deal to release the Norwegian Grammy-winning album through Columbia. The influence of the extreme end of metal in System's sound, primarily came from the guitarist's interest in all things dark. If Serj was to be found tinkering with his recently-acquired nose flute ("I don't really know how to use it, I just like making weird sounds with it on my face," he reasoned), it was Daron who was coming up with the hard-edged riffs inspired by a legion of truly underground bands. "I really respect the black metal scene a lot," he said. "It's the closest we've seen to punk rock, with that kind of integrity." Since then however, EatUrMusic has remained strangely quiet. Perhaps Daron realised that playing guitar is more fun than all the paperwork that goes on behind the scenes.

Meanwhile, in late 2003 System Of A Down played a clutch of shows, apropos of nothing other than because the demand was there, including two storming sets at the Reading and Leeds festivals, the most established hard rock gatherings in the European festival calendar. Uniformly clad in black and with Daron sporting a large beard and wearing some dramatic black metal-inspired spikes round his wrists, the band took the festival by storm. Taking to the stage before Metallica's headlining slot, the set at Reading that I witnessed was furious, fun and full of 'the hits', a performance that no doubt won over a lot of floating voters who otherwise might not have seen the band at one of their headline shows. The image of Daron's gurning face blown-up on the huge TV screens as he ran around the stage like a wild man from the woods who had just come down into the town is one that will stay with me for some time, the inherent other-worldly weirdness of it all provoking reactions in the crowd ranging from laughter to unease to lifelong devotion. He actually reminded me a little of Jethro Tull's prancing frontman Ian Anderson in his hey-day.

Leeds was even more eventful. A few minutes into the show and the force of the crowd placed a number of fans down the front in danger, resulting in the set having to be halted. "We asked everyone: 'If all 60,000 of you can take a step back' and everyone looked at us as if we were crazy," recalled an incredulous Shavo.

"During the first few minutes of the System Of A Down performance, the front of stage barrier moved approximately half a metre," Mean Fiddler's Festival Director, Melvin Benn said in a subsequent press statement. "This resulted in a young girl trapping her foot. The performance was halted for a few minutes to release the girl and re-pin the barrier. The medical services have reported that 22 people were treated for minor injuries and the whole SOAD and Metallica performances continued with no further incident."

As if there was any doubt that System were the most important metal band on the planet, some members of the band took to the stage with Metallica – the *biggest* metal band on the planet – for a version of the Bay Area band's classic 'Creeping Death'.

A full ten years had passed since System Of A Down had formed, a time in which the musical landscape had changed. Amazingly, the band hadn't had to compromise either their sound or their integrity to get to the lofty position as arguably the most important rock band in the world. Instead the world had come around to their way of thinking. What had been deemed non-commercial and unsignable (as the band had frequently been advised by LA's A&R men) in the mid-1990s was now capable of topping the charts internationally. It was a rare example of a band sticking to their guns and ultimately being vindicated. Furthermore, what had once sounded like the rhetoric of conspiracy-obsessed stoners out to get recognised was now accepted by many as a reality. The topics that the band had been discussing since their earliest interviews – American foreign policy, exploitative regimes, media misrepresentation – were a living reality. Some aspects of their discussion such as the far-reaching power of television had, ironically, been turned to their advantage while the on-going debate about the Armenian genocide and other such recent humanitarian disasters had received new levels of awareness and discussion. System were doing more for the cause than any political mandates or discussion in the Senate.

But when it came down to it, System Of A Down were a band. Are a band. Their job is to make music to lose yourself too, and everything else is a by-product of the artwork. Throughout 2004 Daron embarked on another creative outpouring that would result in the band's most grandiose concept yet. The mad professor of the band was never more comfortable than when at home, getting stoned, writing songs and recording them on his prized old tape player. With Serj engaged in Axis Of Justice activity and John and Shavo enjoying the music of the LA scene, Daron retreated further into his own world of domesticity. At the time he was going out with model Jessica Miller and admitted in an interview that aside from seeing her he could quite easily go three or four weeks without seeing anyone else, such was his obsession with music, his drive to document "the wild sounds in my head" and his anti-social tendencies. Why go outside when there's weed, music and everything else you need at home? *Toxicity* had now sold five million copies worldwide. After that, the only impending question remaining was: where now?

Over the course of a number of months the answer soon revealed itself. Over the course of late 2004 and into 2005 Daron had accumulated scores of songs – maybe a hundred or more. His own listening tastes had expanded to include a lot of Brit bands of the 1960s, electro innovators such as Kraftwerk and plenty of death metal, and the new set of songs drew from the dynamics of such disparate sounds. He was also spending more time considering his vocals within the songs. Only ever really acting as a harmonious aural foil for Serj's abrasive, impassioned roar, the new songs featured a greater contribution than ever from the guitarist.

By the time Daron presented his new material to his band mates it was becoming obvious that they had more than enough material for a clutch of albums. The new songs sounded more expansive – simultaneously harder, faster, slower, dafter. More serious, more silly, more 'quacky'.

"I bring in a song and me and Serj jump lyrics off each other," said Daron. "Even if Serj doesn't know exactly where I'm coming from, he writes stuff that fits perfectly without even knowing."

"Sometimes we put in an idea with another idea that doesn't belong next to it, and see how they dance together and what comes out of it," agreed Serj, referring to their writing technique as 'ping-ponging'. "It's interesting. Everything that already has relationships with each other has been tried and tried again. It's good to find new relationships."

These 'new relationships' Serj refers to are not merely just the hippy-speak that he's prone to using, but the reality of a band who spend long intense periods of activity together – both in the studio and touring the world – only to then go their separate ways for similarly lengthy periods, as happened during these down-time periods.

"For a long time, we didn't see each other outside of System," John told *Rolling Stone*. "After being on tour for so long, you get on each other's nerves. We were either going to get a divorce or come closer together. So now there's a new camaraderie. We go to dinner and clubs together, and we're having a great time onstage. We have our arguments but not to the point that it's just frustrating and everybody leaves. Sometimes we fight. But after a couple hours on the phone or yelling at each other, we resolve it. However, we never argue about musical stuff. It's always about stupid shit, like why some T-shirt was approved."

For the latest recordings the band were back on familiar territory with familiar faces – Rick Rubin's Mansion studio in Laurel Canyon, with the bearded one co-producing alongside Daron and Andy Wallace mixing again. In fact, throughout their career System have only ever really recorded in LA, within commuting distance of their homes, a factor which may explain the influence of the city in their music: the next album would contain not one but two songs with 'Hollywood' in the title. As with the *Toxicity* sessions the songs came thick and fast.

Since the earliest days Daron had written much of the music, some of the lyrics and contributed vocals so the portrayal of him as a member seizing control of the band as depicted in the press at the time was erroneous. The only difference now was that some of the pressure was deflected from Serj who, as frontman, many naturally assumed was the leader.

"I knew that wasn't Serj's fault so I wasn't ever angry with him," said Daron. "It never really caused any bad relationship between us because how could I blame him? It's not like he plays up to being a rock star. He's happier for me now because he's always wanted people to know what I do in the band and he's never tried to hide that… I'm not about to start calling it 'The Daron Malakian Show.' Serj plays a big part in what happens with System Of A Down. What he and the other guys bring to the table is important and I don't want to discredit anybody. I don't have any reason to have it be a solo project to cater to my ego. I dig being with those guys, even kind of being the quiet one. I know that's tough to believe after seeing me on stage, but it's true."

As the sessions progressed a concept of sorts began to emerge – or at least, the idea that the band had more than enough material to conceivably release a double-album. Though the idea was touted, as

Daron explains, there was concern that a double-album might be too much, even by System's standards. So they settled on a slightly different approach.

"We were worried about people's attention spans these days," said Daron. "In America especially, and the world increasingly, it's very much an 'I want it now' culture. No one seems to have any patience any more. This is a generation of iPods and quick fixes. If we were in the 1960s, people would drop acid and quite happily listen to a double album in its entirety. So we decided to do two separate albums and have a six-month gap between them. That was so people can assimilate the songs on [the first album] *Mezmerize* before [the second] *Hypnotize* comes along."

"Another influence was the two *Kill Bill* movies. I thought that was really clever and cool. I find some similarities between Quentin Tarantino and System Of A Down, because Tarantino movies are horror movies, happy movies and drama movies all in one. It's kind of the same with System Of A Down's music."

So, two albums it was to be if only, as Serj said "for digestive purposes." A short fifteen-minute promotional film made by the band's friend and film-maker Garine Torossian showed the band at work carefully piecing together their ideas. In a studio decorated with skulls and flags it depicted a band at a creative peak, comfortable in their own strange niche, confident that they were making not one but two almighty records. It also illustrated some of their more unconventional techniques, such as Daron's request to point a set of speaker cabs to a custom-built wall of a dozen or so cheap acoustic guitars with their strings removed so that "the sound jumps into the guitars, then out of them – organic and grainy." Actually, the idea came from many hours spent trying out guitars in Hollywood's Guitar Centre (Serj's former place of employment), where a wall of acoustic guitars seemed to accidentally enrich the sound of the room.

In between footage of the band recording and goofing around playing table tennis on Rubin's balcony, snippets of conversation revealed some of the general themes of the twin albums – what John surmised as 'mental atrophy.'

"I don't want this to be a political agenda against this person or that person, but a political agenda against the way the world is, if anything," Daron was seen explaining as his band mates nodded in agreement.

"Revolution/evolution to me means you've got to change shit to evolve into a better society. That's hopefully what people will get out of it. Because … dirty television, the fucking 'reality' [TV] phase … we're like the Romans. We like people to suffer."

As with all their albums, anticipation was high as the time approached for the release of System's first (proper) album in nearly three years. The band had planned it well. Throughout 2002-2004 they had remained highly visible through extensive touring, festival appearances and the release of singles, so much so that their fanbase had expanded further still by the time *Mezmerize* dropped.

The usual rounds of promotion began in earnest as journalists were treated to the customary playbacks in sterile Sony boardrooms the world over. Paranoia in the corporate world surrounding downloading and the leaking of songs onto the internet was reaching new highs and just to hear *Mezmerize* involved the confiscation of bags, mobile phones and recording equipment and someone lingering nearby keeping a watchful eye on those crafty critics. But, unlike with most other bands, it was worth it.

The album intro of 'Soldier Side' was a cyclical piece of music that closed *Mezmerize's* follow-up, *Hypnotize*, a clever device that drew the two albums together as one. Set to a gentle, maudlin melody it also worked as a stand-alone song, recalling an image of a lone solider adrift in place and time. It could have been about a US soldier currently engaged in Basra or Baghdad or Falujah, but it could have just as easily have been about a solider in any struggle contemplating the solitude and futility of war. It was the same timeless ambiguity, the mixing of the Biblical with the modern, the antiquated with all things contemporary and plastic, that the band had achieved on earlier works.

Either way, as with war, the silence was broken as the music dissipated away to a brief silence before – boom! – the jagged guitars of 'B.Y.O.B.' exploded in the listener's face like a landmine. The opening minute of the song was nothing short of elephantine, a heartfelt battle cry of galloping drums and vocals like a wronged warlord seeking bloody revenge.

"Before the lyrics or music comes an initial thought about something, and that then triggers the lyrics," Daron told me just after the album's release. "'B.Y.O.B.' came out of a television commercial that I saw for army recruitment – and that pretty much triggered everything about this song."

Though the lyrics brimmed with curious images of "hypocritic [sic] and hypnotic computers" just when you had it pinned as another System thrash work-out, the change in tempo revealed a chorus that was pure pop party music with an R&B swing in its step. The simple feet-to-the-dance-floor refrain was dumb to an extreme, but deliberate and knowing with it, as if the band were laughing at the Britney/Christina/J-Lo clones who need vast teams of songwriters to come anywhere as radio-friendly as *this*. Then the song was off again, sprinting through a Daron rant to a climax that was heart-stopping, symphonic, as sharp and fast as you can get without losing coherence. Idealistic, simple, but essentially based on basic truths.

"I don't see it as a political song," said Daron. "The lyrics sing, 'Why don't presidents fight the war?...' but that's not a thought for politics or anything else. That's just a viewpoint. That's just a question. And I think, more than politics, we try to spark questions that the powers-that-be don't want you to ask. It's more about a social commentary. I think it's about a few different things as opposed to being pointed at one thing."

The song's title was a play on the acronym for a party invitation – Bring Your Own Bottle – changed to fit the theme of the song. It was not bottles System Of A Down wanted, but bombs. The lead single from the album was one of their best yet.

Like *System Of A Down* and *Toxicity* before it, *Mezmerize* went straight for the throat, bludgeoning with an assault of opening songs, in this case straight into the power-metal guitars of 'Revenga' where the rapid-fire words flying from Serj's mouth only relented for the chugging chorus. It was another pop song dressed with weird signatures and repeated screams. An MP3 download of the track had already been widely circulated and quickly became known as the song with the immortal opening line *"My cock is much bigger than yours!"* A comment on the ruthlessly competitive methods of modern consumer culture? Maybe, or maybe more good old rock star machismo.

"I'm not really singing about my cock, I'm singing about an ego-based attitude that's out there," countered Daron. "Why does one person have the right to go out and kill, and when another person kills he's a terrorist? Is it because I have a bigger army than you? How do we differentiate that? Some people will take it in a sexual way and some people will think about it a bit more."

Another blazing comet shower of sound and surrealistic colours, the song's "cigaro, cigaro" chorus referenced, in Daron's words, "the vibe" of Mozart's comic-opera 'The Marriage Of Figaro' (which was once banned in Vienna for its mockery of the upper classes) before spluttering to a halt. A wry song loosely about fame and success, 'Radio/Video' was another album highlight. Its deceptively mellow guitar intro led to a self-referential boast about being on the radio with "Danny and Lisa". The two names weren't just plucked from the ether, but were in fact Daron's two closest childhood friends. Looking beyond the initial jauntiness it appeared to be a song about clinging to images of innocence and childhood as a way of coping with adulthood.

"I haven't seen them since I was ten," says Daron. "This album is somewhat dear to me because there are moments from my childhood on it. They are not blunt, but there are pictures in my head that I see when I sing the songs. I couldn't even tell you what they are exactly about. Sometimes I sing them as happy songs, but they're not happy songs. We do that a lot. Most of our funniest songs are about the saddest moments in my life."

While celebratory, the song also possessed a plaintive quality during the musical breaks that were System's most Armenian-sounding yet, the affecting folk music – actually in a Russian time signature – and quasi-yodelling (what do you call that anyway?) capable of stirring something deep inside, regardless of nationality.

Despite such inherited influences, System Of A Down are true Americans too. Which might explain the mind-set songs such as the 'This Cocaine Makes Me Feel Like I'm On This Song' and 'Violent Pornography', two distinctly Western songs. The former was tightly-wound and nonsensical, a musical delirium of putrid, sexually transmitted images such as *"gonorrhoea gorgonzola"* (delivered in a pipsqueak cartoon voice) that warned "don't eat the fish", the latter a *Sesame Street*-style nursery rhyme rap with thrash falsetto and funk-filled drums. Actually, the song's contents were pretty grim, depicting violent pornography as one more example of TV's desensitising effect. You could almost have called it puritanical had Daron not spent most of the late 1990s declaring his affection for porn.

It was almost all too much to take in, so fortunately 'Question!' was a less frantic affair. Far earthier than the songs that preceded it, it was bordering on classic rock – epic and vaguely pompous, recalling Cat Stevens' spiritual simplicity once again as it questioned the big issue of life after death. The song elevated itself into a powerful finale to make neck hairs stand to attention.

"The song kind of asks *you* to ask the question," explained Serj. "Please question! To me, it's been interesting – people who have had life-after-death experiences that have been reported and written down for scientific experiments with quantum theorists and what-not. It's generally [about] going into some tunnel of white light or some type of natural crossing. Being confronted by non-judgmental beings in a world that's more green and musical than ours. Infinite harmonies abound. Knowledge gained in an instant without a body to necessitate it."

Playing on the image of the Statue Of Liberty as representative of America, 'Sad Statue' projected the idea of the empire after it has crumbled. The metaphor of the sinking statue as representing the fall of man recalled that of the same statue in the original version of *Planet Of The Apes* where only a decaying Liberty's torch and upper body protruded from the sands of time.

With its electro vocal samples, 'Old School Hollywood' was something of a departure for the band, musically and lyrically. The song was inspired by a Hollywood All-Stars charity baseball event held at the Dodgers stadium and which Daron was invited to take part in. Though not exactly enamoured with celebrity culture – or a natural sportsman – he was a huge fan of baseball and pleased to be invited.

Taking to the field on a Saturday afternoon with the temperature in the high 90s, Daron struck six consecutive hits and also played centre field but was uneasy to find himself rubbing shoulders with 'celebrities' including *Who's The Boss?* star Tony Danza and aging crooner Frankie Avalon. Not his usual scene.

"It has been my life-long dream to get heckled by fans while playing at a sporting event," he sarcastically told reporters on the day. "I feel like I lived out a submissive sexual fantasy. Striking out at Dodger Stadium was a big turn on."

Lyrically simplistic, the result was an electro-tinged rock song, not the best on the album but a much needed nod in a different direction. "It has a different vibe for us, because we used keyboards and synths on there, but ones which worked in our world," explained Daron. "We don't want to recreate anything we've done in the past. If we're not pushing boundaries we won't be releasing records and we wouldn't be releasing two albums in one year if we didn't think they showed artistic growth. That's the way we think. We're not going to keep repeating ourselves."

Sticking in the same neighbourhood, album closer 'Lost In Hollywood' was a stronger track. If 'Old School Hollywood' was a spurious commentary on the lifestyles of the rich and (barely) famous and the passing of Hollywood – as an industry and a community – into a 'has-been' cliché since its creative heyday, then 'Lost in Hollywood' viewed the territory from street level.

"All these Hollywood songs!" laughed Daron. "I was really proud when I wrote this song because I really felt like it was going to take the band some place else. That's the main goal for us: to do things that we haven't done before and still make it work in the System Of A Down world. The song is just scenes and pictures, partly from my childhood growing up in Hollywood and partly from my adulthood in LA too. Honestly, if I was own critic I would say that this is one of my best pieces of work. I feel very close to it."

With Daron taking lead vocals it depicted the reality of Hollywood, one that anyone who has been to the place will recognize, the sheen of the silver screen sliding away to reveal a world of street kids, dealers, hookers…societies lost. Slow-paced and high on emotion, the song read like a open letter to the generations of starry-eyed wannabes drawn to Hollywood like production line pins to a magnet from which they'll never be able to extricate themselves; a more thoughtful flipside to Guns N' Roses' 'Welcome To The Jungle' with a vague nod towards early Radiohead. The finale of Daron and Serj harmonizing was nothing short of elegiac, a funereal-feel fading away to nothing …

It was another musical triumph.

As part of the grand scheme of releasing two interlinked albums and keeping everything within the System family, Daron's artist father Vartan created the art concept for the *Mezmerize/Hypnotize* project.

Daron had revealed as far back as 1999 that "he's the greatest artist of the century. Not just because he's my father – even if he wasn't I'd look at it and say 'You're pretty good, dude. Wanna smoke a bubble?'"

The cover for the first instalment depicted an expressionless theatrically-masked face watching over its own repeating reflection with the pendulum of time ticking onwards, while the CD depicted a clock without arms – a concept that came from Shavo so that "the revolution occurs when the arms of a clock fall." (The cover also actually recalled the artwork of 1980s prog rockers Marillion.) Inside were black and white distorted interpretations of the four band members and the image of a clock forming the centre of an eyeball.

"I'm probably more scared than I am excited, to be honest with you," said Daron of the grand project. "But I'm confident people are gonna like it. At the same time, it would be just as important to me if no one ever heard it. You've got to understand that my dad's been an artist my whole life and he's never shown people his art. And that's where I come from. I don't care about whether or not anyone is going to accept it. What it comes down to is having that emotion come out of me and being true to the art."

Mezmerize was released on May 17, 2005 to general acclaim. Though System still continued to divide critics and as such had become the Marmite of the rock world – you either loved their surreal sonic attack or hated them for the very same reason – their stature was unavoidable; with a vast worldwide fan base they had almost transcended criticism. Interestingly, no-one seemed to comment on their misspelling of the album's title.

Still, confusion and general attempts to pigeon-hole this strange sound still reigned, as Daron explained during a conversation with the *Houston Press*. "Lately, we've been doing interviews, and people have been like, 'You guys are really leading the way for the new prog movement,' and I'm like, 'What?' Because a couple of years ago, these guys were comparing us to Limp Bizkit and Korn, and now that we're still here and those bands aren't, they're talking about prog. It's just kind of aggravating that people always have to have something to compare us to, or bunch us up with. I'm not saying we're the most original band in the world, but I don't really feel that we fall into a heavy-metal category or a pure rock category. There's a lot of stuff mixed up into one."

Whatever you called it, it worked. *Mezmerize* debuted at Number 1 in the US, where it sold a staggering 453,000 copies in the US in its first week (twice as many as *Toxicity* sold in the same period, which had now sold six million copies) and a total of 800,000 worldwide. The statistics kept piling up: *Mezmerize* also reached the top spot in Australia, Canada, France, Greece, Austria, Switzerland and New Zealand. It reached

Number 2 in the UK, Norway and the Republic Of Ireland plus various creditable positions in Italy, Hungary, the Czech Republic and Spain.

The cause was helped by a heavy duty promotional campaign across the globe, the band members – black-clad and looking heavily styled in their latest promotional photos – conducting scores of interviews, playbacks and press conferences. Shavo and Daron got through the process of answering the same questions over and over by smoking vast amounts of marijuana throughout.

When the album's most immediate song, 'B.Y.O.B.', was released as a single it gained huge amounts of airplay and made for one of the oddest hit singles of the year. It was released with an accompanying video as dramatic as the song demanded, the band lit in evil-looking red and performing amongst dozens of malevolent-looking jackbooted extras. It also showed the band in a party scene, a pastiche of the aspirational, booty-shaking sexualised pop, hip-hop and R&B videos that ruled the airwaves. Nonetheless this was as slick and big-budgeted as the very videos it was pastiching.

The band also premiered 'BYOB' on *Saturday Night Live*, where the show's producers neglected to bleep Daron's use of the F-word and, in fact, highlighted it by focusing in on the guitarist; another small battle of subversive school boy humour over the evils of nullifying modern TV.

None of this commercial success would have been achievable however without the band touring once again, which they did for most of the year. Though System Of A Down had been touring for large chunks of time for over eight years, it had been interspersed with long periods off. Each band member handled leaving home for a huge worldwide trek in their own ways. "In some ways you have to mentally prepare yourself for going off on long tours, but in some ways you don't," Serj told me, relaxing at home on the eve of the tour in the summer of 2005. "My way of preparing myself for a long tour is to try not to think about it until I'm on it. That way when I'm home I can enjoy it more, and then when I go away I can sink my teeth into it. So it's about living in the moment."

"I'm always such a nervous wreck before I leave to go on tour," said Daron, the same day. "I don't know, I'm such a homebody I get all stressed out and shit. Once I get out there I'm fine, but when I'm getting ready to leave home and packing my stuff it's always a weird feeling. A bit depressing, sometimes. I guess it's just because I'm very comfortable at home and moving from hotel to hotel can be a drag but it's really the only thing about what I do that can produce a slightly negative feeling. Once I'm out there I'm fine though."

By 2005 System Of A Down had expanded from four members into a wider organisation that, aside from the usual hired crew members, also included various friends and relatives. Some on the payroll, others just along for the ride. Vartan Malakian, a healthy-looking, handsome man with a similar build to his son was often to be seen hanging out at shows in a System shirt, saying "Hi" to fans and revelling in his new role as the band's aesthetic director. Similarly, Shavo's mother had long since got over any concerns that in picking up a guitar he was on the road to ruin and accepted that he might not become a lawyer (though as the bassist revealed, it wasn't until the band were receiving Grammy nominations that she truly approved of their success – and even then she wasn't so keen on his ever-present goatee!). Serj's even more impressively bearded brother Sevag Tankian was another familiar face in the entourage – largely because he looked almost exactly like Serj.

It was to be a busy summer. With 'BYOB' riding high in the charts, for their first North American shows since 2002 the band embarked on a 'guerrilla club tour' in April, a favoured practice of big bands going back to the clubs to hone their new live set in front of devout fans upfront of months of shows playing theatres, arenas and festivals. It also meant that after time away from touring, demand for tickets would naturally far outweigh supply and only serve to raise levels of anticipation for the bigger shows.

Starting at San Francisco's Fillmore, the band played ten club shows to crowds averaging a thousand fans each night, all under the title 'An Evening With System Of A Down'. They stuck to the same twenty-four song set, opening each night with their newest single and closing with their oldest.

"We wanted to play shows in the kind of small venues that we used to before we were signed, before our first album came out," said Daron on www.metalunderground.com. "We want to create an environment that is just one big party, not the band on stage separated from our fans in the audience. We're very excited about making this happen."

During this brief tour, further live plans were announced including a month-long US tour in August with the excellent prog-jazz-punk experimentalists The Mars Volta in support and dates in Europe. In May System Of A Down arrived in Europe fresh from the clubs to play what many consider some of their most memorable shows yet, a string of career defining dates across the continent. "When they played Milan [2005] it was one of the most amazingly brilliant shows I've ever seen," remembers manager David Benveniste. "The crowd went berserk, the band was on fire and it was one of the most energetic shows they've done. I think they were in a very aggressive state of mind on stage that night. There was also something really fantastic about the Festimad show they did in Spain where they went on at 3.30am because there had been a wind storm that had taken off the roof of one of the stages. Incubus went on before them at 2.45am and by the time System played no one had moved. There was this very surreal energy in the crowd. A very weird, but very cool vibe."

Their three shows the following week at London's Brixton Academy provided a surreal comedic moment of Spinal Tap-style proportions. If the story is to be believed, after soundcheck Shavo decided that his trousers needed cleaning and ironing so dispatched them to a local dry-cleaners. As stage time approached he went to locate his favoured strides only to find that the emporium in question had closed for the night. Where others might make do with another pair, as a sign of the band's stature and rock star-style eccentricity, Shavo managed to track down the dry-cleaner so that they might re-open the shop and retrieve his trousers. Which, unbelievably, after "a few tense hours" they did. Band of the people they may be, but it didn't stop System Of A Down occasionally getting special treatment. The trousers were returned, everyone breathed a sigh of relief and the band took to the stage late to play another belter, as described in *The Guardian*: "System of a Down are right on the money, underpinning the horrendous volume with a hybrid sound that incorporates hip-hop's focus on social issues along with the usual caterwauling guitars. Singer Serj Tankian, nu-metal's best Billy Connolly lookalike, is certainly the right man for the job...his biggest challenge is 'Aerials', which demands perfect pitch on guttural choruses that sound like a madrigal. Tankian's resonant voice and a preponderance of minor chords produce a sense of gloomy foreboding."

The Brixton show was in itself a warm-up for something bigger and better the following week when the band headlined the main stage on the closing day of the Download festival, the UK's premier festival for metalheads. With Black Sabbath headlining the previous night, System's Sunday slot elevated them into the realms of the truly élite – they were now headlining over not only Slipknot but *Slayer*, the very band who brought them to these shores in the first place.

In between international band obligations, Serj was busy on extra curricular projects again, this time spending his spare hours working with his friend Buckethead, a man better known for being the some-time guitarist with Guns N' Roses during Axl Rose's long protracted attempt at recording the *Chinese Democracy* album, and for wearing a KFC bucket on his head and an anonymous mask. Serj and Buckethead's friendship stretched back a number of years and the singer appeared on his album *Enter The Chicken* alongside a dozen other guest vocalists, and released on Serjical Strike.

With previous bands Deli Creeps and his work with innovative producer Bill Laswell, Buckethead had established himself as a highly inventive and unconventional guitarist with a near-robotic playing style. That he and Serj were firm friends and kindred spirits was no surprise. They were making music, one interviewer noted, that cannot be "chicken-holed into any one category."

"We met a while back, during Ozzfest '99," explained Serj. "Bucket was playing onstage with Primus every night, doing some crazy solo stuff and playing with the band as well, I think. So we met and we've jammed together and done a bunch of stuff together and improvised together before. We've even played an improvisational live show at a high school, unannounced a couple of years ago which was amazing. I think it was a natural, organic thing that this just happened. Bucket's always making a lot of records, he does a lot of different types of music with a lot of people I respect, actually. I've always wondered how it would sound with a bunch of different singers that have different tonalities and different vibes and colors and creativities. So all of that just kind of came together."

Serj's contribution was of both a vocal and economic variety – he appeared on the track 'We Are One' from the album *Buckethead And Friends*, as well as releasing the album on Serjical Strike in October. Serj even acted as spokesman for Buckethead during occasional interviews. A practical necessity given that the guitarist never speaks publicly.

Serj's involvement with Buckethead was a typical move for a member of System Of A Down. Though they remained a tight-knit collective of a band and their inner circle, when members did break out they approached whatever project with gusto and enthusiasm, regardless of commercial potential. As witnessed with Serart and *Cool Gardens*, they were more interested in being involved in interesting projects than money-making schemes.

In August the band embarked on their huge US tour starting with a show in nearby Long Beach, home, incidentally, to support band The Mars Volta. Born out of pioneering hardcore band At The Drive-In, The Mars Volta was the brain-child of guitarist Omar Rodriguez-Lopez and singer Cedric Bixler-Zavala, two Texas-raised Americans of Puerto Rican descent. The pair had been in bands since their mid-teens, forming first The Fall On Deaf Ears, Phantasmagoria, The Dregtones, then the hugely influential At The Drive-In.

Now as The Mars Volta, their music was ambitious, grandiose, hectic and all the other adjectives critics grasp blindly around for to describe music that is often indescribable. It was unique music that drew from punk, salsa, 1970s stadium rock, progressive rock, jazz, literature and poetry, Krautrock and dub to create a heady, brilliantly executed bilingual new millennial hybrid as heard on their two albums, *Deloused In The Comatorium* and their new release *Frances The Mute*, which had recently debuted at Number 5 in the US charts. Though they had their fair share of critics, equally they also had many friends and supporters – during their opening show of the tour they were joined unannounced by Red Hot Chili Peppers' John Frusciante, who regularly jams with the band. Naturally, System Of A Down saw something in The Mars Volta. Something called originality.

"They didn't do anything to be on the radio, the radio just accepted them, like us," Shavo said. "I've jammed with Omar in England. We had a soundcheck and he was just there and he grabbed the guitar and we jammed for like two hours non-stop. That's when I knew they had it. A band is a real band if they can play not just their songs, but they can just play."

With a Number 1 album and another one in the bag ready for release, System were able to pull out all the stops for the tour, including taking Serj's buddies Bad Acid Trip along for the ride as opening act. The stage and lighting for the tour was designed by Shavo, who had very particular tastes, right down to the smallest details.

"Our light guy is like a fifth member," he said. "He has to know every move, 'cause I don't like programmed lights. I love strobes and I hate pyro. Lights and colour and vibe and art, whatever is classy."

System and The Mars Volta was a dream coupling for many fans who like their rock music loud and wired, but with an intelligence and intent behind it too. The August leg took the bands south out of California, through Arizona to Texas then across to Florida, then up the Eastern states, each night playing in arenas that held between 15,000 and 20,000 people. It was the type of tour that the big rock bands of the 1980s would undertake, a schlep through the heartland of America playing to fans young and old, recent and long-standing, left-wing, right-wing and no opinion at all. It was a tour that transcended all the boundaries that previously stood in the band's way − genre, ethnicity, politics and so forth. Where the band had decided to play only a few new songs on their guerilla tour, audiences now had had time to devour *Mezmerize* and the band opened each night with its opening three songs, a dramatic 'Soldier Side' performed from behind a black curtain that dropped as the song segued into 'B.Y.O.B.', then straight into 'Revenga'. Large angled mirrors were also placed to give the impression of each member being somewhat larger than life. Before the opening show in Long Beach − where Rick Rubin and members of the Deftones watched from the side of the stage − they claimed that they had only rehearsed some of the new songs live once, the night before. Not that you could tell.

One other timeless signifier of System Of A Down's − or indeed any band's − status: each member had the luxury of performing on his own rug.

In August, the band released 'Question!' as the second single from *Mezmerize*. Though it wasn't the best song on the album by a stretch it was arguably the most accessible, a word rarely associated with the band. The UK release of the single came back with live versions of *Toxicity* tracks 'Forest' and 'Prison Song' recorded at the Big Day Out festival in Sydney and the 'Question!' video, which was once again directed by Shavo, though he had initially declined to direct, claiming to have run low on aesthetic inspiration.

"I was just, like, 'I'm gonna let this go' because I didn't have any ideas," he told MTV. "Then we were in Europe and I woke up startled by this crazy dream. I paged Serj [Tankian] right away and said, 'Dude, I think I've got something for 'Question!'" I was like, 'All this could be done as an opera, 'cause this song has an operatic feel, it's very triumphant and epic. Then I'm like, 'What if opera singers sing the song along with us?'"

System Of A Down *did* have an operatic quality that few had really remarked upon before. A mixture of introspective acoustic tones, power metal and such operatic undertones, 'Question!' was brought to life on screen with a dazzling video depicting the band dressed in formal wear, with theatrical sub-plot. Though 'Question!' went Top 10 on US radio playlist charts, for the first time since 'Sugar' it failed to make the UK Top 40 (charting at Number 41). Luckily System Of A Down have never been a 'singles' band; both band and record label merely viewed them as calling cards for their more complete works: the albums.

And there was another one due any minute …

Chapter 8: Hypnotize

"It starts off like you want to kick somebody's ass, and then it ends with you wanting to hug your mom..." was Daron's description of *Hypnotize*. Though it was an accurate one, the guitarist neglected to mention all that went on in between these two polar opposites of emotion.

Opener 'Attack' was System at their blunt effective best. With Daron's guitars jerking and twitching like snapped electrical cables, John's hissing hi-hat spitting venom and a raging inferno of vocals from Serj it was, quite obviously, an all-out musical attack about man as creator and, ultimately, destroyer. Though it was a violent-sounding song, it was as much about resistance and fighting back against attackers. It was a response to the unnecessary and indiscriminate warmongering of the US military in recent history and their years of propaganda.

"When 'Attack' comes in, and there's that big growl, you want to go hit someone," said Daron. "'Attack' is more like straightforward punk rock, a 'bring it on, but let's dance' song." 'Dreaming' began equally as hard before clicking into a melodic, swooning chorus. The lyrics were a baffling stream-of-conscious mess of images and alliteration about bottled water and "sexy people". 'Kill Rock 'n' Roll' was comical and seemed to stretch the band's sound in all directions, not necessarily to the best effect – Daron's vocal break was perhaps a little too quirky to stomach. But it was at least short.

"The influences are all across the board," Daron said. "In 'Kill Rock 'n' Roll' the choruses came about at the moment I was listening to a lot of The Supremes, and if you listen to that part you can hear a melody and a harmony there that's not too far away from what The Supremes would probably be doing, but there's heavy guitars in the back."

Title track 'Hypnotize' was the first song with any real depth and meaning beyond the usual war-mongering. In fact, it was quite brilliant, easily one of their best songs to date. Listening to Serj's steady, impassioned singing on the opening verses you could almost feel the influence of the voices of those singers such as his father who inspired him at a young age, the weight of his heritage resting easy on his shoulders. The musings of someone sitting in his car waiting for his girlfriend (as jotted down by Daron), the song's lyrics were almost incidental to the magnificent musical flourishes, such as Daron's impressive guitar solo.

"That song takes on a real complex matter and brings it down to a real simple level," explained Daron. "It shows a chaotic world, but I like to personalize it. 'Yes, the world is crazy, but how am I a part of it?'. That's just a reflection of society right now: it is a mesmerised society. Whether it's propaganda for war or to buy toothpaste, it's just a hypnotised, mesmerised society." 'Hypnotize' was wisely selected as the lead single and when released in November 2005 went to Number 1 in the US Modern Rock chart but again missed the UK Top 40.

'Stealing Society' initially recalled the pogo-friendly *Toxicity* tunes such as 'X' and 'Bounce' yet painted a pretty grim picture of urban disillusionment, the same narcotic-deadened Hollywood malaise that had informed earlier works.

Listened to in isolation 'Tentative' was another strong song, but you somehow got the feeling that it was a little lost amongst the twenty three new compositions that the band had released within six months. Subject-wise it worked alongside 'Attack' as the voice of those caught up in conflict – in this case the voice of the persecuted rather than the persecutor.

Comprised of a few select lines, 'U-Fig' tackled the notion of supremacy and was another rallying cry song that was low on reason but high on optimistic visceral energy and quick-fire, snare-cracking beats. 'Holy Mountains' was System Of A Down at their biblical best, Serj merging a harmonious Benedictine monk-like baritone with a breathless, close-up whisper layered over the creeping atmosphere. The song also made reference to the river Aras, which runs along the Armenian-Turkey border, its inclusion symbolic of the historical barrier between the two countries and the mountainous area that has seen much bloodshed over the years. The 'Holy Mountain' was believed to be Mount Arafat, which though geographically was Turkish, many Armenians believed to be rightfully theirs. "That's one of our national landmarks, like the Armenian soccer team is called Ararat," said Shavo in an MTV interview.

'Vicinity Of Obscenity' was one of the 'quacky' songs Daron spoke so fondly of. Their quackiest yet in fact. Similar in approach to a number of oddball artists – Captain Beefheart, The Cardiacs and John Zorn being but three examples – yet a unique entity, it was the band at their most unashamedly schizophrenic. It was a surreal, sexualized ultra vivid song about a mythical pie. As if baked by Salvador Dali and served by Frank Zappa. And it was good! One online review noted: "I don't think the band is that into mind-alerting substances, but anyone listening to 'Vicinity of Obscenity' will be left feeling like they had something slipped into their drink."

During an old interview I conducted with Daron, the guitarist once said he was most excited about one of his recent as-yet-unheard compositions, 'She's Like Heroin', which he described as one of the best songs he'd ever written. I'd be inclined to disagree. The song was certainly a curio with a slightly lighter sound than usual, though the guitarist's squeaking vocals and declarations of *"Ass!"* were just that little too grating to make it wholly palatable. With references to "Chinese tricks" and "ghosts of hooker girly dudes" it was a comically-inclined piece of jerk-pop that considered the heroin-like allure of a beautiful woman.

'Lonely Day' also offered a new take on the System *oeuvre*. A gentle, meandering introspective ballad it had a similar down-and-out-in-LA feel as Red Hot Chili Peppers' 'Under The Bridge'. The song's strength lay in its simplicity, the content inspired by nothing other than an inescapable feeling of abject loneliness. "I actually fuckin' wrote that the moment shit was going down," explained Daron. "It was a relationship issue. I was stuck between two phone calls, two different people, two different exes. It was just a miserable day."

The song that closed the band's ambitious two-album set was the same one that opened it, 'Soldier Side'. Expanded from the lilting intro of *Mezmerize*, it was a haunting war tale for history's many 'unknown soldiers' and was in its own way as lyrically evocative as renowned war poets like Wilfred Owen. Three minutes in and the song subtly reverted back to an uplifting version of that very first intro, with Serj and Daron in fine dual-vocal form. The circle was complete.

"I swear to God, the first time I played 'Soldier Side' to my mom – on my honour, I tear-ed up," said Shavo. "I had to walk out of the room. It's just that it affects me. I have a younger brother [who could go to war] and it's just really harsh, you know? Cause it's pretty freaking blunt, the way we put it."

So, *Hypnotize* had many moments of beauty, power and absurdity. Vartan Malakian's artwork certainly contributed to the concept, his sleeve design enabling people to conjoin the two albums into one complete work as it was originally intended. But the latter album also suffered from the inclusion of a couple of weaker songs (which seem to vary, depending upon who you ask). By anyone's standards it was a great rock record, but by System's it didn't quite match the completeness of *Toxicity* or the depth of *Mezmerize*. Or maybe perhaps we'd had too much of a good thing; maybe the aforementioned absurdity was expected whereas previously it always leapt out of the speakers. Perhaps the element of surprise had dissipated?

Not that it mattered too much. Handily, the album had already been well promoted in interviews at the same time as *Mezmerize* and a heavy tour schedule kept the band in the public eye. Accordingly when *Hypnotize* was released on November 22, 2005, it debuted at Number 1 in the US, giving them two consecutive Number 1 studio albums in the same year. The last band to achieve this feat in the US was some band called The Beatles. It also reached Number 1 in Canada, Number 3 in Australia, Number 11 in the UK and Top 10 in another ten countries. Another major success all round.

The final months of 2005 were action-packed as the band used their position to benefit both themselves and their causes. Most notably, in September the band continued the on-going mission for the acknowledgement of the Armenian genocide when they headlined an awareness-raising political rally outside the office of US House Speaker Dennis Hastert's office in Batavia, Illinois. Though the senator was conveniently not in town on the day, Serj himself delivered a letter to Hastert once again calling for a House vote on two controversial resolutions that would recognize the massacres as genocide; Hastert has said that both the Democratic Clinton administration and the Republican Bush administrations have previously opposed the resolutions because of an alliance with Turkey.

"By allowing this vote, and allowing the will of Congress to be freely expressed, you will be doing the right thing morally and, at the same time, encouraging Turkey to deal honestly with its past and more openly with its future," Serj said through a megaphone to the assembled crowd that included fans, members of the ANCA (Armenian National Committee of America), Axis of Justice and the Armenian Youth

Federation. Many rock stars have dabbled in politics and taken on short-term causes to little or negative effect, so it's to Serj and the band's credit that in their tenth year of existence they were still flying the flag for Armenia's oppressed. And if you still think politics and music aren't natural bedfellows – as many do – why not re-read this in two or three decades time and see whether System Of A Down's on-going campaigning through music, using the media in interviews and playing such rallies will have paid off. I'll wager it does.

Strangely, even by the time of the release of *Hypnotize*, System Of A Down remained the world's 'smallest' huge band. Or, put a better way: one of the least known multi-million selling rock bands. It took the release of two albums selling undeniably huge amounts of records in one year for large sections of the media to catch on to what the rock press had been hyping for a good five or six years.

Finally then, the critical plaudits were far and wide. Reading the press coverage of the time you still got the sense that the critical old guard who rule the broadsheet newspapers and dusty monthly magazines didn't fully understand who or what System Of A Down were about, but they knew it was something special, something culturally significant. Maybe that's one of the most attractive things about this band, their music seems to lever a generation gap: between those who just get it instantly, who feel the force of the music and let the often cryptic lyrics wash over them to create a lyrical portrait of the world; and to those who analyse and deconstruct the band as if they were an old V8 engine whose many parts need to be laid bare to be fully understood. It's not an age thing, for their fans span all ages, but very much a taste thing. For System have never really worked on paper, their sum has always been greater than their parts: a death, glam and rap-inspired metal band with Eastern European polka rhythms, singing surrealist protest songs about economic imperialism? Sounds great. To a few dozen mad fuckers worldwide, perhaps.

Reviewing the album for a magazine after another high-security playback session deep in Sony's offices in London, it was a point I was keen to mention – "What can be said about System Of A Down that hasn't already been covered during a recent deluge of press coverage summed up in the band's own description of their music: 'quacky'? No matter how much you describe their music, it never quite comes across on paper."

Elsewhere others similarly grasped for metaphors to sum up such an expansive sounding album in their allotted word count. "The fast bits are like falling down a spiral staircase dressed in full medieval armour," enthused critic Ben Thompson in a '5 out of 5' review for *The Observer Music Monthly*, who awarded the band their 'Album of the Month' over the likes of Madonna, Robbie Williams and Babyshambles. "The slow bits swirl and pulse like giant phosphorescent jellyfish…there is a restless intelligence at work in System Of A Down's apparently scattershot polemic which supersedes the work of many of rock's more self-conscious social commentarists."

A month later and Serj wasn't just talking about Armenia – he was there, along with his fiancée, an LA-based Armenian young lady. The trip was part-business, part-pleasure. One particular highlight involved Serj being received by Armenia's Foreign Minister Vardan Oskanyan. During the meeting the Minister expressed his respect and appreciation of the band and in particular Serj for his continued endeavours to raise awareness about the country's past, calling System Of A Down "the true ambassadors of Armenia"

"You encourage the self-consciousness of the young generation of the Armenian diaspora and maintenance of the Armenian identity," Oskanyan noted. As subsequently reported on a number of Armenian and band fan sites, during the friendly conversation Serj (dressed down in jeans and trainers for the occasion) and Oskanyan exchanged many thoughts about the Armenian diaspora. That a high-ranking government official would not only meet but personally thank and encourage the singer of an American heavy metal band is almost unthinkable. The nearest equivalent would be US Secretary Of State (their version of the Foreign Minister) Condoleezza Rice hanging loose with, say, The Clown from Slipknot. Never gonna happen … But then this was System Of A Down and if we've learnt anything then it is that this band do things differently.

Shortly afterwards the band reconvened to complete their final obligations of 2005, including a couple of high-profile performances. In November they flew into Portugal to play at the MTV Music Awards at the expansive Atlantic Pavillion, Lisbon, hosted by Sacha Baron Cohen's politically incorrect Kazakhstani alter ego, Borat Sagdiyev. Despite their stature, seeing System performing alongside artists such as Coldplay, Foo Fighters, Green Day, Robbie Williams and The Black Eyed Peas still seemed an incongruous inclusion; maybe because it's hard to accept that System Of A Down have boldly musically gone where others have never dared – or at best were destined for a cult-appeal only. Yet here they were, not only getting love and respect from the same industry that warned they would never get signed but from their contemporaries too. The band beat Beck, White Stripes, Bloc Party and Goldfrapp to receive the accolade 'Best Alternative Act' by MTV viewers worldwide. The band also closed the evening's proceedings with a ferocious rendition of 'B.Y.O.B.'

"This is where my mom accepted us, and accepted me, as in this is what I'm supposed to be doing, because for the Armenian people, we've done more than anybody else in America," Shavo told hosts MTV. "I think we put Armenia on the map, and I'm not trying to pat our back or anything like that, but we have. No joke. It was so funny. We were hanging out with the guy from the Black Eyed Peas [another band born out of LA's multi-cultural diaspora, in this case Jamaica, the Philippines and Mexican/Native American] at the MTV thing, because we were friends from high school. We got signed the same week and our albums dropped the same day. Well, I see them in Portugal for the European MTV awards, and we're just hanging out, and [vocalist] Will.I.Am hasn't seen me in forever, so he got comfortable and he's talking about us. He was talking to one of the guys from Interscope and he said something that really touched me. He goes, 'What other band do you know that is backed by a nation? A whole nation has this band's back. Like, anywhere in the world you go and you see an Armenian, they know who System Of A Down is, and they pump it.'"

In December, System were back home to play another corporate rock event when they appeared at KROQ's annual acoustic show, alongside other such big-hitters as Nine Inch Nails, Coldplay and Korn at LA's Gibson Amphitheatre. Over a charged ninety minutes they delivered another mind-blowing hit-filled set, Daron diving into the crowd, Shavo climbing the speakers and Serj, in a rare break from his Zen-master air of tranquillity, kicking over instruments and gear on stage. Another truly memorable evening to crown the band's most successful year yet.

One other point of interest that came out of the success of the *Mezmerize/Hypnotize* musical cycle was the increased discussion about

Daron's role within the band. Some suggested that he was the musical driving force of the band (true to an extent, but not exclusively so), some argued that the songs he sung were either the best and/or worst in the System canon, while others speculated about his future within the band. And it was all just speculation, the down-side to having a far-reaching fanbase with dozens of websites and chat rooms devoted solely to the band and everything about them. If half the rumours about the band that I have unearthed while researching this book were indisputable fact rather than loose-tongued gossip tossed into the cyber ether, it would be a very different tale.

One rumour seemed to be based in truth though. During interviews in January 2006 the band spoke of a forthcoming hiatus that was wholly deserved given how much they had crammed into the past twelve months. And while John, Shavo and Serj surely looked forward to a much-needed break, rather than do less, Daron (who had declared he could release "ten solo albums tomorrow" if he wanted, such was the wealth of material he had written) expressed a desire to work on another project that he was tentatively calling Scars On Broadway. Actually it was nothing new. As early as 2003 the guitarist had mentioned the name in relation to music he hoped to record with Amen's Casey Chaos, describing it in *Kerrang!* as "a little bit of both of our worlds coming together, with his rock edge and my eclectic edge. I wanted to stay away from System. It's a vision I have for this sound and I feel like a voice and a character like Casey's fits into the vibe really well." More recent discussions of the Scars project were a little more vague as Daron publicly pondered his options.

"I don't want to sit around [doing nothing], so I'm going to make an album," he said. "I haven't decided if I'm going to make it a revolving door of musicians or one solid band but it all revolves around my writing. We all want to take a little bit of a break. But I don't want to sit around, so I'm going to make an album. Serj did Serart. We're always doing things outside of System that come back to System in a positive way."

Shavo meanwhile was enjoying all-night jams with Wu-Tang Clan members RZA and GZA for a proposed collaboration. "We all hit it off, so we'll be working on a solo project soon," the bassist said, as reported on the Wu-Tang's website. "GZA's writing beats and all of the lyrics, RZA's writing beats and I'll be playing all the bass and writing most of the music. It's not written in stone, but we're talking about it. I want to get Serj to play drums, maybe sing on some songs. We have a few ideas for songs and it's going to be really cool. It's going to be a really crazy album, but it's not going to be like Wu-Tang or System. It'll be wherever I'm at in my head and wherever they're at in their heads."

Naturally, despite Daron's disclaimer that non-System projects only strengthened the band as an entity, rumours nevertheless circulated that all was not well with System Of A Down, that they may have already made their last record. At the time of writing though it's pure conjecture. You suspect that despite the accolades, the sold-out arenas, the awards, the magazine covers, the tens of millions albums sold, the festivals headlined and the new bands inspired, System Of A Down have still got so much more to achieve. Not because they need the money or the adoration. But because music – hell, the world – needs them.

Next stop: the White House?

Which bring us up to the here and now. The present fleeting moment. Soon it will pass but for now the sun is shining over LA. The Hollywood sign still oversees its domain. Up close it's cracked, chipped and fading but from here it still stands proud, drawing people to it like moths to a flame. All chasing the dream. And some of them actually getting it.

"Someone dropped the ball somewhere with System Of A Down," Daron whispered conspiratorially, breathless and sweaty backstage somewhere in Paris in 2005. "They actually let us be heard. The machine wants every band to play by the rules. And usually the machine gets its way. But not with us. They haven't managed to control us yet."

Sources And References

Interviews with the band were conducted by the author at various points between 1999 and 2005. Special thanks should be extended to the band's UK publicist Simon Hargreaves at James Grant PR for allowing me unlimited access to the band's archives.

The ever-expanding online encyclopaedia-for-the-people known as www.wikipedia.org was an invaluable resource in the writing of this book, particularly for the verification of historical dates and details relating to Armenia and the Middle East. The following magazines and websites also provided further material: various articles by Morat, Josh Sindell, Ian Fortnam, Tom Bryant, Dave Everley, James Sherry and the news pages in *Kerrang!, Spin, Metal Hammer, The Washington Post, NME, Rock Sound, Rolling Stone, Q, The Guardian, The Big Issue, The Boston Phoenix. The LA Times, The Village Voice, CMJ, Mean Street, Rhythm, Guitarist.*

The following websites and web articles were invaluable:
www.allmusic.com
www.drownedinsound.com
www.suicidegirls.com
www.mtv.com
www.homestead.com
www.armeniapedia.org
www.undeercover.com
www.songmeanings.net
www.blabbermouth.net
www.armeniandiaspora.com/archive/27652.html
www.burieddreams.com/attitude/issue5/drev.htm
www.mrl.nott.ac.uk/~dxl/reviews/NARS/Vol1/system-int.html
www.digitalprosound.com/Features/Interviews-Discuss/RickRubin4.htm
www.homestead.com/scottperham/Manager_Profile_-_David__Beno__Benveniste.mht
www.shoutweb.com/interviews/soad0901.phtml
www.timmcmahan.com/SOAD.htm
http://prefixmag.com/features/S/Serj-Tankian/Genre-Defiance/11

www.roadrun.com/blabbermouth.net/news.aspx?mode=Article&news
itemID=7998
www.metalunderground.com

Specific articles that were excellent resources include:
The Guardian, article by Adam Sweeting, May 27, 2005
NY Rock interview by Gabriella, November 2000
Spin.com, 'My Life In Music' by Greg Milner, June 2003
Metal Hammer, 'My Life Story', John Doran, Jan 2006
Metal Hammer, 'Welcome To My Gaff', April 99)
Total Guitar, July 2005
Rolling Stone, Neil Strauss, June 2002
Sunday Times Eye magazine, Gavin Martin, May 2005
Rhythm, Teri Saccone, June 2002
NY Rock, interview by Jeanne Fury, Nov 2001
Music Connect, interview by Scott Perham,
Music Channel, interview by Dan Epstein
Rock Sound, Nick Smith, 1999
Boston Phoenix, 'Rock in a Hard Place: System of a Down's struggle to be themselves', by Matt Ashaare, August 26, 2005
The Daily Telegraph, Ben Thompson, Sept 2001
CMJ.com, articles by Kory Grow
Classic Rock, Geoff Barton album review, June 2005
The Guardian, 'Moshpit Masterminds', Adam Sweeting , May 27 2005,)
The Guardian, Caroline Sullivan, June 7, 2005
Q live review, Luke Lewis, May 2005

There are many System Of A Down fan websites in existence, far too many to document. However, the following have proved to be particularly useful sources:
www.systemofadown.com
www.www.soaduk.co.uk
www.soadonline.net

Discography

Given the number of variations of System Of A Down releases and the different exported or repackaged copies currently available, this discography is biased towards the UK market. It is not a complete discography of every format with the band's name on it but rather an overview of their most significant releases. To this end, I have also excluded the many different promotional versions of singles. The vinyl formats of each release have all been released as limited editions. Apart from the early demos, unless otherwise stated all releases are on American Recordings / Columbia.

<u>Demos</u>

Demo 1
Released 1996
Suite-Pee / Sugar / Dam / P.L.U.C.K

Demo 2
Released 1997
Honey / Temper / Soil

Demo 3
Released 1997
Know / War? / Peephole

<u>Singles</u>

Sugar
Released: May 24 1999
CD / seven-inch vinyl
Sugar (Clean Version) / Sugar

Chop Suey!
CD1
Released: August 14 2001

Chop Suey! / Johnny / Know (Live)

Chop Suey!
CD2
Released: August 14 2001
Chop Suey! / Sugar (live) / War? (Live) / Chop Suey! (video)

Chop Suey!
seven inch clear vinyl
Released: August 14 2001
Chop Suey! / Johnny

Toxicity
CD1
Released: March 11 2002
Toxicity / X (live) / Suggestions (Llive) / Toxicity (video)

Toxicity
CD2
Released: March 11 2002
Toxicity / Marmalade / Metro (explicit version)

Aerials
CD1
Released: July 8 2002
Aerials / Toxicity (live) / PLUCK (live / Aerials (video)

Aerials
CD2
Released: July 8 2002
Aerials / Streamline / Sugar (live)

Aerials
seven-inch vinyl
Released: July 8 2002
Aerials / Snowblind

B.Y.O.B.
CD1
Released May 2 2005
B.Y.O.B. / Cigaro

B.Y.O.B.
DVD
Released May 2 2005
B.Y.O.B.

BYOB
Seven-inch vinyl
Released May 2 2005
B.Y.O.B. / Cigaro

Question!
CD1
Released August 29 2005
Question / Sugar (live)

Question!
CD2
Released August 29 2005
Question! / Forest (live) / Prison Song (live) / Question! (video)

Hypnotize
CD
Released November 14 2005
Hypnotize / Science (live)

Hypnotize
Released November 14 2005
seven-inch vinyl
Hypnotize / Forest (live)

Albums

System Of A Down
Released June 30, 1998
Suite-Pee / Know / Sugar / Suggestions / Spiders / DDevil / Soil /
War? / Mind / Peephole / Cubert / Darts / P.L.U.C.K.

International versions of the album also featured 'Marmalade', while the
Japanese release also featured 'Marmalade' and 'Storaged'. A special 2CD
version was also released featuring a bonus live CD, the 'Sugar' video and
an EPK EPK (electronic press kit).

Toxicity
Released September 4, 2001
Prison Song / Needles / Deer Dance / Jet Pilot / X / Chop Suey! /
Bounce / Forest / A.T.W.A / Science / Shimmy / Toxicity / Pyscho /
Aerials / Arto (bonus/hidden track)

An initial 2CD version of the album was also available internationallu.
The second disc featured the instrumental piece 'Arto' and also doubled
as a DVD featuring an about of the making of the album. A second
2CD version was also available – the second disc was a DVD that
featured the video for Toxicity and live footage of three tracks. The
Japanese release also featured 'Arto' and 'Johnny' whilethr Australian and
French versions contained a 6 track live CD.

Steal This Album!
Released November 26, 2002
Chic N' Stu / Innervision / Bubbles / Boom! / Nüguns / A.D.D /
Mr. Jack / I-E-A-I-A-I-O / 36 / Pictures / Highway Song / Fuck The
System / Ego Brain / Thetawaves / Roulette / Streamline

This was also released as four limited editions versions with the on-CD
artwork designed by each band member.

Mezmerize
Released May 17, 2005
Soldier Side – Intro / B.Y.O.B. / Revenga / Cigaro / Radio/Video / This Cocaine Makes Me Feel Like I'm On This Song / Violent Pornography / Question! / Sad Statue / Old School Hollywood / Lost In Hollywood

Hypnotize
Released November 22, 2005
Attack / Dreaming / Kill Rock N' Roll / Hypnotize / Stealing Society / Tentative / U-Fig / Holy Mountains / Vicinity Of Obscenity / She's Like Heroin / Lonely Day / Soldier Side

Also released on December 20 2005 on vinyl on Rick Rubin's Soda Profit label imprint.

Compilation appearances
System Of A Down have appeared on numerous compilation albums including a number of giveaway   CD's via a variety of outlets (including *Ozzfest, Metal Hammer, Kerrang!, CMJ*), which for the sake of simplicity have been ommited here.

Diabolus In Musica
Released: 1998
Rare tour cassette sampler featuring 'Suite-Pee' along tracks from Slayer and Clutch,

Strangeland Soundtrack
(TVT)
Released September 15 1998
Featured 'Marmalade'

Chef Aid: The South Park Album
(Sony / Columbia)
Released November 3 1998
Featured the band collaborating with Mase, P Diddy and Lil Kim on 'Will They Die For U?'

Heavy Metal 2000 Soundtrack
(Restless)
Released April 18 2000
Featured 'Storaged'

MTV: The Return Of The Rock
(Roadrunner)
Released July 12 2000
Featured 'Suite-Pee'

Loud Rocks
(Loud)
Released September 5 2000
System Of A Down and Wu-Tang Clan featured on this album of metal and rap couplings with a reworked version of the Wu-Tang's 'Shame'.

Strait Up
(Virgin)
Released November 7 2000
This tribute to Snot singer Lynn Strait featured Serj Tankian singing on 'Starlit Eyes'

Dracula 2000
(DV8/Columbia/Sony)
Released December 5 2000
Nu-metal-heavy soundtrack featured a cover of Berlin's 'Metro'

Not Another Teen Movie
(Warners)
Released December 4 2001
Featured 'Metro'

Pledge Of Allegiance
(Columbia)
Released May 26 2002
This live album of the tour package of the same name featured 'Chop Suey!', 'Bounce' and 'Toxicity'

The Scorpion King Soundtrack
(Universal)
Released May 26 2002
Featured 'Streamline'

The Osbourne Family Album
(Epic)
Released June 4 2002
This cheap cash-in compilation on 'The Osbournes' TV show included a cover version of Black Sabbath's 'Snowblind'.

Ozzfest 2002
(Epic/Comubia)
Released August 27 2002
Featured 'Needles'

Songs And Artists That Inspired Fahrenheit 9/11
(Epic/Sony)
Released October 5 2004
Featured "the artists Michael Moore listened to as he created the motion picture 'Fahrenheit 9/11'", including System Of A Down's 'Boom!'

Genocide In Sudan
(Waxploitation)
Released November 3 2004
Featured 'Nüguns'.

'Shimmy' featured on the computer game 'Tony Hawk's Pro Skater 4'
'Science' featured on the game 'ATV Offroad Fury 2'

Side projects and miscellaneous appearances

Serart
Serart
(Serjical Strike)
Released May 5 2003

Arto Tunçboyaciyan (also featured an appearance from Shavo Odadjian)
Intro / Cinema / Devil's Wedding / The Walking X-Periment / Black
Melon / Metal Shock / Save The Blonde / Live Is The Peace / Leave
Melody Counting Fear / Gee-tar / Clautrophobia . / Narina / Zumba
/ Facing The Plastic / If I Can Catch 404 / I Don't Want To Go Back
Empty Handed

Amen
Death Before Musick
(EatUrMusic)
Released April 13 2004
Produced and released by Daron Malakian

Zoolander
Shavo made a cameo appearance as one of 'Hansel's Friends' in the 2001
Ben stiller/Owen Wilson movie. As 'DJ Tactic' Shavo also regularly
makes public DJ appearances.

Various Artists
Axis Of Justice: Concert Series Volume 1
(Serrjical Strike / Columbia)
Released November 2 2004
Aswell as organizing the event. Serj made a number of appearances on
this Axis Of Justice llve album/DVD, including 'Piano Improvisation',
'Charades', 'Speak On It' (with Knowledge) 'Chimes Of Freedom and
'Jeffrey Are You Listening' (both with Tom Morello).

Buckethead (featuring Serj Tankian)
The collaborative track 'We Are One' appeared on the 2005 'Masters Of
Horror' soundtrack on Immortal Records.

Buckethead & Friends
Enter The Chicken
Released October 25 2005
(Serjical Strike)
Featured musical and production contribution from Serj Tankian and
was released on his label

Tribute records

Various
A Tribute To System Of A Down
(Big Eye)
Released June 11 2002
Strangely accurate cover version of System Of A Down songs. Only not quite as good.

Various
The String Tribute To System Of A Down
(Vitamin)
Released July 1 2003
Strange but recommended chamber music versions as played on violin, viola and cello

Richard Cheese
Tuxicity
(Ideatown)
Released November 25 2003
Lounge music cover versions of alterative rock classics by comedian Mark Jonathan Davis' alter ego, including 'Chop Suey!'

Visit our website at *www.impbooks.com* for more
information on our full list of titles including books
on My Chemical Romance, The Killers, Dave Grohl,
Muse, The Streets, Green Day, The Prodigy
and many more.